Journeys through mental illness

Journeys through mental illness

Clients' experiences and understandings of mental distress

Juliet L. H. Foster

First published in 2007 by
PALGRAVE MACMILLAN
Houndmills, Basingstoke, Hampshire RG21 6XS and
175 Fifth Avenue, New York, N.Y. 10010
Companies and representatives throughout the world.

PALGRAVE MACMILLAN is the global academic imprint of the Palgrave
Macmillan division of St. Martin's Press, LLC and of Palgrave Macmillan Ltd.
Macmillan® is a registered trademark in the United States, United Kingdom
and other countries. Palgrave is a registered trademark in the European
Union and other countries.

ISBN-13: 978–1–4039–8625–2 hardback
ISBN-10: 1–4039–8625–8 hardback
ISBN-13: 978–1–4039–8626–9 paperback
ISBN-10: 1–4039–8626–6 paperback

This book is printed on paper suitable for recycling and made from fully
managed and sustained forest sources. Logging, pulping and manufacturing
processes are expected to conform to the environmental regulations of
the country of origin.

A catalogue record for this book is available from the British Library.

A catalog record for this book is available from the Library of Congress.

10 9 8 7 6 5 4 3 2 1
16 15 14 13 12 11 10 09 08 07

Printed in China

Contents

Acknowledgements

Thanks are due to so many people who have helped this book come to fruition in one way or another. For academic inspiration and guidance in various forms, I am indebted to Uwe Flick, Denise Jodelet, Rob Farr, Sandra Jovchelovitch, Martin Stefan and, above all, to Gerard Duveen, whose support has been especially significant. Many thanks also to the consultants and staff at the three services who participated in my own study of client understanding. I would also like to thank Catherine Gray and everyone at Palgrave for their help, support and interest.

Ultimately, however, this book is dedicated to all the clients of the mental health services who took part in my research, giving so generously of their time, expertise and friendship, often at particularly difficult points in their lives. I hope that the following discussion goes some way to raising the issues that concerned them and to doing justice to the richness of the conversations that I had with them.

Part of Chapter 7 is reprinted by permission of Sage Publications Ltd from Foster, J. L. H. (2003) Beyond Otherness: controllability and location in mental health service clients' representations of mental health problems *Journal of Health Psychology* 8(5) pp. 632–644. (©Sage Publications, 2003)

1 Allowing madness vox

CLOWN: *Truly, madam, he ...*
        ... has here writ a letter to you; I should have given't you
        to-day morning, but as a madman's epistles are no
        gospels, so it skills not much when they are delivered.
OLIVIA: *Open't, and read it.*
CLOWN: *Look then to be well edified when the fool delivers the*
        madman.
        [Reads]
        'By the Lord, madam,' –
OLIVIA: *How now! art thou mad?*
CLOWN: *No, madam, I do but read madness: an your ladyship*
        will have it as it ought to be, you must allow Vox.
                                        (*Twelfth Night*, Act V, scene i)

Divine retribution, possession by evil spirits, the effects of a degenerate lifestyle, societally sanctioned role playing, societally unsanctioned rule breaking, a chemical imbalance, the result of difficult life experiences, an alternative lifestyle, an organic failure in the brain. At different points throughout history, in different cultures, and to some extent still today in Western society, mental ill health has been defined and regarded as all of the these: discussion and controversy abound when it comes to understanding 'madness' or mental health problems. Indeed, we need only look to the plethora of paintings, literature, poetry and drama depicting madness to find support for Foucault's (1961) assertion that '*On all sides, madness fascinates man*' (p. 23).

The social sciences, too, have focused on the way in which we try to understand mental ill health and to make sense out of what has often been regarded as the ultimate in confusion and unfamiliarity. In Western cultures, where the ideology of the individual is especially strong (Marková et al., 1998), this seems particularly pertinent. Lukes (1973) claims that here the individual

1

self is regarded as being located entirely within the mind. An illness of the mind, therefore, threatens the individual self (Morant, 1996); irrationality threatens modern societies that value rationality above all else (Tew, 2005a). How, then, do people understand something that, culturally, seems to represent the most frightening thing that could happen to a person, the idea of the loss of the individual self? How do we understand what seems to embody the very antithesis of understanding? Psychologists, psychiatrists, sociologists and anthropologists have sought the answer to these questions as much as artists and writers.

The theme of this book, however, is the understanding of mental ill health held by individuals who have used mental health services, been labelled mentally ill or have considered themselves to suffer from mental health problems. It focuses especially on people who have been in regular and/or recent contact with the mental health services, and who might therefore be considered to be experiencing more severe mental distress, whether chronic or acute in nature.

Until recently the focus of much work in the social sciences and elsewhere has been almost exclusively on public understanding of mental ill health, with some concessions towards consideration of professional views. Outside autobiographies and other writings, in the realm of academia, the voices of those who have been diagnosed with and considered to have mental health problems have been conspicuously absent. In this book I will review some of the few, but important, areas in which client understanding has been considered, in particular focusing on more recent work, including that conducted within the mental health service user movement and on my own study of this topic. I will argue that examining client understandings of mental health problems is, in fact, crucial and has significant implications for the mental health services and wider society, and also for social scientists interested in the development and interaction of different forms of knowledge. However, before addressing the issue of client understanding, I would like to explore some of the political, historical and ideological reasons for the imbalance in existing literature and for the way that society has traditionally ignored the understanding of those considered to have mental health problems.

Silencing the voice of the Other

Historically, the process of segregating those considered 'mad' can only have contributed to a devaluing of their views, and a fail-ure on the part of wider society to listen to what they had to say (Porter, 1987). While there is some debate as to exactly when this 'great confinement' (Foucault, 1961) began (Porter, 1987), the Bethlem hospital in London was founded in 1247 and was used exclusively for the care of those labelled mad from 1377; records also show other asylums being established elsewhere in Europe around this time, for example a madhouse was founded in Elbing, Germany, in 1310. By the eighteenth century, private madhouses were relatively common in England, and the so-called trade in lunacy began, as more establishments were set up to care for the 'mad' away from their homes. A cursory glance at the relevant stat-istics shows how far this process took off during the nineteenth century: around 5000 individuals are thought to have been in institutional care in England in 1800; this figure had leapt to 100,000 by 1900, as additional, larger asylums were built (Rogers & Pilgrim, 2001).

These out-of-town asylums remained part of the geographical and cultural landscape of the United Kingdom for some time: lit-tle societies in their own right, with farms, ballrooms, laundries, furnaces and the ubiquitous water tower, they were a well-known sight and entered into local myth – 'You belong in [insert name of local asylum]' was a familiar playground taunt. However, although well recognised, these asylums remained mysterious, set apart from the rest of the local community and deliberately designed to function independently.[1] This separation has import-ant practical and psychological consequences: practically, it iso-lates those who are institutionalised from the wider community, making it almost impossible for their views to be considered. Psychologically, it reinforces the 'Otherness' of mental ill health already found in public understanding: mental health problems, and people suffering from them, are seen as less comprehensible and more distant from the rest of society.

Although recent developments in the mental health services have seen the closure of these water tower asylums, many of which have (perhaps somewhat ironically) been converted into luxury flats or business parks, and a move towards mental health facilities being located within the community, it would not appear that any real shift in the segregation of people with mental health problems has taken place. Indeed, research tends to show that individuals living in areas close to community mental health facilities first may not be aware of the existence of these facilities (Brockington, Hall, Levings & Murphy, 1993; Huxley, 1993a), and second that their views about mental health problems and those experiencing them do not differ substantially from individuals living in an area further away from such facilities (Brockington et al., 1993; Taylor & Dear, 1981; Wolff, Pathare, Craig & Leff, 1999).

The media debates surrounding the potential danger that individuals using mental health services might pose (Rose, 1998) do little to encourage integration and acceptance: indeed, most people seem to believe that mental health facilities downgrade an area (Office for National Statistics, 2003), and attitudes have doubtless been affected by the very few rare, yet often-highlighted, tragedies in which members of the public have been murdered by so-called care in the community patients. Such cases have received enormous media attention (Foster, 2006a; Rose, 1998), and there are now high-profile campaigns aimed at persuading the government to review their mental health policies and to provide more hospital-based care: SANE and the Zito Trust are particularly active in this area. A recent government report on attitudes to mental illness found that since mental health policy shifted from hospital to community-based care, attitudes at first remained fairly stable (1993–2000) but have most recently become less favourable, although it is important to point out that they remain sympathetic in the main (Office for National Statistics, 2003). The same study also suggests that fear of individuals with a mental illness has increased since 1990 (ibid).

Consequently, individuals deemed to be suffering from madness or mental health problems have long been physically segregated from the rest of society, and continue to be so despite changes in their geographic location. The situation is exacerbated by the few opportunities afforded to individuals with mental health problems to reintegrate themselves into society: Bracken and Thomas (2005) detail the many and varied ways in which mental health service users in today's society lose their rights as citizens, including exclusion from various social and economic spheres, restrictions on migration, on parenting and so on.

This physical segregation may also mean that mental health service users have been harder to access for social scientists than other populations, such as the general public. While several classic studies have been conducted in psychiatric institutions – Goffman's (1961) famous study of life in a total institution and Rosenhan's (1973) infamous pseudopatient study, for example – few focus exclusively on the patient perspective. Many of these earlier studies were conducted covertly, and while the introduction of ethics committees has addressed the important issues inherent within such studies, other barriers to working with individuals diagnosed with mental health problems have doubtless arisen, such as questions over capacity to consent. Certainly, if negotiations with the ethics committee relevant to my own study that will be discussed later in this book are anything to go by, problems of access and gate-keeping may well mean that some studies on client perspectives are thwarted at the outset, thereby tipping the balance in favour of more accessible populations, such as the general public.[2]

However, there are other important reasons why people who use mental health services may not be listened to within society, even if they have the physical opportunities to present their cases. It has been suggested that this failure to ask the mental health service user for his or her views and assessments stems from the idea that the 'mental patient' is incapable of giving rational answers (Rogers, Pilgrim & Lacey, 1993). An integral part of several diagnoses is that the patient's understanding and ideas are questioned: a diagnosis of schizophrenia, for example, rests on the presence of delusions and/or hallucinations, bizarre thought patterns and beliefs that are not shared by the majority of the population. Service users are often seen as lacking insight into themselves and their conditions (Furlong, 1991; Weinstein, 1981), as a result of their psychopathology. Indeed, the weight given to a professional interpretation of an individual's situation or experience over that individual's own interpretation is enshrined in our legal system. This, for some, can make it hard to see any value in what an individual diagnosed with a mental health problem might have to say: people might ask how we can ever be sure that this is what a client would say if she were not ill. Are her ideas merely the product of faulty psychopathology? How can we separate out what is actually the case from what she wrongly believes to be the case? This notion of lack of insight is an important reason for the lack of consideration of client views and understanding (Beresford, 2005), and is likely to be the reason why the mental health services have lagged behind other health services in seeking patient and client views (Rogers et al., 1993). Client views have long been invalidated (Sonn, 1977) and can be seen as a form of subjugated knowledge (Foucault, 1976).

There is now substantial evidence that, rightly so, this situation is changing, both in the social sciences and in the mental health services. Beresford (2005) claims that the past few years have seen unprecedented levels of interest in user perspectives, including at governmental level. Certainly, in the social sciences we have seen the rise of interest in narrative approaches within health (Kleinman, 1988), which challenge the dominance of biomedical understanding; similarly, approaches based on theories of social construction call for an appreciation of the multiple voices within society and the variety of different forms of understanding that stem from these. In parallel, the health services in the UK have been influenced by consumerism (Rogers & Pilgrim, 2001) and democratisation (Beresford, 2005): the NHS plan of 2000 details the rights of patients as citizens. How far this process has extended to the mental health services remains something of a moot point: Bracken and Thomas (2005) contrast the NHS plan with National Services Framework for Mental Health of 1999, which they claim deals much more in issues of the risk posed by clients of the mental health services and in improving public confidence than in issues of the rights of the client.

Another factor that has had a major impact on the increased interest in client perspectives is the rise of the mental health service user movement, which, as will be discussed in Chapter 3, has promoted greater research into client opinions and understanding, challenged assumptions regarding mental health problems and provided a forum for clients and former clients whose voices might previously have been silenced or ignored.

A note on theoretical perspectives

Work using a wide variety of theoretical perspectives and methodological approaches to study understandings of mental ill health will be reviewed in this book. However, the main theoretical angle which will be adopted, and which was used in the course of the study that forms part of the discussion of this book, is one of social constructionism. Consequently, I make the assumption that people actively make sense of the world around them, drawing on socially shared stocks of knowledge, and that the meanings that they construct then come to constitute their realities. This is not to deny the possibility of the existence of 'mental health problems' (or 'bipolar disorder', 'depression' etc), but to say that it is not possible for us to step outside our culturally and socially derived understandings of these concepts, nor consequently to state that we can identify them objectively as matters of 'fact'.

There are, of course, a number of constructionist theories and positions (see Burr [2003] for a more comprehensive discussion). One that I believe to have particular relevance to the issue of understandings of mental health is the theory of social representations (Duveen, 2000; Marková, 1996; Moscovici, 1984a). Briefly, social representations theory maintains that members of social groups create, develop and maintain representations about various concepts in order to orientate themselves towards those concepts and to communicate about them (Moscovici, 1973): as such, representations can be seen as codes (Moscovici, 1973) or networks of ideas (Moscovici, 1998). Social representations theory maintains both the importance of cognitive processes within representation, in the form of anchoring and objectification – the naming and association of a concept with that which is already familiar and known (Moscovici, 1984a), and the social context of meaning-making: representations are not created anew as an individual enterprise, but are re-presented as a social process.

Consequently, the theory emphasises the social context of responses to the social world. The relationship between subject and object is at the heart of social representations theory: indeed, it is in many ways the central problem of social psychology (Jovchelovitch, 2006). Traditionally, many forms of psychology, including social psychology, approach this issue by relying on the Stimulus → Response model: for example, within attitude theory we assume that an individual responds to the idea of mental health problems based on the attitudes he/she holds when such problems are made salient to that individual. Theorists who adopt the perspective of social representations theory have argued that this approach creates a false separation between the subject and the object (Farr, 1987), and fails to sufficiently consider the complexity of meaning-making within the social world. In social representations theory, the emphasis is shifted to a consideration of the way in which meanings are socially constructed, by members of social groups, and how these meanings are recreated and represented within interaction, both with other members of the same social group and with other groups. Schematically, this has come to be represented as a triangle, Subject–Other–Object (Jovchelovitch, 2006): this inclusion of the Other, or Alter, is a central feature of social representations theory (Marková, 2003).

In social representations theory, then, individuals within a social group not only take a position with regard to an object within society–for example, responding to the idea of mental health problems but they are also engaged in relationships with one another. Sharing similar, socially derived representations about a concept enables the members of any group to communicate about that concept, and also, reciprocally, strengthens their social identity (Duveen, 2001): sharing ideas and representations helps to define who belongs to the social group, and is recognised as belonging by others, in the first place, and who, in contrast, does not share those ideas and therefore represents the out-group (Moscovici, 1987). Given the multiplicity of social groups that exist in any society, then, there are multiple knowledges about any concept in that society, and these knowledges come into contact with one another, clashing, influencing one another and developing in the process.

Bauer and Gaskell (1999) have also highlighted the importance of the dimension of time within this consideration. Consequently, instead of seeing the two-dimensional triangle described above between members of a social group, others and the representational object, we should see a three-dimensional triangular structure (Subject–Other–Object–extending through Time), rather, they suggest, like a toblerone chocolate bar. This allows us to consider the way that individuals within the same social group, who share common representations, are engaged in a particular 'project' with regard to the object of representation, a project that has both developed during the past and extends and develops into the future. This project involves sharing mutual goals, interests, activities and so on regarding the object of representation.

This conceptualisation emphasises several important points within social representations theory: first, it focuses attention upon the change and development within any representation and any social group. Representations and ideas are not static, but are altered and developed as time goes by, as the aims and needs of individuals within a social group, and their experiences, change, as new information is incorporated by the group, for example, from the media, and as groups act and interact with one another. Consequently, representations guide and influence our actions and communication; indeed, this is the main function of social representations (Moscovici, 1984b): we do not subscribe to particular ideas in the abstract, but instead respond to situations in our daily lives according to the thoughts and beliefs that we have about the concepts with which we come into contact. In addition, this model emphasises the issue of multiple knowledges within a society and of the way that power affects the actualisation of any representation: given that, as discussed above, different social groups hold different representations about the same object or concept, and that they will act and interact with other groups based on these representations, it is possible to imagine how the representational projects of different groups fit together around the same object of representation. However, since not all social groups within society are equal, these projects will not exist in uniform harmony: instead, some will squash others, dominate others, or be suppressed by others (Foster, 2003). For example, a group of mental health service users may hold representations about mental ill health in common, sharing that understanding and drawing on their own and one another's experience in developing active 'projects', involving ideas about mental ill health, and strategies for dealing with it, as they journey through mental illness. In this way, their ideas about mental health problems will guide their actions and interactions with other service users, with professionals, with members of the public and so on. However, clients do not hold these ideas about mental health problems in isolation: other groups, such as mental health professionals and the general public, will also hold representations about mental ill health, which may well differ from those of the group of clients. Given the stigmatised position of mental health service clients within society (Sayce, 2000), these other groups may be in a significantly more powerful position than the clients themselves: as already discussed, psychiatrists' versions of mental ill health, for example, have a legal and symbolic weight that clients' versions often lack. How far clients are therefore able to act on their representations within their own journey, or project, through mental illness might therefore be determined as much by the opportunities afforded them to do so by professionals and the public as anything else. This will be a recurring theme in this book.

However, in addition to operating at the microgenetic level of the social group, being evoked in conversations between individuals and so on, social representations also operate on a wider societal level, and are evoked in broader contexts such as within the media, or in institutional practices and rituals: this has been referred to as the sociogenetic level (Duveen & Lloyd, 1990). They also have something of an ontogenetic effect (ibid): that is, we are socialised into representations (Moscovici & Hewstone, 1983) as we grow up as members of various social groups and can come to take for granted the representations to which those groups subscribe as matters of fact, or as an ontological reality (Marková, 1996). A good example of this is representations of gender: we grow up in societies which have very clear, well-defined ideas about what it means to be male and female, and what is expected of men and women, and an important part of any child's development is taking on board these representations and beginning to act in accordance with them. Institutions, such as school or nursery, the practices and traditions within these institutions, adults and other children will all play a role in this process (Lloyd & Duveen, 1992).

There are several additional reasons why social representations theory is especially suited to examining understandings about mental health problems in particular. First, as Flick (1998a) has pointed out, health is not an individual matter: definitions of what it is to be healthy or ill are instead socially negotiated, and health problems are then communally approached and discussed by families, friends, professionals, the media and so on. The social emphasis on the process of representing, and its consequences, is therefore both relevant and important.

Second, social representations theory is a theory which aims to rehabilitate common-sense thinking (Moscovici & Marková, 1998) and to examine it in its own context, rather than comparing it with other forms of knowledge to create any kind of hierarchy of understanding. Indeed, the very basis of the theory is that different social groups hold different representations of a concept and that these differences should be examined in context, rather than one form of knowledge being regarded as inferior to another (Foster, 2003); what is taken for granted as a matter of fact must also be examined as a matter of course. This is a crucial facet of the theory when we consider representations of mental ill health: in understandings of mental health, a clear hierarchy has been established in practice which places professional understanding in a superior position, privileging psychiatric understanding in particular over other theories. As already discussed, other ways of understanding mental ill health, especially those held by clients or former clients of the mental health services, are often denigrated and held to be inferior. Adopting the perspective of the theory of social representations allows us a framework within which to take client understanding seriously and to examine it in context and in relation to other forms of understanding (Flick & Foster, in press).

The theory of social representations will therefore be discussed at various points within this book. However, it will not be used inflexibly: other theoretical approaches also have important contributions to make when it comes to examining client understandings of mental ill health, and these will also be considered.

Personal perspective

One of the themes that will emerge in this book is that of identity. The identity of the researcher in studies of the understanding of mental ill health is of increasing interest (Foster, 2006b), especially when, as will be discussed in Chapter 3, so much research is now designed, carried out and analysed by clients themselves. For some, the question has become '*not which is the most suitable method or design, but who uses it*' (Bracken & Thomas, 2005, p. 70). Similarly, for theorists working from a constructionist position and using qualitative methods, it is important to examine the reasons for undertaking a project, in an attempt to clarify biases and perspectives (Flick, 1998b; Truman, 2000).

My own perspective stems mainly from academia, and a long-standing interest in clients' understandings of mental health problems and why, historically, they have been somewhat ignored. I have also spent time working as a support worker with people with long-term mental health problems and, on a personal level, was treated for anxiety, panic attacks and depression over a three-year period by my GP, a counsellor and a clinical psychologist. I introduced myself to the clients I met in the course of this study telling them that I was a social psychologist interested in client perspectives of mental health problems and was open about more personal information in conversation.

This raises an important question within mental health research: is it necessary for the researcher be a part of the mental health service user community, or is there a role for those who do not share the experiences of mental health service users? As the service user movement grows in size and influence, and the amount of research undertaken by users and survivors themselves increases (see Chapter 3), is it enough for researchers to identify themselves as allies (Sayce, 2000), or as academics with 'attitude' (Barnes & Bowl, 2001, p. x)? Given that some sections of the user movement argue that allies should not be included in the struggle for change and recognition (O'Hagan, 1993), where does this leave other interest groups?

Clearly, I do not share the experience of using mental health services, of hospitalisation (often involuntary), of regular use of medication or of the profound levels of distress and disruption about which clients in my own study spoke to me, and to try to claim any conscious partiality (Mies, 1983) with them would, I believe, belittle their experiences and stories. Instead, I presented myself as a learner (Howarth, Foster & Dorrer, 2004; Flick and Foster, in press), interested in engaging in a dialogue about different experiences and understandings. I argue that there is consequently still a role for others in research into mental ill health, as long as an awareness is maintained of the differing perspectives that this affords, and an empathetic and open approach is taken, allowing participants the opportunity to fully engage with the research. Indeed, given some of the current debates regarding how representative the mental health service user movement is of users of mental health services in general, and how far most service users feel that they are part of the wider service user movement (Wallcraft, Read & Sweeney, 2003), it seems unwise to limit research exclusively to that which is conducted within the mental health service user movement: in doing so, we may address some of the problems of power within the research situation, but also risk exchanging one set of preconceptions for another.

Additionally, there can be benefits of *not* sharing participants' experiences: as researchers we bring our own set of skills to the research situation (Condor, 1997), and, as 'outsiders', can learn from participants, questioning as a newcomer might, and seeking clarification of things that might otherwise be taken for granted or ignored (Flick & Foster, in press). As Repper and Perkins (2003) conclude, 'knowing things and having skills is good. There is nothing wrong with expertise per se, nor is there any-thing wrong with seeking confirmation of our expertise. It is the way in which this expertise is used, and the places in which we look to confirm it, that can be problematic' (Repper & Perkins, 2003, p. 74). This last sentence is crucial: if 'outsiders' are to con-tinue to engage with mental health service clients in research, then an awareness of the problems of imbalances in power relations must be maintained, and participatory approaches to research used as far as possible (Tones & Tilford, 1994).

A note on language

As Scheff (1966) has pointed out, the terms used to refer to the phenomenon of 'mental illness' in society prejudge the issue. Beresford (2005) maintains that although terms such as 'mental illness' and 'pathology' may have been replaced by the euphemistic 'mental health' and 'mental health problems', ultimately their origins, meanings and legal basis are the same. Indeed, Repper and Perkins (2003) ask exactly what is a 'health problem' if it is not an 'illness'? Similarly, whatever language is used to refer to people who use mental health services – patients, service users, clients the implications are the same, and employing a different term is unlikely to encourage other members of the community to interact with those clients (Penn & Nowlin-Drummond, 2001). In other words, changes in professional language and jargon may not reflect changes in ideology or practice.

Throughout this book, I have chosen to employ the terms that were used by the clients of the mental health services who participated in my own research. Consequently, although I will tend to use the phrases 'mental health problems' or 'mental ill health', I will also refer to 'mental illness' and, on occasions, 'madness'. This does not mean that I regard these terms as interchangeable, as, of course, they can have important semantic differences. They will, however, all be used, given their currency in my own research. Similarly, I will employ the terms 'service users', 'clients', 'survivors' and 'patients', again because all these terms were used by participants in my own research.

Structure of the book

This book will draw on work examining clients' perspectives from a number of different areas. First, Chapter 2 will review some of the existing literature from various disciplines in the social sciences that examines understanding about mental ill health per se, from the perspectives of the public, professionals and clients of the mental health services. Chapter 3 will focus more exclusively on clients' understandings, in particular examining the development of the mental health service user movement and the opportunities it has afforded to promote client understandings of mental health problems in greater depth.

Chapter 4 will move on to consider how clients of the mental health services define and understand mental health and illness: drawing on my own work, and on other research, it will consider, in particular, the way in which clients define mental ill health by and through experience and how they actively engage in their own journeys through mental illness. Chapter 5 will draw further on relevant empirical data as key themes in these journeys through mental ill health are examined. Chapter 6 seeks to consider the effects of being diagnosed with a mental illness on the identity of an individual, in particular considering the role of the client's conceptualisation of their journey in maintaining a positive identity.

Many of these themes are drawn together in Chapter 7, which focuses on the main ways in which clients in this study represented mental health problems: these representations occur along two dimensions of controllability and location. These will be discussed in greater depth. Chapter 8 aims to draw some conclusions, in particular considering the implications of work on client understanding for the mental health services and on what studies of client understanding might contribute to our understanding of the interaction between different perspectives and different forms of knowledge.

2 Perspectives from psychology, psychiatry and other disciplines

Introduction

As highlighted in the previous chapter, a large number of studies in the social sciences have considered the understandings of mental ill health held by various groups. This chapter will review some of these studies, the conclusions we can draw from them and, perhaps more importantly, consider where the gaps lie.

One of the most important distinctions that can be made between these studies is that of whose understanding is being considered. Here, I intend to consider three main perspectives: (1) that of the general public (2) that of mental health professionals and (3) that of those who have been defined as 'mentally ill', by whatever criteria. It is perhaps symbolic of the boundaries that exist between these communities that few studies attempt to examine the perspectives of more than one of these groups. It is also significant that, historically, psychology and psychiatry seem to have been less concerned with the views expressed by individuals considered to have mental health problems themselves, creating something of a gap in the literature. This gap is now partially being filled by work in areas outside mainstream social sciences, especially that undertaken by the mental health service user movements: this will be discussed in the next chapter.

Broadly speaking, the main area of interest of this book is the representations of mental health and illness held by those diagnosed with a mental health problem: however, studies on the beliefs of the public and of mental health professionals also have important implications. What is the relationship between client, professional and public views? Are they as divergent as has been suggested (Round, Bray, Polak & Graham, 1995), or is there a more complex interaction at play?

The ideas of the general public might be of particular relevance. A person might be diagnosed with a mental health problem at any point in their life, perhaps after years of exposure to, and subscription to, the kinds of views about mental ill health found amongst the general public. Is diagnosis likely to change the ideas that such an individual might have had overnight? Clients of the mental health services are, of course, subject to the same representational influences regarding mental ill health as the general public. They are party to the same media coverage, the same dominant images found in society and the same representational resources. This has led some theorists in the past to argue that clients' ideas remain closer to those of the general public (O'Mahony, 1980). Labelling theory (Scheff, 1966) would seem to support such a view. It holds that mental illness is merely a demonstration of behaviour in-keeping with the learned societal stereotypes of mental illness, thereby implying that those labelled mentally ill and those not labelled mentally ill hold the same beliefs and understandings of mental illness, and employ a common frame of reference. Johnson and Orwell (1995) claim that acceptance of the label 'mental illness' may not depend on 'insight' or severity of condition but result from the cultural perceptions of mental illness in that individual's society and the stigma associated with the label itself. Littlewood and Lipsedge (1989) similarly argue that the extent to which patients see themselves as 'mentally ill' varies with culture, an increasingly important point in today's multi-cultural mental health services. As Brockington et al. (1993) note, if, as has long been recognised in psychiatry (Leff, 2001), family situations can contribute to the prognosis of an individual's mental health problems, so too can the situation in the community in which a person is living: understanding the different ways in which groups in society understand mental illness, and the relationship between these understandings and those held by clients, is therefore crucial.

Other work, however, suggests that the views of mental health professionals have more relevance when considering the views of mental health service clients. Users of mental health services come into regular, sometimes daily contact with mental health professionals, and interact with them within a largely biomedical model of mental illness, that tends to favour professional, psychiatric interpretations and knowledge over any lay interpretation

(Schurmans & Duruz, 1999). Individuals with a diagnosis of a mental health problem therefore have additional sources of information less readily available to the general public, and might use the professionals with whom they come into contact as extra resources. Weinstein and Brill (1971) and Krause Jacob (1992) both claim that the views of all clients come to mirror those of the professionals who work with them.

Consequently, public and professional representations of mental illness require examination if we are to discover how clients accept, develop or reject the existing representations of mental illness found elsewhere in society.

Public perspectives

Of the three groups considered here the views of the public have been sampled most widely, in a variety of disciplines and using a variety of methods, from interviews and questionnaires to media analysis, and experiments.

Within all of this work, however, the same major themes recur: the mentally ill are regarded with fear by the general public (Maclean, 1969; Miles, 1987; Nunnally, 1961), a fear which can lead to distrust of any research or programmes associated with mental illness (Cumming & Cumming, 1957). This fear stems partly from the notion that the mentally ill are violent (Scheff, 1966; Maclean, 1969) and unpredictable (Miles, 1987). Although it is clear that this fear of violence has long been an important feature in the public's beliefs about mental ill health (Gilman, 1988), recent media reporting seems to play a key role in reflecting and perpetuating this belief: Philo, McLaughlin and Henderson (1996) report that by far the most pervasive reference to mental illness in the tabloid press and on television involves the notion of violence towards others, despite the fact that statistical analysis reveals such cases are unusual (Taylor & Gunn, 1999).

In particular, the media's increasing focus on recent changes to mental health care (Anderson, 2003) and on several high-profile violent crimes and tragedies (Hallam, 2002) may have strengthened the link between violence and mental illness in the public mind. Using evidence from a study that sampled the views of 1963 people before and after the event, Appleby and Wessley (1988) argue that the tendency to see extreme violence as resulting from mental illness became stronger after the Hungerford massacre in 1987, when Michael Ryan shot 16 people before turning the gun on himself. Although there was much speculation in the press at the time about Ryan's mental health, he had no history of contact with the mental health services, nor of any diagnosis. This speculation alone, however, seemed enough to convince many of the link between mental ill health and violence. This trend has continued (Cutcliffe & Hannigan, 2001), and perhaps even increased, since this event: Rose (1998) traces the reporting of the case of Christopher Clunis, a young man with a diagnosis of schizophrenia and a long history of contact with different mental health services, who killed a stranger, Jonathan Zito, in 1993, a case which has become iconic for the press (Hallam, 2002). Rose (1998) argues that following this tragedy a new narrative appears in the press, that of the failure of the mental health services and neglect of individuals with mental health problems living in the community leading almost inevitably to those individuals committing violent crimes.

The shift from institutional care to community facilities plays an important role in this. The government's recent plans to reform the Mental Health Act[1] were also widely debated in the media: here, interestingly, most of the reports provided a more sympathetic picture of individuals with mental health problems and lamented the proposed changes as a knee-jerk reaction and an infringement of human rights. However, certain examples of violent crime, namely Clunis and Michael Stone, a convicted murderer with a diagnosis of personality disorder, are used frequently, and vocabulary often continues to perpetuate the link between violence and mental illness, albeit often implicitly (Foster, 2006a).

Fear is also a major part of public representation of mental ill health, perhaps because individuals with mental health problems are seen as different and incomprehensible. They represent the Other (Gilman, 1985a; Gilman, 1988; Littlewood & Lipsedge, 1989), as such might also be regarded as easily recognisable (Miles, 1987), or as looking and acting differently from other people (Nunnally, 1961). Gilman (1988) claims that this is because we need to believe that we can recognise, and therefore avoid, the 'violently insane', thereby maintaining a sense of control over our world. Otherness is often the predominant theme in studies that take the theoretical perspective of social representations: in a collection of studies edited by Bellelli (1987a), the mentally ill person is found to be constructed as strange and unpredictable (Di Giacomo, 1987; Serino, 1987) and clearly differentiated from the 'normal person' (Amaturo, 1987).

Gilman's (1985a; 1985b; 1988) work highlights just how deep-seated this construction of the mentally ill as Other is. In a fascinating study that details the depiction of madness and the mentally ill in art through the ages (Gilman, 1985b), he demonstrates how images of strangeness and difference predominate. Interestingly, such images are also replicated when the lay public is asked to draw pictures of people with mental health problems. Drawing on the theory of social representations, De Rosa (1987) asked Italian children and adults to draw pictures of and as 'madmen'. Three categories of picture were evident and roughly followed the developmental trajectory: consequently, younger children tended to produce pictures that drew on magic-fantastic elements, slightly older children focused on the criminalised and finally older children and adults emphasised medicalised aspects. However, elements of each type of drawing overlapped, and the themes of Otherness and deviance recurred in all phases. By comparing the drawings with art from the Middle Ages onwards, De Rosa (1987) was able to demonstrate the tenacity of many of these ideas.

Other forms of visual media portray similar images. Rose (1996a; 1998) analysed portrayals of mental ill health in British television programmes and found that in addition to the language used and action portrayed, other visual techniques such as camera angles were used to reinforce the notion that the mentally ill character was strange and alone. Research examining film presentations of mental ill health found similar results (Wahl, 1995; Wahl, 2003).

However, the line between Self and Other is not always regarded as distinct and unchanging in public representation. Outside the social sciences in literature this theme is perhaps even stronger (Feder, 1980). The recurrent themes of duality in many of these works (Jekyll/Hyde; the madwoman in the attic and so on) emphasise the fragility of the boundaries that we might construct between Self and Other, Sanity and Madness. Perhaps we need to engage more constantly in representational work to maintain the divide.

An excellent example of the construction and maintenance of physical and psychological barriers between the mentally ill Other and the non-mentally ill Self comes from the exemplary research of Jodelet (1991), who conducted an ethnographic study of a French community in which patients from the local psychiatric hospital 'lodged' with 'foster families' in the surrounding villages. Although (or perhaps because) the villagers lived in such close proximity to individuals diagnosed with a mental health problem, they maintained that they understood little about mental health problems and organised their lives around rituals of separation, often seemingly at a non-conscious level. The lodgers therefore ate from different crockery, which was washed separately from that of the other householders. Laundry was done separately, and some houses had even been specially adapted so that living quarters were minimally communal. Jodelet (1991) traced these rituals back to a fear of contagion, especially through bodily fluids, resulting in a need to maintain separation as far as was possible. However, even these rituals could not provide as much protection as some families would like, and Jodelet (1991) discusses the fact that four-fifths of mothers from one town participating in her study had consulted a psychiatrist about one of their children or asked her for her own opinion on the child. Interestingly, Gittins (1998) details similar rituals of separation, especially around issues of patient and staff laundry, in her study of Severalls Hospital.

Despite the predominance of images of violent mental illness, more positive or neutral representations are also evident. In Philo et al.'s (1996) study of the tabloid press and television programmes, although violence to others was by far the most prevalent category out of the five that they found, other categories such as criticism of accepted definition, and advice were also found. Bastounis (1996) examined the representation of madness on Greek television and claimed that a new representation of 'mental illness', which can be treated with psychotherapy and is regarded sympathetically, is emerging in opposition to representations of other kinds of madness, which continue to be seen negatively, paralleling Pradeilles' (1992) findings. Other works also emphasise a more sympathetic representation of the mental health service client as more sad than bad (Räty, 1990), a dualism that has existed in ideas about mental illness throughout history (Gilman, 1988; Porter, 1987). In a study of Finnish students, Räty (1990) found two main social representations of mental illness: the first, naturalistic, highlighted many of the themes already discussed, laid most emphasis on pathology and saw mental illness as a threat. It promoted fatalistic, rejecting attitudes towards mental illness, which was seen as leading to deviant behaviour and violence. The mentally ill were regarded as distinctly different, even inferior to other people. The second representation was based on a criticism of civilisation: mental illness was thought to have socio-ecological causes, and the mentally ill were cast as 'victims of society'. Portrayals of people diagnosed with mental health problems as passive, pitiful and in need of sympathy and support were also found in the study of the British media coverage of proposed changes to the Mental Health Bill, discussed above (Foster, 2006a).

In addition to more sympathetic representations, some theorists also suggest that there might be positive elements associated with mental ill health in the public mind: in particular, the notion that it might entail an element of creativity or even genius, a link highlighted by Foucault (1961), and reviewed by Repper and Perkins (2003), among others. Jamison (1996) discusses the link between creativity and bipolar disorder in some depth, reviewing the cases of numerous writers, artists, composers and their families.

While it is clear that these themes predominate in public understanding of mental ill health, it is important to know how the public actually defines the concept in the first place, and what they consequently consider to be mental illness. The accepted view in most research is that deviance is accepted by the public as long as it is not named 'mental illness' (Rabkin, 1974) and that a far wider range of eccentric behaviour is considered normal in society than mental health professionals imagine (Crocetti, Spiro & Siassi, 1974; Cumming & Cumming, 1957; Hall, Brockington, Levings & Murphy, 1993). The latter studies all employ the Star vignettes (Star, 1955, unpublished, cited in Cumming & Cumming, 1957), a selection of short descriptions of people defined by mental health professionals as 'paranoid schizophrenic', 'obsessive', 'delinquent' and so forth. Cumming and Cumming (1957) found that such behaviours were generally seen by the public as the result of experiences, and not mental illness. Crocetti et al. (1974) observed that the only vignette consistently labelled a mental illness was that of 'paranoid schizophrenia', although more recently Hall et al. (1993) found that only one quarter of respondents picked 'mental illness' out of a list of possible causes for the same vignette, preferring explanations such as childhood experience and stressful life events. The other vignettes were even less likely to be seen as mental illness. This difference in understanding between public and professionals leads some professionals to highlight the large amount of undiagnosed mental illness in society: individuals may not seek help because they do not see themselves as having a problem, and nor do those around them (Leff, 2001). Other research has found a lay confusion between what would be divided into mental illness and mental handicap by professionals (Reda, 1996).

Work on public ideas about the causes of mental illness suggests that the public are divided as to the aetiology of mental health problems: as suggested by the work above, the majority of studies find that the public tend to see mental ill health as rooted in social problems or experiences (MORI, 1979), with stress cited as the most common cause (Leff, 2001). This explains the overriding belief amongst the public that talking treatments are more successful in treating mental ill health than medication, which is inherently mistrusted (ibid).

Other recent work, however, conversely suggests that the public have come to mirror professionals in their views of the causes of mental illness, in what has been termed 'protoprofessionalism', and name a mixture of social and biological factors when asked about the causes of mental ill health (Rogers & Pilgrim, 1997). Supporting this, Rippere (1977; 1981) argued that the general public tend to display 'accurate' beliefs regarding the causes and coping strategies appropriate to depression.

The latter study highlights an important issue within research in this area, that of differentiation of mental ill health. Volumes such as the *Diagnostic and Statistical Manual of Mental Disorders* (American Psychiatric Association, 2000) and the *International Classification of Disease* (World Health Organisation, 1992) demonstrate the level to which professionals make distinctions between different kinds of mental health problem, yet, in contrast many research studies in the social sciences employ the more generic terms 'mental illness', 'mental health problems' and so on when examining public understanding, something which has been highlighted as a flaw in research in this area (Cormack & Furnham, 1998; Nieradzik & Cochrane, 1985). The issue of differentiation in public understanding is therefore sometimes masked.

However, some research has divided mental illness up, usually into its medical labels (e.g. Levey & Howells [1995] on schizophrenia). The results of such work suggest that the public makes some distinctions: Nunnally (1961), for example, claimed that people with neuroses are seen as weaker, and those with psychoses are liked less. Levey and Howells (1995) suggested that people diagnosed with schizophrenia are seen as different, unpredictable and often violent. This apparent parallel between the attitudes expressed towards mental illness in general and to schizophrenia has led some theorists to suggest that schizophrenia is in some senses the prototypical mental illness in public perception (Morant, 1996; Rabkin, 1974).

Stockdale and Purkhardt (1993) used multi-dimensional scaling to investigate differentiation within social representations of mental illness; they found that mental illnesses were divided up according to their effect on the sufferer's reasoning, the possibilities of treatment, how easy it is for others to deal with and how aware the sufferer is of his or her condition. Subsequent analysis revealed four distinct groups of mental illnesses (paedophilia, kleptomania, obsessive-compulsive disorder, agoraphobia; alcoholism, anorexia; paranoia, hysteria, anxiety, depression; psychopathy, multiple personality, schizophrenia). The latter was clearly separated from the others. However, content analysis of responses did not match these results entirely.

The topic of differentiation in representations of mental illness has also been considered in qualitative work: Pradeilles (1992) found that participants differentiated between more serious mental illness and 'nervous depression'. They referred to friends, acquaintances and those living in the community using the latter term, reserving 'mentally ill' for people needing hospitalisation, who remained 'Other'. Another study with student populations found that while different representations of mental illnesses do exist, both along medical lines and also along other continua, such as whether the individual is harmful or not, mental illness is also unified in representation: any condition that can be labelled mental illness is therefore affected by a representation of generic 'mental illness', which is seen as unpredictable, violent, incurable and Other (Foster, 1998; Foster, 2001).

To talk about the public as an undifferentiated group, however, might be similarly facile. Some studies have examined whether different groups within society have different attitudes towards mental illness. It has been suggested that education has an effect, the more educated being more tolerant and accepting (Brockington et al., 1993; Hall et al., 1993; Nunnally, 1961; Rabkin, 1972) but this has been disputed (Maclean, 1969). Similarly, some evidence has been found that positive attitudes towards mental illness are more common amongst the higher socio-economic groups (Brockington et al., 1993; Hall et al., 1993; Hollingshead & Redlich, 1958; Rabkin, 1972) or those with higher status (Taylor & Dear, 1981). The recent study undertaken by the Office for National Statistics (2003) supported this, finding that people from lower socio-economic groups and also people over the age of 55 were more likely to be in favour of greater restrictions on people with mental health problems, especially early hospitalisation. The same study also concluded that younger people are more likely to believe that there are sufficient existing mental health services. Lastly, Farina (1981) claimed that women are more likely to hold more positive, tolerant attitudes towards the mentally ill than men. Angermeyer, Matschinger and Hotzinger's (1998) work on German attitudes towards people with schizophrenia supported this, although a Finnish study found that men held more positive attitudes than women (Laine & Lehtinen, 1973). There seems, then, to be considerable confusion over which groups, if any, within society hold more negative attitudes towards people with mental illness.

The question of change over time in attitudes and opinions about mental illness is an equally contentious one. Crocetti et al. (1974) claimed that attitudes towards mental illness are becoming increasingly tolerant, and this is supported elsewhere (Bentz & Edgerton, 1971; Farina et al., 1978; Lemaku & Crocetti, 1962). In a more recent study, Brockington et al. (1993) echoed these results, although another part of the same project did not support this level of tolerance (Hall et al., 1993). The shift from institutionalised to community-based care has promoted several studies on this topic, as, perhaps following contact theories in the social psychology of prejudice, many theorists have hypothesised that attitudes might have become more positive towards individuals who use mental health services now that these services are situated within the community, and, to some extent, demystified. Taylor and Dear (1981), however, still found negative attitudes towards the mentally ill amongst those living near community mental health facilities, although other studies suggest that increased education and attempts to integrate staff and patients into the local communities may lead to greater attitude change and a more positive outcome (Wolff et al., 1999).

Other studies are less positive: an attempt to replicate the Crocetti et al. (1974) study failed (Olmstead & Durham, 1976), whereas the more negative studies by Cumming and Cumming (1957) and MORI (1979) have been replicated by D'Arcy and Brockman (1976) and Huxley (1993b) respectively. Similarly, as already briefly mentioned, the Department of Health has tracked attitudes towards mental ill health since 1993, using samples of around 2000 people in each study. Although the vast majority of people display sympathetic attitudes towards individuals with mental ill health, there has been an overall increase in intolerance of such individuals since 1993, as measured by items that focus on social distance, such as whether a respondent would be happy to live next door to someone with mental illness (Office for National Statistics, 2003). It could be concluded that negative attitudes towards mental illness are remarkably tenacious and historically grounded, something which is disappointing for organisations that try to mount campaigns to destigmatise mental health problems (Byrne, 1999).

Professional perspectives

Professional ideas and beliefs about mental illness obviously abound in both diagnostic manuals (American Psychiatric Association, 2000; World Health Organisation, 1992) and textbooks of psychiatry (Gelder, 1983) and psychology (Davison & Neale, 1994), although they are often not regarded as representations, but rather accepted versions of the truth about mental ill health.

Taking a social constructionist perspective, however, as high-lighted in Chapter 1, requires us to examine these professional notions in the same way that we would examine any form of knowledge. These texts, unsurprisingly, subscribe in the main to a biomedical model of mental illness, in which mental illness is highly differentiated into various groups and subgroups. There is, of course, fluidity in that certain diagnoses are included and excluded from one edition to the next, depending upon current thinking and research, and other developments: it is important not to underestimate the influence of the thinking, politics and ideology of wider society in these changes, as Kutchins and Kirk (1999) point out, especially in relation to their discussion of the removal of homosexuality from the *DSM-II* in 1974. Schoeneman, Clark, Gibson, Routbort and Jacobs (1994) also show how this process of development can then be adapted to present a particu-lar picture of professional thinking: numerous textbooks on abnormal psychology use the same pictures in historical chapters, perpetuating an ideology of the mentally ill as low status Others, and a 'Whiggish' interpretation of the history of mental health care as one of progress brought about by heroic figures.

Professional journals are also useful sources of information on professional understanding: Schurmans (1990) analyses the images found in adverts for psychiatric medication, finding repetition of polarisations between light and dark, bestial and human, rising and falling. She supplements this analysis with a consideration of the way in which the history of psychiatry is presented in medical thinking, demonstrating how professionals present a progression from religious speculation to scientific understanding, paralleling some of the arguments made by Schoeneman et al. (1994).

Some of the more interesting work which details professional views and beliefs about mental health and illness comes from research that was designed to challenge the psychiatric profession. Two famous examples are the studies by Rosenhan (1973) and Temerlin (1968). Rosenhan (1973) sent 8 research confederates to 12 psychiatric hospitals as 'pseudo-patients', falsely claiming that they had heard voices. All were admitted, at which point they reported no longer hearing voices and answered all subsequent enquiries truthfully. Despite this, all the pseudo-patients were kept in hospital for periods ranging between 9 and 52 days, and their 'normal' behaviour (such as keeping a diary) and responses to questions about relationships and past history were seen as confirmatory of their diagnosis and psychopathology. Interestingly, the other patients on the wards were not taken in.

Temerlin (1968) found that psychiatrists in particular were more likely than clinical psychologists or students to diagnose a normal actor with some kind of mental health problem, and that this was especially the case if the situation were manipulated so that they were 'allowed' to overhear an eminent professional making a diagnosis before the tape was shown.

These examples show how deep seated many professional beliefs are and how mental health professionals have the power to define the normal and the abnormal (Morant, 1998a; Repper & Perkins, 2003), often with far-reaching consequences: in Rosenhan's (1973) study, not only were all pseudo-patients hospitalised, but they were labelled 'schizophrenic in remission' on discharge. Studies like this also challenge the idea of objectivity in diagnosis, demonstrating the relevance, often implicit, of other factors that might come into play.

Another important study, again using social representations theory, was carried out by Morant (1995; 1996; 1998b), who found that mental health professionals represent mental illness as a polymorphic category, which is thus not clearly defined. Similarly, professionals preferred to maintain an agnostic stance with regard to the causes of mental illness. However, despite this there was evidence that psychosis and neurosis were differentiated: while neurosis was seen as more understandable, more likely to be a reaction to events and more a possibility for anyone, psychosis was set apart, seen as more likely to be organic in nature and as more irredeemably Other. Schizophrenia and manic depression were regarded as prototypical psychoses, depression inhabited a grey area, and phobias, anxieties and obsessions were all viewed as neuroses. In addition, professionals did not express the fear so ubiquitous in public representations.

Zani (1993) similarly found that students and professionals in the field of psychology expressed less social distance between themselves and the mentally ill than those with no connection with psychology.

Some research into professional understandings of mental health problems and people diagnosed with them takes the form of comparisons between results of semantic differential tests with staff and patients in mental hospitals, much of it undertaken in the 1960s. For example, Imre (1962) reported that mental hospital staff and volunteers were, perhaps unsurprisingly, more positive towards hospitals than patients, whilst Imre and Wolf (1962) found alcoholic patients, as well as staff, more favourably disposed to mental hospitals than non-alcoholic patients. Delange (1962) found considerable heterogeneity in attitudes to mental illness amongst staff, some of it dependent upon the category of staff member. Staff have also been found to have less authoritarian attitudes towards mental illness than patients (Mayo & Havelock, 1970), although older staff might hold more custodial attitudes than younger professionals (Bates, 1968). Ethnographic work from the same period found similar results: in particular, nurses have more custodial attitudes to mental illness and tend to be less optimistic about the outcome of mental ill health (Caudill, 1958; Caudill, Redlich, Gilmore & Brody, 1952; Stanton & Schwarz, 1954). The finding that nurses have more negative attitudes towards mental illness than doctors is echoed in some more recent work in other countries (Sevigny et al., 1999). In particular, work in Italy using similar methodological techniques, but drawing on social representations theory, comes to similar conclusions: Bellelli (1987b), for example, considered the representations of a variety of mental health professionals and students, finding that the views of psychiatric nurses were closer to those of the public than to psychiatrists and psychologists and that overall a cyclical model of mental illness was preferred to an acute one. Petrillo (1987) found similar divisions between nurses and other kinds of professional, the former being less ready to discriminate between the 'mentally ill person' and the 'mad person', in what Petrillo (1987) terms 'pre-medical thinking'. Serino (1987) explained these results with reference to the difference in goals and professional cultures between the groups and the asymmetrical power relations that exist between social groups. However, professional differences might also extend beyond the nurse/other divide: Zani (1987) claimed that psychologists tend towards a more socio-relational conception of mental illness, whereas psychiatrists prefer the more medical-biological.

Manktelow (1994), a social worker, studied numerous aspects of the psychiatric system and the ideas he found within it: he claimed that younger doctors were more moralistic than their elders about mental illness. He also found differences between psychiatrists and general practitioners (GPs): while psychiatrists divided their clients into 'deserving' and 'undeserving', GPs were closer to the general public in their acceptance of disruptive behaviour and their avoidance of labelling. This latter point is supported by Leff (2001), who regards GPs as gatekeepers, claiming that they intentionally only refer 1 in 20 patients diagnosed with a neurotic illness to a specialist, and unintentionally fail to recognise the presence of such an illness in 1 in 3 patients. Guimelli (2000), in another Italian study, found fewer differences: although GPs saw medicine as more effective and depression as easier to diagnose than psychiatrists, both professional groups were unified in their conviction that depression could be differentiated into more serious and more benign cases.

Mental health service user/client perspectives researched within the social sciences

Historically, several key figures within psychiatry have gone against the general trend of failing to consider the views and ideas of mental health service clients. I will briefly highlight two important movements here – psychoanalysis and anti-psychiatry. There is much to be said on both these movements, but the focus of this discussion will be on the opportunities they have afforded people diagnosed with mental health problems to speak out and to put forward their own views of their experiences.

Sigmund Freud, and his followers, played an important role in listening to the voice of people with mental health problems. Prior to Freud, so-called mad doctors and other professionals had made little attempt to talk to their patients (Porter, 1987). As Prior (1991) says, however, in contrast, in Freudian analysis patients were seen as having minds of their own and were located at the centre of the therapeutic process. The reliance within psychoanalysis is on inviting the patient to free-associate, to remember their dreams, to engage in the kind of long-standing, lengthy talking treatment so famously described by Anna O, one of Freud's first patients as the 'talking cure' or 'chimney sweeping'[2] (Freud & Breuer, 1955, p. 83). However, although the patient is treated as a whole in the psychoanalytic encounter, symptoms are still degraded: the content of patients' understanding becomes important, but only from the point of view of the unconscious elements behind it, not for what is being said by the patient per se. Again, the opportunities for the patient to really speak out are limited: the trained analyst is the privileged one and the key to interpreting the patient's problems, labelling any disagreement on the part of the patient as resistance. This has led to significant criticism of the psychoanalytic movement (Gellner, 2003).

Some of the most famous opportunities for those labelled mentally ill to speak out came in the 1960s through the so-called anti-psychiatry movement,[3] made up of a number of psychiatrists in the United Kingdom and the United States who challenged accepted definitions and modes of treatment and drew attention to the wider context of 'mental illness'.

One of the most prominent of these was R. D. Laing, who maintained that mental illness has to be understood in its existential context (Laing, 1960). He claimed that the standard clinical interview was insufficient to establish the real meaning of the 'mental illness' exhibited, and his works are littered with dialogue from those labelled mentally ill and their families (e.g. Laing & Esterson, 1964). Indeed, Laing even reinterprets other famous examples of 'dialogue' between psychiatrist and patient, such as that of Kraeplin in 1905, ridiculing the professional's role and their inability to hear what was really being said in the encounter (Laing, 1960). In this way we are given the opportunity to hear the 'mentally ill' person's voice and are encouraged to see their 'mental illness' as a means of expression of problems in their situations and circumstances, such as within their family and other relationships. Laing was partly responsible for the foundation of a therapeutic community in the east end of London. Mary Barnes co-authored a book detailing her own experience of 'going down' into madness in this environment (Barnes & Berke, 1971).

The above theorists, and many others such as Szasz (1961), then, all attempt to encourage a more critical stance towards accepted theories and ideas about mental illness and the mentally ill, and often give more opportunity for those diagnosed as mentally ill to speak through their work. There is still, however, the issue of power to contend with: however much the person labelled 'mentally ill' is allowed to speak, the majority of text is still constructed by the theorist, and it is their interpretations, not those of the person labelled mentally ill, that are proffered. Barnes' story presents a slightly different case, but it is still backed up by the more authoritative voice of Berke. Szasz, for example, continues to present the mental health profession in a privileged light: it is still required to interpret the symptoms expressed by the service user (Rogers et al., 1993). In addition, there is a tendency in early anti-psychiatry, in its rush to see mental ill health as largely socially fabricated, to fail to acknowledge the distress that mental ill health can cause a client (Miller & Rose, 1986).

In other areas of more mainstream psychiatry and psychology, and in parallel with many studies on professional understanding, a large proportion of the work undertaken on service users' views stems from 1960's America and relies on semantic differential or Q-sort testing. Typically, this work involves patients at mental hospitals being asked to rate concepts such as 'Mental patient' or 'Insane man', 'Psychiatrist', 'Me' and so forth on adjectival scales such as dangerous-safe, and boring-interesting. These results are then compared with the same scales as filled in by people without diagnoses of mental health problems or by mental health professionals. The results of such studies are strikingly similar. The 'mental patient' is seen very negatively, as dirty and dangerous, by both patients and the lay population alike (Giovanni & Ullmann, 1963; Johannsen, 1969; Rabkin, 1972). Crumpton, Weinstein, Acker and Annis (1967), however, claim to have found small differences between patient and public views: those with schizophrenia see the mentally ill as not sick, but immoral, safe and inconsequential, whereas the general public see the mentally ill as sick but moral, and to be pitied and feared. As discussed earlier, it has also been suggested that patients subscribe to a more authoritarian model of mental illness than staff (Mayo & Havelock, 1970).

Backner and Kissinger (1963) tested the hypothesis that the patients of different services might have different opinions about mental illness, but this was not supported empirically. Patients from open and closed psychiatric wards, neurological wards, orthopaedic and convalescent wards all rated concepts in a similar way, leading this study to conclude that mental patients see themselves as just as worthless and incomprehensible as non-mental patients. Similarly, Crumpton and Groot (1966) found no differences between more and less disturbed patients: all rated the mentally ill as ugly, dirty, sad and so forth, and preferred to class themselves as 'suffering from nerves', not 'mental patient'. Manis, Houts and Blake's (1963) study is an exception and does emphasise differences: those on closed psychiatric wards were more moralistic in their views of mental illness; those diagnosed with schizophrenia saw mental illness as particularly hopeless, whereas those diagnosed with depression saw it as more serious. This study also found that patients who held views similar to those of their therapists had a better prognosis.

Not all work from this era employs semantic differential tests, however. Jones, Kahn and MacDonald (1963) used a questionnaire survey to study all aspects of the psychiatric patient's experience. In particular, they considered the causes assigned to mental illness and suggested that mental health service users see mental illness in psychological terms, as a mixture of the unavoidable and things for which they are responsible, but not as a condition of the mind per se (Jones et al., 1963).

Other studies find patients predominantly citing marital conflict in explanations for their hospitalisation (Wood, Rakusin & Morse, 1960), or other external factors as opposed to internal ones (Mills, 1962). This is paralleled in Molvaer, Hantzi and Papadatos's (1992) more recent work on attributions for psychosis. Unsurprisingly, much work finds a multiplicity of causes cited, and diverse explanations for psychotic experiences (Coursey, Keller & Farrell, 1995; Greenfeld, Strauss, Bowers & Mandelkern, 1989) and for depression (Lewis, 1995).

Labelling theory, which is often associated with the anti-psychiatry movement and will be discussed in greater detail in Chapter 6, has also prompted numerous studies that focus on the views expressed by mental health service users themselves. In developing his theory, Scheff (1966) did not actually conduct any research directly with participants with mental health problems: instead, he relied on existing studies, and conducted research himself on the labelling process with psychiatrists and through observing judicial hearings regarding hospitalisation. Although this was something that Scheff himself recognised as a problem, it has, among other criticisms, led to considerable discussion in subsequent literature as to the accuracy of his theory and prompted further research. Weinstein (1983) is highly critical of labelling theory and uses a meta-analysis to claim that studies that actually seek the views of participants with mental health problems fail to support Scheff's (1966) idea that mental illness is learned rule-breaking and role-taking. Instead, they show that mental patients have less stereotyped ideas of mental illness as a result of hospital-isation and that on leaving hospital they successfully move away from a deviant career, giving credence to the theory that client understanding of mental ill health does in fact differ significantly from that of the general public.

Self-concept and self-esteem are also particular foci in main-stream psychology and psychiatry. Some studies, again, employ semantic differentials to compare the concepts of Self and signifi-cant Other held by the patient himself[4] and someone close to him. One study suggests that patients both have a lower self-concept than their spouses' concept of them, and see themselves in more negative terms than they see their spouses (Harrow, Fox & Detre, 1969). A study of adolescents and their parents paralleled these results (Harrow, Fox & Markhus, 1968), thereby suggesting that diagnosis and mental health service use have some kind of negative impact on self-esteem and self-image. Kennard (1974), however, found that patients saw themselves as closer to an ideal version of themselves than their significant Other did and that this was especially true for those diagnosed psychotic.

However, in addition to the obvious lack of consistency in these different findings, there are also significant methodological issues surrounding the use of semantic differentials in the study of service user beliefs about mental illness. Apart from the fact that there is no opportunity to probe, ask for qualification or discover what the concepts being rated may really mean to participants, there is also the issue of labelling. In some of the studies discussed earlier, there is the assumption that 'mental patient' will be a term that patients in a mental hospital will readily assign to themselves, when this may not necessarily be the case. These studies are of limited value, then, in trying to understand the meanings given to mental illness by users of mental health services.

Clients' attitudes towards mental health services are currently, and quite rightly, something of a vogue topic in the mental health services, but studies have focussed on it for some time: Weinstein (1983) cites 12 in his review, which mainly employ questionnaires and scales as a means of sampling attitudes. Such studies vary somewhat, but these, and later projects, report that the majority of patients feel positive towards hospitals (Chastko, Glick, Gould & Hargreaves, 1971; Kotin & Schur, 1969), their treatment (Freeman & Kendell [1980] on ECT; Wolfson & Paton [1996] on clozapine use) and towards staff (Weinstein, 1981). This satisfaction is not, however, universal: some studies report greater heterogeneity (Linn, 1968) or dissatisfaction, (Mills, 1962; Sonn, 1977) and users are frequently forthcoming with suggestions for improvement (Jones et al., 1963). Gynther and Brilliant (1964) claimed that differences in attitudes towards hospitals are functions of class and education, those with less education and from lower socio-economic groups having more custodial attitudes. This finding parallels studies discussed earlier in which the general public participated, providing further evidence that public and user views of mental illness may coincide to some extent. A more likely explanation, however, which will be addressed in Chapter 3, is that the results of such studies depend significantly on who is conducting them, and how, and that this has a greater influence on how clients respond.

More recently mainstream psychiatry has begun to show more interest in the effects of beliefs and ideas about mental illness on service users' careers through the mental health services. As discussed in Chapter 1, this is due partly to the rise in consumerism (Rogers & Pilgrim, 1993) and democratisation (Bracken & Thomas, 2005) in the health services, and partly to an increasing recognition that what a client thinks about his or her health and treatment might influence behaviour and attitude. The Royal College of Psychiatrists has recently spear-headed a campaign to counteract the stigma of mental illness (Byrne, 1999), and there is a growing awareness that one of the potential ways of doing this is to increase understanding about the experience of mental illness from the client's point of view (Chadwick, 1997a).

An example of this increasing interest in client perspectives is that of the journal *Schizophrenia Bulletin* which carries an occasional feature entitled 'First Person Account', in which users are encouraged to detail their thoughts and experiences (e.g. Bowden, 1993). However, the introduction states that accounts are more welcome from 'articulate' users, and it could be argued that professionals are encouraged to act as gatekeepers, suggesting to certain users that their accounts might be appropriate. This has often been the case in other professional journals in which users are encouraged to tell their stories: one is often conscious of the voice of therapy speaking through the text (e.g. Anon, 1955).

The sub-discipline of social psychiatry has often paid more attention to the views of the mental health service users than more mainstream psychiatry has. Bastide (1972), however, noted that social psychiatry struggled both to define itself and to establish its credibility. He claimed that there has been resistance towards it because of its implication that society plays a role in mental health, something that psychiatry can be unwilling to accept. Leff (2001) has more recently pointed out that, despite an increased awareness of the social context of mental health problems, funding for social psychiatry has plummeted over the past few years, in the wake of increased interest in the biological basis of mental health problems. However, Bracken and Thomas (2005) claim that this emphasis on the biological (and concurrent links with the pharmaceutical industry) is more obvious in academic psychiatry, while in practice, psychiatrists are more open to models of mental ill health that emphasise social context.

Despite these problems, social psychiatry has provided some useful insights into client understanding. Most notably, it focuses on patient satisfaction studies and on 'quality of life' measures. In many ways, much of the work on the views clients have about the services they use and the studies on quality of life have methodological parallels and stem from similar psychiatric perspectives. They rely heavily on various scales and standardised questionnaires developed in recent years (e.g. Fitzpatrick & Hopkins, 1993). Callan and Littlewood (1998) believe that the rise in such patients' satisfaction studies stems both from a shift in emphasis in the health services towards compliance with treatment, which can be problematic (Williams, 1994), and also from the rise of the mental health service user movement, which presses for change. 'Quality of life' work draws largely on scales, such as the Lehman quality of life survey to measure the 'subjective' quality of life experienced by mental health service clients. In general, such work finds fairly high levels of quality of life, despite adverse conditions (Trauer, Duckmanton & Chiu, 1998). Some aspects of service use are associated with higher quality of life scores, such as using new anti-psychotic medication (Awad & Vorugarti, 1999) or attending a clubhouse (Warner, Huxley & Berg, 1999).

While such studies are certainly useful, and go some way towards redressing the current imbalance in mainstream psychiatric and psychological literature in terms of user views, they are perhaps less useful than work on user views that has gone on outside the area, for example in the service user movement itself. This will be discussed in the next chapter. In addition, as Crawford & Kessel (1999) point out, quantification of satisfaction is somewhat simplistic and masks a great deal of dissatisfaction with services; they note the importance of a broader methodological approach, including interviewing and ethnography. Letendre (1997), for example, casts doubt on quantitative satisfaction studies, claiming that by using qualitative 'focused accounts', he found that patients in hospital complained of everyday boredom and showed ambivalence towards their medication.

Work considering the views of clients of the mental health services has also gone on in other areas of the social sciences, such as social psychology. In general, studies taking the perspective of the theory of social representations have paid relatively little attention to the understandings of mental ill health held by users of the mental health services. This is an interesting omission, given the strong tradition of research into social representations of mental ill health among the public discussed earlier, and the fact that researchers using social representations theory are more usually interested in the understanding of people directly affected by an issue/concept: for example, in studying representations of HIV/AIDS, Marková (1990) interviewed families affected by haemophilia, while Joffe (1996; 1999) talked to sexually active gay and heterosexual men in the UK and South Africa.

A possible exception is the work of Fainzang (1995), who focused on alcoholics' representations of the effects of alcohol on the body. Despite substantial heterogeneity, central themes did exist, such as the role of the nerves in aggression and loss of self-control. The blood is represented as transporting alcohol around the body to the organs which consequently become infected. By ceasing drinking, the organs can be purified, and this state can be maintained through abstention. However, Fainzang (1995) does not discuss whether alcoholism is seen as a mental illness by her participants. Another interesting study is that of Maia de Nobrega (1999) in north east Brazil: although the majority of this study focuses on the representations held by the families of people with mental illness, which tend to centre again on the animalistic and child-like elements of the family member with a mental health problem, a small sample of patients were also interviewed about their ideas. Nobrega (1999) found that patients focused in particular on how little they could remember about their experiences, their past and themselves; they demonstrated an '*oubli de soi*',[5] but at the same time tended to maintain that they were not mad, but suffering from nerves, in contrast to the other patients in the hospital who were mad and should be feared.

In addition, many of the studies in Bellelli's (1987a) collection, referred to earlier in this chapter, include patients, or those who have experienced mental illness, amongst their participants. However, most make little reference to any differences in representations found between patients and other groups (e.g. Bellelli, 1987b), although on occasions specific mention of client understanding is made: Ayestran Etxeberria (1987), for example, claimed that patients in psychiatric hospitals and their relatives see the mentally ill person as further from normality than patients in mental health centres and their families; Paez Rovira (1987) stated that patients are more likely to label various vignettes as normal than their families or 'normal' participants would.

In the related area of subjective theories, Angermeyer (1992) discusses the attributions patients diagnosed with psychosis give for their problems, finding an overwhelming emphasis on social elements in causation, especially stress, at the expense of the biological. Krause Jacob (1992) focused on the change over time of clients' subjective theories, showing how they come to parallel those of their therapists.

In sociology, Erving Goffman (1959a; 1961) conducted an ethnographic study of life in an asylum, focusing on the 'moral career' of the mental patient, as he/she becomes an increasing part of the total institution of the mental hospital and consequently loses his/her sense of self. Goffman (1968) also analysed stigma, including the stigma of mental illness, concentrating on the ways in which individuals manage stigmatised identities. Although useful, Goffman's work is limited by the fact that he acts as mediator between the reader and clients, who speak directly only rarely, and by lack of methodological transparency. It has, however, inspired many other studies, including Karmel (1969) who states that, contrary to Goffman's claims, sense of identity and self-esteem actually increase over the duration of the hospital stay. Swanson and Spitzer (1970) suggest that 'post-patients' (i.e. those who have left hospital) feel less stigmatised than in-patients, as they possess discreditable, rather then discredited, identities. Barham and Hayward (1991), however, found it was all too easy for the ex-patient to be discredited as a P(mp) (Person-mental patient) for the rest of their lives. This work will be discussed in more depth in Chapter 6.

There is also a wider sociological literature focusing on disability which sometimes touches on issues relevant to mental health. Recently, for example, studies have been carried out on the views of people with dementia (Proctor, 2001; Reid, Ryan & Enderby, 2001) and of people with autism (James, Zahl & Huws, 2001). These studies show the importance of listening to people traditionally thought of as 'incompetent', or incomprehensible, and the valuable results that can be obtained.

Moving on: some conclusions

There are, then, clearly gaps in social science literature when it comes to a comprehensive understanding of the meaning of mental illness for those who might be labelled mentally ill, although there have long been calls to consider this topic from psychiatry (Guzé, 1957; McIntyre, Farrell & David, 1989; Mechanic, 1962; Sonn, 1977), anthropology (Wallace, 1972), sociology (Weinstein, 1972) and psychology (Kahn, Jones, MacDonald, Conners & Burchard, 1963). It is also clear that, although those who use mental health services are defined as 'mentally ill' in the representations held by many groups within society (Foster, 1998; Jodelet, 1991; Morant, 1996), mental health service clients themselves have often been given little opportunity to express their ideas in social science research.

This chapter has aimed to demonstrate several points. First, that in any study of the understanding of mental illness held by users or clients of mental health services, the representations held by public and mental health professionals must be taken into consideration: knowledge does not develop or exist within a social vacuum; nor do mental health service clients exist in total isolation from other social groups and their ideas. While this review provides evidence of the diversity within public and professional representations, some themes emerge. Work in a variety of areas on public understanding of mental illness finds negative and historically enduring representations of mental illness as 'Other', while work with professionals finds greater differentiation, with elements of Otherness contained within representations of particular conditions, especially psychosis.

Conclusions regarding the themes within clients' representations are harder to draw, first because of the comparative paucity of studies on the topic, and second because of their overall focus on opinions about services rather than about mental illness itself. Conflicting evidence suggests that clients might see mental illness either in similar terms to the general public, or to mental health professionals. In addition, much academic work in the area of service user understanding relies on somewhat limited methodology, usually quantitative testing of some kind, while work on public and professional understanding has employed a much greater variety of qualitative and quantitative techniques.

Another important issue, already briefly mentioned in this chapter, is the issue of who is conducting the research: how far does the researcher mediate what is said by clients when presenting their views and beliefs? Indeed, how far does what a client says in a research project in the first place depend on who is asking the questions? This leads us to arguments raised within the mental health service user movement, and to the research that has gone on into client and survivor understandings within these organisations: this significant development will be the focus of Chapter 3.

3 Perspectives from clients and the mental health service user movement

Although, as the previous two chapters demonstrate, society's habit of not listening to the views and ideas of those diagnosed and labelled as mentally ill is both culturally deeply engrained and historically enduring, this does not mean that they have been silent. We may have to look harder, and to turn, at least until recently, outside academic work, but individuals with mental health problems tell of their experiences and beliefs in many places. This chapter will review some of this work, taking a historical perspective and firstly discussing autobiography and similar writings, before moving on to discuss more recent work undertaken within the mental health service user movement and to consider this very important development.

Autobiography and other writings

Although it is perhaps not customary to do so, social scientists might have much to learn from art and literature (Moscovici, 1972). Repper and Perkins (2003) claim that such personal accounts of mental health problems offer insights that cannot be obtained through descriptions that rely on symptoms and diagnoses. Sommer and Osmond (1960) maintain that more use should be made by mental health professionals of the numerous autobiographies written by those labelled mentally ill and have produced two bibliographies of relevant works (Sommer & Osmond, 1960; 1983). Psychiatrists themselves, they suggest that such texts may not have been attended to in the past because 'It is almost as if we really did not want to hear our patients' opinions of the care we provide' (p. 649).

41

The failure to consider autobiography may, of course, stem from the same reluctance to include those considered to be mentally ill in wider research. However, it is also possible that the autobiography is thought to be too tainted with notions of bias, dramatisation or fiction to be considered useful to social scientists and mental health professionals. Certainly, its utility can be questioned on one level: it seems unlikely that all mental health service users are equally likely to write an autobiography, and have it accepted for publication, although the ways that the service user movement has challenged this will be discussed later. The establishment of organisations like the Survivors' Press, based in Glasgow, has certainly made publication more of a possibility for any client.

It does, however, seem more than coincidental that the authors of many autobiographies are often learned and respected, sometimes academics (Sutherland, 1976), medical professionals (Jamison, 1995; Wield, 2006) or writers (Styron, 1991), *before* the onset of their mental illness. Other autobiographies are clearly written by people with money or power in the first instance (Barrymore & Frank, 1957; J. T., 1904). Many of the autobiographies available contain editing or commentaries by mental health professionals (e.g. Barnes & Berke, 1971; Bateson, 1961; Coate, 1964; Read, 1989): it seems that this is a way of lending to the story an authority and credibility it might otherwise be seen as lacking.

However, a very large number of books written by individuals considered to have a mental health problem have been published, testifying to their enduring appeal: some have become cult classics, and turned into films (e.g. the recent examples of Elizabeth Wurtzel's *Prozac Nation* [Wurtzel, 1996] and Susanna Kaysen's *Girl, Interrupted* [Kaysen, 2000]). This is not the place to review all these autobiographies, but, given their importance in filling a glaring gap in our knowledge of understandings about mental health problems and the fact that they highlight certain themes which are also to be found in the research into client understanding undertaken by the mental health service user movement and within academia, it is important to emphasise their potential.

One of the easiest ways to access older writings is through some of the edited collections that have been published that aim to bring together the writings of those with mental health problems down the years (e.g. Peterson, 1982; Porter, 1991). However, while certainly making such writings more accessible, they are still mediated to a large extent: Porter (1991), for example, selects passages to illustrate particular themes and includes them alongside writings about madness by other individuals, including professionals, thereby limiting the opportunities for any thorough consideration of the views of those labelled mad or mentally ill.

Collections of more recent writings have also been published, drawing together a variety of pieces by clients and former clients of the mental health services. Some of these are very short: many of the contributions in Read and Reynolds (1996), for example, are less than a page, while other collections tend to feature longer pieces (e.g. Curtis, Dellar, Leslie & Watson, 2000). Similarly, while some focus on a variety of experiences and diagnoses, others invite contributors to tell their stories about specific conditions and experiences, including stories from people with eating disorders (Shelley, 1997) and sexual abuse survivors (Walker, 1992).

An early, and important, autobiographical text is that of John Perceval, who published his treaty on his incarceration and treatment for madness in the nineteenth century and founded the Alleged Lunatics' Friend Society in 1845, often regarded as the forerunner of the British service user movement. Perceval details the onset of his 'lunacy', his delusions and his 'unnatural treatment' at the hands of lunatic doctors (Bateson, 1961, p. 69), before suggesting improvements that should be made to our understanding and treatment of insanity.

In common with Perceval's narrative, many texts written by individuals diagnosed with a mental health problem seem to be written with the aim of re-dressing the balance and putting across a client's own perspective, challenging the professional views that he or she has been subject to. Some of the more high-profile autobiographical texts include those written by Daniel Schreber (Schreber, 1988) and Sergius Pankejeff (Freud's Wolf Man) (Pankejeff, 1972), both of which attempted to provide alternative or complementary views to those written about them in Freud's case studies.

Inevitably, conflict with mental health professionals is a continuing theme in many autobiographical texts, further supporting the notion that people diagnosed with mental health problems are far from passive receptacles for psychiatric knowledge but instead form their own ideas and opinions, and feel the need to voice these.

There is also a strong tradition of poetry written by people who have used mental health services, including some published collections (e.g. Smith & Sweeney, 1997; Bethlem and Maudsley NHS Trust, 1997). Many user organisation newsletters contain poetry sections, and there is a national organisation, Survivors' Poetry, which is also made up of smaller local groups who organise regular readings. This provides another resource for people interested in understanding clients' perspectives on the experience and actuality of mental health problems.

The mental health service user movement

A brief history

The development of the mental health service user movement over the past 20 years has, in many ways, radically altered the possibilities that clients and former clients of the mental health services have to speak out about their ideas and experiences.

A recent report on the mental health service user movement by the Sainsbury Centre for Mental Health (Wallcraft, Read & Sweeney, 2003) shows that many of the activities that mental health service user groups engage in centre on the dissemination of client ideas and beliefs, both to other clients and other parties, in the form of support and self-help, education and training, campaigning, advocacy and so on. A particularly important development has been user-led research, a topic which will be discussed in some depth later in this chapter.

Given the importance of the mental health service user movement in promoting client understanding of mental ill health and that it is only relatively recently that there has been a concentrated consideration of the growth of the movement (see, e.g. Barnes & Bowl, 2001; Campbell, 2005; Rogers & Pilgrim, 2001; Wallcraft et al., 2003), it is worth focusing on its history in a little more detail, before considering the findings of some of the studies that have been conducted within the movement.

Although certain forerunners of the mental health service user movement, such as John Perceval's Alleged Lunatics' Friend

Society, set up in 1845, and the Mental Hygiene movement of the early twentieth century, have been identified, there was little organised user/survivor activity in the United Kingdom until the 1970s, when two organisations, The Community Organisation for Psychiatric Emergencies and the Mental Patients' Union, were established. The latter organisation published the 'Fish Pamphlet' in 1974, detailing the need for a Union, and the ways in which such a group should fight for the rights of mental patients. The document was recently reproduced in *Mad Pride: a celebration of mad culture* (Curtis et al., 2000). However, despite the background of anti-psychiatry and hospital scandals against which these groups developed, they received little media attention. The Mental Patients' Union went through various transformations, ending up as the Campaign Against Psychiatric Oppression in the 1980s. Around this time, the movement began to diversify as more groups sprang up. In particular, the growth of the advocacy movement in the United Kingdom began, although it was already fairly well established in countries such as the United States and the Netherlands by this point. In addition, the organisation Survivors Speak Out was also founded in the late 1980s, and the first national conference of mental health service user activists was held at Edale Youth Hostel in 1987, agreeing on a 'Charter of Needs and Demands' which highlighted the importance of a non-medicalised service that valued first-hand experience and the rights of mental health service clients (Beresford, 2005).

This diversity has continued to be a theme in the mental health service user movement (or perhaps, more appropriately, movements): several organisations attempt to represent the interests of more than one group, and debate continues as to how effective this can be. For example, MIND, formerly the National Association for Mental Health, is made up of a variety of individuals with an interest in mental health, including professionals, carers and users. A user network, MindLink, was set up as a result of the MIND 1988 conference, Common Concerns, but some people remain wary of the role of professionals within MIND (Rogers and Pilgrim, 1991). A similar situation exists with regards to Rethink, formerly the National Schizophrenia Fellowship: as Rogers & Pilgrim (1991) say, although they too have a branch specifically for users, the National Voices Forum, the National Schizophrenia Fellowship's initial role was to provide support to the carers of people with schizophrenia; this 'collusion' has caused some tension with other more user-focused organisations. Shepherd, Murray and Muijen (1994) point out that trying to accommodate both client and carer perspectives can be problematic, especially when work suggests that their views and needs can diverge so significantly (Cleary, Freeman, Hunt & Walter, 2005).

However, one should not assume that even if an organisation concentrates on clients or former clients of the mental health services there will be an automatic commonality of views. Wallcraft et al. (2003) highlight four issues on which the 318 groups surveyed in their study agree on: these are the need to be treated as an individual, dissatisfaction with mental health services, opposition to any extension to compulsory treatment, demands for an end to discrimination and prejudice, and for services based on social inclusion and the notion of recovery. There are also, however, four main issues on which opinion diverges: these con-troversial issues are forced treatment, the biomedical versus social models of mental illness, the need for the mental health service user movement to work with the wider disability movement and the relationship between groups and drug companies. Repper and Perkins (2003) maintain that there are broadly two categories of user organisation: on the one hand, the more 'radical' anti-psychiatric organisations that seek to challenge the status quo, and on the other, the more reformist or consumerist groups that seek to improve existing services.

Part of my own study detailed in this book examined material written by clients and former clients of the mental health services in newsletters produced by mental health organisations: several of these differences were evident in the way in which different groups approached issues of treatment, medication, power and so on. For example, *A Single Step*, the magazine of Depression Alliance, included many readers' experiences and recommendations for self-help, but would always include a caveat 'Please note that you should never change or alter your medication, or start to take any other preparation or herbal remedy, without first consulting your GP' (A Single Step, Summer 2000). Similarly, they received sponsorship from Priory Healthcare Ltd,[1] who both supported the publication financially and commissioned some articles by professionals to appear in it.[2] In comparison, Pendulum, the magazine of MDF – the Bipolar Organisation, focused in depth on self-management programmes, inviting readers to share their understanding and challenging psychiatric practices on the basis that MDF members were 'experts by experience'; no caveats were included in this, and the independence of the MDF from the medical establishment was emphasised.

One major difference often lies in the origins of the organisation: once again, there is substantial diversity here. As already mentioned, MIND was formerly known as the National Association for Mental Health, which grew out of the amalgamation of three Mental Hygiene organisations (Central Association for Mental Welfare, National Council for Mental Hygiene and Child Guidance Council) in the mid-1940s. Consequently, its membership and outlook over the years are likely to have been influenced by these more mainstream, health service-based origins, although users are now involved to a much greater extent. In contrast, the grassroots level of organisations such as the UK Advocacy Network (UKAN) or Survivors Speak Out, that have grown up outside the health service or voluntary sector often reflect different attitudes and present more of a challenge to the medical model of mental illness and to accepted ideas and definitions.

An interesting development in the past ten years has been the appearance and activities of two other related movements, Reclaim Bedlam and Mad Pride. Both of these organisations approach issues of mental health and illness very much from outside the mainstream. They are less sympathetic towards the involvement of 'allies'[3] in their activities and focus explicitly on challenging the mental health establishment and on political activism. Reclaim Bedlam was set up in 1997 as a direct response to what some survivors saw as the hypocrisy of the Royal Bethlem and Maudsley Hospital celebrating its anniversary as '750 years of health in mind'. It focused instead on highlighting the abuses within the psychiatric system and organised various demonstrations and protests: Reclaim Bedlam marched on the headquarters of SANE (Schizophrenia a national emergency), the organisation headed by Marjorie Wallace that is associated more with carers and campaigns for increased hospitalisation (Rogers & Pilgrim, 2001), and was also present at the Hutton Report in 2004 into the death of Dr David Kelly as part of its ongoing campaign to highlight suicide.

Mad Pride grew out of Reclaim Bedlam in 1999, originally intended more as the entertainment wing of the survivor movement, although it now engages in a variety of activities. The organisation explicitly models itself on the Gay Pride movement (Bracken & Thomas, 2005). The importance of language is paramount here, with many (although not all) individuals within the organisation seeing 'Mad' as a term of abuse that needs to be reclaimed and redefined by those who have been labelled with it. There is much debate on the organisation's website (http://www.ctono.freeserve.co.uk/) surrounding the use of this word: in fact, the site contains results of a questionnaire survey designed to sample these views, and a great deal of concern is expressed by survivors of the mental health service user movement. However, the organisers defend their decision to continue using the term 'Mad', in particular citing the importance of the capitalisation to emphasise the political point that is being made.

Recent work has sought to assess the successes of the mental health service user movement, concluding that while there has certainly been significant progress in areas such as campaigning and increasing user involvement (Campbell, 2005), there is still a need to consolidate and extend much of the work that has gone on (Wallcraft et al., 2003). In particular, as already mentioned in Chapter 1, there are questions over how far clients and former clients feel that they are fully represented by the movement, with suggestions that up to 90 per cent of users may know nothing about the user movement and that Black and other ethnic minority clients are particularly under-represented. It has been suggested that groups are more effective at local level (Campbell, 2005).

Research

However, regardless of the diversity within the mental health service user movement, and its possible limitations, it has unarguably provided a supportive forum for service users and survivors to express their views, and increasingly to promote these views to a wider audience. As early as 1975, the National Schizophrenia Fellowship produced a volume of seven narratives called *Schizophrenia from Within* (Wing, 1975), and a similar volume on anorexia by anorexics has been published by Survivors Speak Out (Pembroke, 1992). Many groups also produce newsletters containing articles, letters, poetry, and even cartoons and other artwork produced by service users or survivors.

In addition, research conducted by the service user movement has played a hugely important role in addressing the absence of work on client understanding. Early studies tended to rely on sympathetic academics and professionals to conduct the research, but increasingly research projects now involve users, or are even fully user-led. Reception of this work has not been without its problems: as Faulkner and Thomas (2002) point out, there has been political resistance to seeing psychiatric patients as experts and to involving them as partners in research. However, its significance is manifold: Bracken and Thomas (2005) go as far as to maintain that there is no equivalent of user-led research in any other branch of medicine; it adds both to our knowledge of client understanding and to an ideological shift in notions regarding clients' capabilities.

One of the earliest studies, published in association with MIND in 1993, was conducted by Anne Rogers, David Pilgrim and Ron Lacey (Rogers & Pilgrim, 1993; Rogers et al., 1993). This study, entitled 'People First', challenged the assumptions that service users were incapable of giving valid views, and claimed that views that did not coincide with those of professionals had been suppressed in the past. The survey discussed the views of 516 clients and former clients: in particular it noted substantial dissatisfaction with in-patient treatment, the problems of a lack of continuity of care between in-patient and community care, and clients' feelings towards treatments. Many reported polypharmacy and the problems of side effects of medication; there were higher levels of satisfaction with talking treatments and a polarisation of views regarding ECT.

The Sainsbury Centre for Mental Health (SCMH),[4] although not itself a mental health service user organisation, has been central to establishing and developing research in this area. In addition to running its own research programmes, many of which are user-focused, and will be discussed later, it has also aided numerous other organisations to conduct research, and published the results. In one such collaboration with MDF (Hill, Hardy & Shepherd, 1996), it published the results of a study of nearly 2000 members of the organisation, some with a diagnosis of bipolar disorder and others who were friends or relatives of someone with a diagnosis. The research team included four members who had manic depression themselves. The results of the survey found that respondents felt that psychiatrists were largely helpful although this view was not found in data collected from focus groups.[5] Those with bipolar disorder reported seeing friends and family as most helpful, and the attitudes of the general public as least helpful, whereas friends and family themselves saw lithium as most helpful.

Similar disparities between different interest groups were reported in another SCMH study (Shepherd et al., 1994), which sampled the views of 400 users, carers and professionals on services for people with schizophrenia in the community, although overall agreement was greater than disagreement. Users rated practical aspects of care, counselling and social networks as more important than professionals and saw professional intervention as less important. Carers rated all of the 11 key areas they were asked about as important. Users requested a greater level of respect, empathy and understanding from the public and professionals. Interestingly, a substantial minority of users valued the support of other users and non-professionals more than that of professionals.

This theme is picked up by a study conducted by the Mental Health Foundation on the strategies clients employ to help themselves (Mental Health Foundation, 1997). A user-led project, it reviews data provided by 401 respondents to a questionnaire focusing on what people felt was helpful to their mental health. Again, medication was regarded with some ambivalence, with side effects being a particular concern. In contrast, talking treatments were seen as helpful or helpful at times by 90 per cent of respondents. In addition, the importance of religious and spiritual beliefs, and personal coping strategies was underlined. The study suggested that these aspects were often overlooked within the mental health services.

A key feature of these studies is the increasing involvement of clients of the mental health services in the research itself. This significant development has arisen in line with both increased involvement for users in all health service areas, and an increasingly consumerist model within the health services in general. Guidelines have been issued for user-involved research in general (McIver, 1991a; McIver, 1991b).

However, there is also an important political angle to the increased role of users in research undertaken by the mental health service user movement, mirroring a similar move towards participatory or 'emancipatory' approaches to research in the social sciences (Humphries, Mertens & Truman, 2000), which aim to move beyond traditional research practices in which the seemingly omnipotent, omniscient academic conducts research on more powerless subjects. User-led and user-focused research aims to move 'from research on users to research by and for users'(Rogers et al., 1993, p. 11), in which users set their own agendas, and conduct their own research, and often to implement change for the better for service users as a result of this.

The SCMH has been integral in promoting this approach, undertaking its first User Focused Monitoring (UFM) project in Kensington, Chelsea and Westminster in 1996 (Rose, Ford, Lindley & Gawith, 1998), extending this work to five other sites across the United Kingdom at a later stage (Rose, 2001). This large-scale UFM study found some significant similarities between users across rural, suburban and city locations: in particular, the execution of the Care Programme Approach (CPA)[6] was partial, and problematic; medication was viewed with the usual mix of appreciation and concern, and half of the users overall reported insufficient access to talking treatments. The study also involved site visits to various in-patient locations, in which clients reported high levels of boredom. This project is in many ways archetypal, and has led to the development of guidelines for UFM studies (Sainsbury Centre for Mental Health, 2003), many of which now operate around the country.

The studies cited so far in this section have all been fairly broad in their focus. Other studies have, of course, taken a more specific topic of study. In particular, the SCMH has published studies on service user views of community care (Rose, 1996b), 24-hour nursed care (Rose & Muijen, 1998) and case management (Beeforth, Conlan & Gravley, 1994). Although the specificities of the results of such studies might vary, there is commonality in the fact that, first, users have important views that need to be taken into consideration if services are to be successfully implemented, and, second, users need to be involved in services, and their own mental health, to a much greater extent than has often been appreciated in the mental health services.

In 2002, a user-led research unit, the Service User Research Enterprise (SURE) was also established at the Institute of Psychiatry at the Royal Bethlem and Maudsley Hospital, co-ordinated by Dr Diana Rose, who, while discussing the importance of such a role, has highlighted some of the tensions surrounding user researchers working in academic environments with mental health professionals (Rose, 2003). SURE has organised a number of research projects into user views, one of which focused on ideas about ECT. This review of studies into patient perspectives found that the identity of the researcher and the methods used had a significant effect on levels of reported satisfaction with the treatment: patient-led or collaborative studies reported less satisfaction (Rose, Fleischmann, Wykes, Leese & Bindman, 2003). This study provides further evidence of the importance of researcher perspective on the results of any study.

User professionals

Another interesting development of recent years is the appearance of a limited number of 'user/professionals', who fall into two categories. First, there are mental health professionals who have themselves experienced mental health problems who 'come out' in public to draw on these experiences to encourage other professionals to reflect on user experience. Some, such as Chadwick (1993; 1997a; 1997b) and Bassman (2001) write in mainstream journals. Increasingly, however, user/professionals might also fall into the second category, that is, individuals who have been employed in the mental health profession precisely because of their experience of mental ill health, rather than having had to hide a diagnosis for fear of discrimination. Researchers in the user-led projects discussed before fall into this category. In 2001, the first conference of survivor workers was held in Manchester. There is, however, much more that could be done in this area to include the expertise of users and survivors into the mental health services in a more formal capacity. In 2004, it was estimated that there were only two user academic teaching and research posts in the UK (Livingston and Cooper, 2004), despite the unique potential role for such individuals in training other mental health professionals.

Conclusions

It is hard to overestimate the importance of the development of the mental health service user movement in the UK in the past fifteen years (Laurance, 2003), and its role in promoting user and survivor views that have often been ignored in the mental health profession and wider social sciences. Several common themes emerge from the wealth of research that has been undertaken, much of it user-led, by the various organisations: in particular, it is clear that clients and former clients of the mental health services have valid and important views, and that they can express these cogently, despite arguments to the contrary (Furlong, 1991; Powell, 1992). In addition, although clients express ambivalence to some aspects of the mental health services, including medication, other aspects, especially talking treatments and therapeutic relationships with professionals, tend to be warmly welcomed.

However, it is still the case that most of the studies conducted by the mental health services tend to focus on user assessments of services, rather than on the ideas that clients might have about mental health problems themselves. While reading autobiographies and poems might convey more of clients' understanding of mental health problems, there are still clearly gaps when this is compared with the work on the representations of mental ill health held by the public and by professionals discussed in the previous chapter.

The remainder of this book will try to go some way towards closing this gap, with discussion of a study that focused explicitly on service user understanding of mental health and ill health. There are, of course, numerous parallels with the work discussed in the previous two chapters, which will also be covered.

4 Defining mental health problems by and through experience

Introduction

In this chapter, I will begin to consider the way in which clients of the mental health services define and understand mental health and illness in more depth, drawing not only on the studies discussed in Chapters 2 and 3, but also on my own research into client understandings.

A full discussion of the methods involved in my own study can be found in the Appendix. In short, it comprised qualitative content analysis of material produced by clients and former clients of the mental health services in four newsletters produced by mental health organisations (Openmind, produced by MIND; A Single Step, produced by Depression Alliance; Pendulum, produced by MDF – the Bipolar Organisation, formerly the Manic Depression Fellowship; Signpost, produced by the Eating Disorders Association), and ethnographic work and interviews at three mental health services, Winter Centre, Spring Ward and Summer Centre.[1]

Winter Centre is a medium-sized urban day centre catering for clients who have generally been in contact with the mental health services for some time and are considered by professionals to have long-term, chronic mental health problems. Spring Ward is a 26 bed acute inpatient ward in an out-of-town psychiatric hospital, dealing with a variety of patients, both voluntary and sectioned,[2] some of whom have had no contact with the mental health services before, and some of whom are so-called revolving door patients. Summer Centre is a large urban day centre which caters for a very wide variety of clients: unlike Winter Centre, where the emphasis is mainly on the drop-in facility, with additional optional group activities, Summer Centre aims to engage clients in numerous group activities, and casual use of the Centre is less encouraged.

Defining mental ill health

A natural starting point for discussion of any form of understanding is definition. How do individuals categorise and name a concept; in the words of social representations theory, how do they anchor and objectify it? This is particularly relevant in studies of the understanding of mental health problems: one theorist (Rose, 1996a; 1998) argues that mental illness proves too difficult to anchor and, as such, represents a failure of representation. According to Rose (1996a; 1998), mental illness is the ultimate in unfamiliarity and, because of the fear associated with it, remains Other, and uncomfortably undefined.

It is certainly true that some clients find it very hard to define what mental ill health is. I would, however, agree with Morant (1996) that this is due more to mental ill health being represented *as* incomprehensible, as we saw in the discussion of public understanding in Chapter 2, rather than it being a failure of representation: it is not that mental illness cannot be defined in any way. We all have an idea of what is meant by the term 'mental illness', even if that idea might entail notions of incomprehensibility, and of unfamiliarity.

What is clear from this study and those discussed in earlier chapters is that most clients of the mental health services work hard to understand and to define, to make meaning out of the concept of mental ill health. In this chapter, I will discuss some of the strategies that clients use in defining mental ill health, and therefore in making sense out of it. Having first focused on some of the ways that clients use diagnosis, reference to physical illness, and to the abnormality or normality of mental health problems, I will move on to discuss the way that clients, ultimately, define mental ill health *by* and *through* their own experiences (Foster, 2004). By this, I mean that clients use their own experience to describe, define and make sense of mental health problems in general, and that their definitions also change and develop as the client's experience changes and develops, and as they interact with other individuals. Essential to the remainder of this book will be the notion that clients embark upon a journey through mental ill health, developing and employing representations actively within these journeys, in 'projects' in which they engage with regard to their mental health. The next chapter will then discuss the journeys in which clients are engaged in greater depth.

For many clients in my own research and elsewhere, diagnosis, and the psychiatric knowledge that goes along with this, is an important part of being able to put a name, and a definition to their experiences: as Tew (2005b) has acknowledged, biomedical understanding has the attraction of claiming to provide answers, established meanings and some certainty. A client, and his or her friends and relatives, might find comfort and familiarity in being given a medical diagnosis, a name for their often distressing experiences, and in the biomedical framework that goes along with this process. When we receive a medical diagnosis from a health professional, we might assume, with some relief, that the professionals who will treat us will draw on the understanding of a condition that they have established from treating others with the same diagnosis, prescribing effective medication and treatment, and therefore making the experience easier to deal with, and potentially short-lived.

This was often important for clients on Spring Ward, most of whom were relatively new to the mental health services.

> Chris talks about how his consultant has still not given him a formal diagnosis. I ask him if things will change if he gets a diagnosis, and he says it might help him to understand what the medication is 'And enable me to look at what I think is good for me', but he also says it might be painful. (Interview with Chris, Spring Ward)[3]

It was also routine for clients to use their diagnosis as a kind of shorthand in introducing themselves in some of the newsletters I examined. It provided writers with a way of defining themselves and their experiences to other readers. However, this idea runs counter to the arguments, often highlighted within some sections of the user movement, which encourage people to avoid identifying themselves through their diagnosis (Tew, 2005a). It has been suggested that in doing so, clients might risk adopting, albeit implicitly, an overly biomedical understanding of mental health and might fail to sufficiently acknowledge other aspects of their identity.

Diagnosis, however, is not seen as unproblematic, and for many clients it fails to provide an adequate definition of experience: it was often treated with some irreverence by clients in all locations, and there was also an awareness that diagnoses could be changed and challenged. In addition to the ambivalence expressed earlier by Chris on Spring Ward, for example, for other clients diagnosis does not make sense, and therefore provides no definition.

I: *So when you went into hospital did they give you a diagnosis, or anything?*

A: *No, they just sort of said I was ... heightened panic attacks with personality disorder. Whatever the heck that means.*

I: *Right. So what do you think it means?*

A: *Well, I don't know what it means. I don't think anybody does, really. I tried to ask them, but ...*

I: *Right ... OK ... so how do you feel about the diagnosis you've been given? Is it something that helps, or doesn't?*

A: *It doesn't make any sense to me. I don't know what it is.*

(Interview, Summer Day Centre)

Others, often clients at the Winter Centre, could not remember being given a diagnosis when they were admitted to hospital, especially as in many cases their first admission was some time ago. Consequently this had not played a large part in the definitions they gave to their experiences.

I: *So when you first went into hospital did they tell you why you were there?*

JONATHAN: *Yeah ...*

I: *Did they give you a diagnosis?*

JONATHAN: *Well, originally they just said that I ... I'd had a breakdown.*

(Interview with Jonathan, Winter Day Centre)

Although these clients were subsequently given a diagnosis, it was not always the case that this aided the process of definition. Discussion of diagnosis was rare at the Winter Centre, although a minority of clients here did seem to regard it as an important part of their identity, and might introduce themselves to newcomers by referring to it. Estroff (1981) found a similar absence of discussion of diagnosis in her study of a community-based mental health project.

Mental illness, of course, can also be defined in relation to physical illness, something which has been encouraged by many health education campaigns that seek to address the stigma of mental ill health[4] (see Bracken & Thomas [2005] and Repper & Perkins [2003] for a discussion of this). However, this process is far from simple. For some clients, mental illness should be regarded in the same manner as any other physical illness: indeed, there is no distinction between physical and mental illness. This view is predominant in A Single Step, the newsletter of the Depression Alliance: depression, it argues, is a physical illness, and to label it in any other terms is both unfair and stigmatising.

Adding further to the idea that mental illness can be defined in the same terms as a physical illness, many clients talk about the experience of mental illness in very physical terms.

I: *OK. And just one last word, what do you think of when I say mental illness?*

MELANIE: *... a complete ... almost physical sort of pain I get often up there [motions to forehead] in my forehead. And you know you're mentally ill, it all goes greasy.*
(Interview with Melanie, Winter Day Centre)

He says he had a breakdown in 1982. When I asked him how he would describe that to someone who didn't know so much about it, he says 'Your whole body goes.'
(Interview with Adam, Winter Day Centre)

The use of the term 'greasy' is particularly interesting here; other words with similar implications were mentioned, such as your mind 'turning to slurry', or being 'sticky' or full of cotton wool. These are vivid, unpleasant images, denoting the way in which mental illness can be seen as changing the physical nature of your mind and altering your perceptions.

Some clients seemed to believe that they *should* see mental illness in exactly the same terms as physical illness but found this hard to sustain, mirroring Sarbin and Mancuso's (1970) results in a study of the public, mentioned in Chapter 2. For some, the analogy between the mental and the physical remained useful.

We chat about the differences in using the terms client, patient and user. Chris says he prefers the term patients, as they are suffering from something that requires hospital treatment, and if he had gone into hospital to have his leg fixed he would be a patient, so it shouldn't be any different if he's come in to have his 'head fixed'. He says he's no less of a patient. (Interview with Chris, Spring Ward)

For others, the notion of a 'broken mind' was hard to maintain and had problematic implications.

I: *How do you think you'd describe mental illness to some-one who'd never heard of it? [pause] ... Like an alien [laughter].*

SIMON: *I do sometimes talk to friends of mine who ... who know me, ... as somebody using the mental health system, ... I do try and explain it to them, but they don't quite under-stand [inaudible] it's like any other illness.*

I: *Yeah.*

SIMON: *Even though it's not quite the same as any other illness, is it? It's like trying to get [inaudible] it's something you can't see.*

I: *Right*

SIMON: *So my doctor says ... you can't say I've got a broken mind like you've got a broken arm. Because you can see that, but with mental illness ... I'm losing track here.*

                    (Interview with Simon, Summer Day Centre)

The difficulty that Simon has with the analogy, and the implications of this difficulty, are clear.

The problems associated with drawing comparisons between physical and mental illness might result partially from the distinction between psychiatrists and other doctors, mental and other health services, that is also maintained professionally: although discussion of moving mental health services into the organisational framework and buildings of general hospitals was mooted as early as 1962, in Enoch Powell's Hospital Plan, the reality has often been somewhat different, and the status of psychiatry has arguably remained the lowest of any branch of the health services (Rogers & Pilgrim, 2001). Clients were acutely aware of continued distinctions.

Jane asks if there is a 'body doctor' here on the Ward as well as 'head doctors'.   (Spring Ward)

Part of the problem also arises from the fact that many clients believe that the general public fail to treat mental illness in the same way as physical illness. The stigma that is unarguably associated with mental illness (National Institute for Mental Health in England, 2004; Sayce, 2000) means that it is not consistently possible to define mental illness in terms of physical illness. The consequences of the ways in which other people see mental health problems will be discussed in Chapters 5 and 6.

The idea of defining mental illness in relation to physical illness is closely linked to the issue of whether mental illness is defined as normal or abnormal, a distinction that is also important in public understanding of mental ill health (Foster, 2001). Two issues are of particular importance here: first whether mental illness is something that happens to normal people or whether a client is abnormal to develop a mental illness in the first place; second, is mental illness part of normal experience, or should it be set apart and regarded as abnormal?

The prevailing idea for most clients in my own study was that mental illness is something which happens to 'normal' people: we are all equally at risk.

There's mentality in everyone, but some people show it more than others. Everyone does mental things, but some show it more.   (Interview with Adam, Winter Day Centre)

In this way, mental illness can sometimes be defined as being part of a continuum between the more normal and the more mentally ill. The difference is not a qualitative one, rather it is a matter of degree. In fact, many more so-called normal people who exist outside the mental health services would be diagnosed with a mental health problem, were they to come into contact with these services.

Anna says she reckons that if you brought in everyone off the street you could find something wrong with them.   (Spring Ward)

In the extreme, clients of mental health services might see themselves as the normal ones and believe it is the rest of society that has the problem, not them.

> Joe says the way he sees it is that 'inside [the hospital]' is more normal than 'out there'. He says it should be that everyone talks to each other in the same way they do in the smoking room of the ward, but at a bus stop people will stand for twenty minutes without talking to each other. He says 'it's more normality in here than it is out there,' and that people don't talk to each other like they do in here out there. (Spring Ward)

This idea is taken one stage further in the consideration of society's role in the creation and maintenance of mental illness. In general, more anti-psychiatric or social constructionist ideas were limited to the mental health service user movement newsletters reviewed here, which sometimes focused on the way in which society might label an alternative lifestyle that was unusual, but unproblematic, as madness or mental illness. Outside this, anti-psychiatric ideas were rare.

However, the idea of a continuum between mental illness and normality is similarly not a universal idea, and was more common on Spring Ward and in the more political newsletters, such as Openmind. At the Winter Centre, some clients referred to other clients as less 'normal' than other people, often in conjunction with the expression of a desire to mix with more 'normal' people outside the day centre. Likewise, there was a feeling within much of the literature from the Eating Disorders Association that sufferers of eating disorders were not normal, although they often tried to appear so. In addition, an alcoholic client might see his/her reaction to alcohol as abnormal, and not something that most normal people would have: there are some parallels between the way in which food is represented in Signpost and alcohol was discussed on Spring Ward.[5]

> I ask how he would explain drinking problems to someone who didn't know anything about them, and he says that most people use alcohol to make them happy, or to cope with a bad

day, and that I could go home this evening and say to my husband that I've had a crap day and I want a drink, and that people like that can have a drink, have a couple of drinks, and then wake up in the morning and start again with their life ... I ask what the difference is between someone who can just drink to make them feel happy, and someone who has drinking problems, and he says that 'someone once told me that some people are just addictive by nature ... You're just born with it, and that it's just in your nature, or your make-up.' (Interview, Spring Ward)

Again, this idea that people with various mental health problems are somehow abnormal compared with the rest of society might be something that is reinforced by the organisation of the mental health services. This was very much a focus of some sections of the user movement: Openmind, for example, took issue with the way in which clients of mental health services were assumed to have different needs from normal people at the outset, and services designed accordingly (see also Repper & Perkins [2003] for a discussion of this).

The additional discussion of the normality/abnormality of mental illness rests on whether mental illness is an experience that can be defined as normal, the implication being that it is therefore more understandable, or whether it remains abnormal and therefore cannot be understood by those who have not experienced it. To some extent, this latter position ties in with discussion on whether a definition of mental illness would make sense to someone who has not experienced it themselves, discussed later in this chapter.

For many clients, mental illness was an experience far removed from normal, everyday life. This representation, however, was not limited to clients who had been diagnosed with some kind of psychotic illness, as one might expect, given the distinction between neurosis and psychosis found in Morant's (1996) work amongst mental health professionals, which found psychosis portrayed as less comprehensible and neurosis as a more everyday experience. For example, members of Depression Alliance were keen to highlight the differences between depression and more mundane sadness, and to emphasise that their experiences were more alien, and by implication more serious, than those of people who merely felt unhappy. The frustration caused by casting depression

as part of normal experience was a recurrent theme throughout in
A Single Step. However, the abnormality of mental illness was
also emphasised by other clients: past and even current experiences
could not always be understood as part of normal experience.

> Well, everything is unreal when you're a schizophrenic. You're
> not leading a life that ordinary people can. (Interview with
> Melanie, Winter Day Centre)

> Joe says he's starting to think about what he believed in when
> he first came in to the ward, how he didn't even mention some
> things to anyone else at first, because he thought they were so
> important, and how much he believed in it. He's starting to say
> that he finds what he thought very frightening. (Spring Ward)

Discussions about panic attacks on Spring Ward also emphasised
their abnormality, and the fact that it was hard for people who had
not experienced them to understand.

Definitions by and through experience

In addition to the strategies of definition discussed here, and
perhaps more significantly, for many clients in all contexts, mental
illness can best be described and defined in terms of experience.
As such, definition develops throughout the client's experience
and journey through mental ill health.

> I ask how she'd explain being unwell to someone who didn know
> anything about it. She says 'mood swings, hallucinations ... it's
> very hard to say, very hard to describe hallucinating'.
> (Interview with Penelope, Summer Day Centre)

In this way, definitions of mental illness are often something quite
personal, and pertain to one's own experience, rather than some
wider, more abstract construct.

I: *Then if I say mental illness what does that make you*
        think of?
JASON: *Well, I suppose I think of my own mental illness that I've*
        had. Really.
                            (Interview with Jason, Winter Day Centre)

Interestingly, this emphasis on the personal is mirrored elsewhere: in 2000, MIND conducted a survey on 'Heroes and Villains' of the mental health world and found that respondents tended to nominate individuals with whom they had come into contact, psychiatrists, nurses and so on, rather than more famous examples, leading Openmind to conclude: 'for many the history of psychiatry was first and foremost their own history.' (Openmind, 102). The findings of this study mirror this: for many clients, the definition of mental health problems seems to be first and foremost their own experience.

This reliance on definition by experience is something that is reflected, indeed encouraged, by some mental health organisations and also professionals: it is common to find 'hearing voices' used as a definition, for example, as in the 'Hearing Voices Network'. Likewise, use of the term 'user' or 'survivor' of the mental health services rests on defining oneself in terms of experience, or in terms of service use, and is seen as more acceptable than defining oneself as 'schizophrenic' or as 'mentally ill', which might imply a greater subscription to the biomedical model of mental illness, and a one-dimensional identity based solely on a diagnosis of a mental health problem.

For some clients, mental illness cannot be defined to others: it must be experienced holistically and as such can only be understood by those who have experienced it themselves, a point also made in other studies (Beresford, 2005). This, for many, is a significant flaw in the psychiatric system: clients are treated by those who, in the main, have not experienced mental health problems and therefore cannot understand what mental ill health is (Repper & Perkins, 2003).

> Chris says that you can tell people what mental illness is like, but they'll not understand ... He says he could explain it to me but 'it's like, I could explain what the internal combustion engine is to you, but it wouldn't make you an engineer.' (Interview with Chris, Spring Ward)

It is for this reason that some sections of the service user movement refer to themselves as 'experts by experience' and see themselves as an important resource for other users and professionals alike.

This point, already discussed in Chapter 3, will be returned to in Chapter 8.

Experience of mental health problems was often likened by clients in this study to experience of a place, in an example of what Lakoff and Johnson (1980) have termed an orientational metaphor. Consequently, mental illness might be a prison (A Single Step) a trap (Signpost) or deep in the woods (A Single Step): this representation of mental illness as a place was particularly common amongst members of Depression Alliance.

This mental ill health 'place' was often understandable in terms of a vertical plane: it was deep in a pit or an abyss (A Single Step), it was a black hole (Openmind) or it was high in the clouds (Kirsten, Summer Day Centre). It can be the very edge of a cliff over which you are being held (Rufus on Spring Ward). In addition, clients referred to their attempts to overcome mental health problems using similar spatial terms: you might sink into it, and had to climb out of it, or emerge from it (A Single Step), or come 'out of the blue' (A Single Step). Many clients with a variety of diagnoses routinely referred to the progression of their mental health problems, their journey, in terms of highs and lows.

> Scott says he feels very drowsy in the morning at the moment, but by the afternoon he's feeling better: he says he knows it's his medication, but if he doesn't take it he goes high, and 'acts like a prat'. (Summer Day Centre)

> Thomas says that when he went into hospital he was very very low. (Summer Day Centre)

For clients with a diagnosis of any kind of mania, this description was even more common. Obviously there are parallels here with the way in which we discuss moods in everyday understanding: we feel down, or low, or feel high.

However, the implication was often that one did not remain in the same 'place' indefinitely: discussion of mental illness as a journey was similarly common; as will be discussed later, this metaphor has long been associated with the experience of mental ill health. Consequently, mental illness is not generally seen by clients as something static, or from a snapshot perspective; instead it is seen as an ongoing process within which the client might play different roles. Definition develops *through* experience.

The journey through mental illness is by no means exclusively represented as an inevitable progression, or simple process. Mental illness is described as like being on a tightrope (Pendulum) or a roller-coaster (Chris on Spring Ward; Pendulum); it can be like a maze (Openmind). It is something that you need to get through, to come through, to fight through (A Single Step; Openmind; Signpost). These metaphors imply a significant amount of work and activity on the part of the client: mental illness is not usually represented as something that happens to an altogether passive client, a point that will be taken up in later chapters.

The very titles 'Signpost' and 'A Single Step' emphasise this journey image of mental illness: these newsletters are specifically constructed around the idea of helping clients on their way with mental illness. Both A Single Step and Signpost refer to the 'road to recovery' on numerous occasions; Openmind discusses the need to find a pathway through the convoluted maze of distress. There is frequent use of the idea of stepping along this journey, although this process may be a difficult one. A Single Step discusses identifying milestones on the road towards more distant goalposts.

Another image that was extremely common in A Single Step was that of a tunnel, with the client travelling towards the light, often very slowly. While road and tunnel metaphors were most frequent in A Single Step, the idea of progression, of a journey, of moving forward, was also presented in other terms in other newsletters. Pendulum, for example, detailed the 'journey through madness' (Pendulum, 15[3]). Clients too discussed the idea of moving forward, or needing to move forward, albeit often in a more implicit fashion.

> Cathy says she's really glad she's back home now, as she didn't like having to tell people she was in hospital. I ask why, and she says it's like saying you're ill and not 'moving forward'. (Winter Day Centre)

> She talks about other friends of hers moving on, but says she just feels like she's standing still. (Summer Day Centre)

Many clients, then, clearly rely on the narrative, linear notion of a journey in defining mental ill health and understanding their experience: they are engaged in an active project of journeying through mental ill health, and mental health problems are often characterised by clients in terms of experience, of process, of a journey or a progression. The idea of the 'mad' as travellers in a strange land is nothing new, rooted as it is in myth and history and exemplified in the medieval portrayal of images of the Ship of Fools (Gilman, 1988); the journey, or process of mental ill health has also been highlighted elsewhere (Lapsley, Nikora & Black, 2002; Repper & Perkins, 2003; Wallcraft, 2005). Indeed, many of the metaphors discussed above have also been found in other studies of clients' ideas about recovery (e.g. Torpor, 2001, cited in Bracken & Thomas, 2005).

Theoretical frameworks

In addition, this representation of the journey through mental health problems has important contemporary theoretical significance: the portrayal of mental ill health as a journey ties in with several key theoretical concepts used in social and health psychology, which will now be briefly highlighted.

The way that an individual might focus on the development or process of an illness is discussed in numerous places: the theory of illness representation (Leventhal & Benyamini, 1997; Leventhal et al., 1997), for example, includes 'timeline' as one of the five components of an individual's beliefs about an illness, the others being identity of illness, causes of illness, consequences of illness and curability. There is, however, little consideration of the social context in which such ideas may develop (Flick, 2000), and including timeline as one among five components seems to fail to capture the way that ideas about definition, consequences and so on also unfold through time, as the individual's illness experience changes and develops. In contrast, there has recently been increasing interest in the use of narrative approaches to understanding the illness experience in health psychology (Bury, 2001; Murray, 2000). Here, the focus has again been on the way in which an individual develops an ongoing story about their health problem, perhaps drawing on core narratives that exist within society, such as that of heroism, or of progression and regression (Bury, 2001). Veracity or fidelity to history is not the issue, rather it is the significance to the individual and those around him/her, and validity in creating a life story, that matters (Kleinman, 1988). The illness narrative, then, helps to make sense of past experience, especially if that experience has involved distress, disruption and suffering (Charmaz, 1999), and serves as a guide for the individual's future actions and interpretations.

The conceptualisation of the journey through mental ill health also has obvious resonance with the idea of the project in social representations theory, discussed in Chapter 1: there has been much discussion about the close relationship between narrative theory and social representations theory (Murray, 2004). From the perspective of social representations theory, clients are understood to hold ideas about mental health and ill health, and these ideas guide their actions and interactions as they approach issues of mental health problems. Clients are active in this process, developing their own ideas about strategies which work for them, goals, aims and so on. However, these projects are not idiosyncratic, however personal they may sometimes seem: instead, as shown in the above discussion, clients draw on communal ideas about mental health and illness, on other clients' experiences and advice and so on. Consequently, there is commonality between the journeys through mental ill health which clients are undertaking.

In my own study, the concept of mental illness seemed to be objectified by clients through the idea of the journey, or project, in which the client engages: in other words, by engaging actively in the progression of their mental health problem, clients can come to better understand mental health and illness, to make sense of it and to define it. As such, mental ill health becomes inextricably linked for clients with the notion of linear activity, with a journey, that involves the client actively, dealing with mental health problems, making decisions, and putting effort into the process of recovery. Using social representations theory allows us a theoretical perspective from which to examine the way in which a client moves through his/her journey, employing and developing representations of mental health and ill health in the process. It also allows us to conceptualise the interactions between mental health service users, professionals and other interest groups: each group is engaged in a communally defined and shared project with regard to mental health, and these projects come into contact with one another, influencing, resisting, clashing and merging.

The way that this journey, or project, is conceptualised, the key moments within it, and the way that different projects might interact with one another will be the subject of the next chapter.

5 The journey through mental illness

Introduction

The previous chapter showed how clients of the mental health services rely on the notion of a journey through mental ill health to understand their experiences, and how, in doing so, they engage in strategies, or projects, with regard to their mental health.

Within my own work, the notion of the journey through mental ill health operates at two levels. First, there is the more global level of all the clients in this study, within both newsletter and mental health service data: at this level, clients in general clearly see themselves as engaged in a progression, a journey through mental illness, which involves activity and responsibility on the part of the client.

However, this should not imply that there were no discernible differences between clients in their journeys. At the more specific level, then, we deal with the particular communally defined projects in which clients from different services are engaged. Although there is commonality between these projects at the three services in this study, which would still broadly fit under the wider journey through mental illness in which all service users are engaged at the more global level, the way that these more particular journeys are conceptualised, the strategies that are employed and the representations expressed within those journeys differed somewhat according to the particular locale within which they were found. This is to be expected, given the different group contexts of particular mental health services, and that representations are, to some extent, a product of particular times, places and participants (Farr, 1993a). These three different journeys will now be discussed in a little more detail.

At the Winter Centre, the journey in which clients were involved was conceptualised as one of coming round and then staying round. Mental illness was constructed as something which takes you away from yourself, and coming round is the process you must go through in order to become yourself again, almost like coming round from unconsciousness. However, in parallel with becoming yourself, you must also come round into the role of mental health service user and accept this new identity.

Coming round was sometimes referred to explicitly, as in the following examples.

And I started the medication and first I was scared to go out of one room, then two rooms, then I branched off down the corridor, then to the dormitory, I was coming round all the time getting better and better.   (Interview with Mark, Winter Day Centre)

She was frightened of me at first, but she's come easy, and she talks to me. She wouldn't talk at first to anyone, but she's come round, and it's all a coming round, gradually. (Interview with Bob, Winter Day Centre)

Alternatively, it may be something more implicit. Coming round involves having an awareness of experiences and problems, and can involve stories about past behaviour, which the client might even regard as amusing now that they have 'come round' and can see things differently: clients see a difference between themselves at the start of their journey, before they have 'come round', while their mental health problem is still more extreme and its effects more profound, and themselves once they have 'come round', embarked on a journey of recovery and are working hard to stay in this state.

At Spring Ward, the journey was conceptualised in different terms. Here, it was seen more as a process of 'getting it together' and 'keeping it together'. At Spring Ward mental illness is something that might scatter the pieces of you, but those pieces are still intact and can be reassembled, not so much redefined. It implies a great deal of personal effort and responsibility in moving away from mental illness.

Richard says he doesn't understand why he can't get it together when he has so much going for him, and Emma agrees. They both say they feel like failures because of their experiences.   (Spring Ward)

Chris talks a bit about how he should probably have come into hospital sooner, but he's been trying to keep it together himself.   (Spring Ward)

There is also a lot of responsibility involved in the idea that you have not managed to keep it together in the first place, and some stigma associated with losing it.

It is interesting to note the personal agency required in the process of getting it together, which exists despite the fact that most clients at Spring Ward see external circumstances as playing an important role in causing their problems in the first place, something which Nugent (2001) also reports in the findings of her small-scale study. However, clients assumed that if they were successful in actively getting it together, and then keeping it together, they stood every chance of returning to their old lives, families, jobs and identities, albeit with a consistent need to maintain their own efforts to stay mentally healthy. Less redefinition of the self and fewer alterations to life in the long term were needed within the journey of getting it together than within the journey of coming round.

Clients at Summer Day Centre were engaged in the journey of 'keeping going'. In fact, this phrase was only used explicitly once by a client at the day centre.

I ask about the future, and she says she'll just keep going the way she is.   (Interview with Penelope, Summer Day Centre)

However, it was an implicit part of the clients' ideas about their journeys at Summer Day Centre in a number of ways. Here, mental illness seems to be constructed more as an ongoing struggle on a number of different levels and involves effort on the part of the client if they are to maintain any kind of life. 'Keeping going' implies the establishment of a routine, which was clearly important for many clients (see also Rollason, Stow & Paul [2000]). Clients also emphasised how hard life was on a day-to-day basis, but they were obviously engaged in strategies to try to keep going, and not give in, as they saw it, to their problems.

In addition, the idea of keeping going incorporates the idea of keeping going to the day centre itself: clients spoke of dwindling numbers at the centre since the emphasis had been shifted from the drop-in to the organised group activities.

> She says that the centre used to be full, and it was a 'buzz'. She says there aren't the people in the day centre anymore, as they've changed the focus, and they just want you to come to the groups now. (Summer Day Centre)

These three different kinds of journeys will be discussed through-out the remainder of this book. Table 5.1 summarises the import-ant aspects of each journey, which will be discussed in the remainder of this chapter, and provides a brief comparison between the journeys, or projects, at the different centres.

Table 5.1 A comparison of journeys

	Coming round	Getting it together	Keeping going
Activity involved on part of client	+	+++	++
Responsibility of client	−	+++	++
Longevity	+++	+	++
Role of hospital	−	++	++
Role of services	+++	+/−	+++
Role of medication	++	+	+
Role of other things (counselling; CBT etc)	−	+++	++
Importance of routine	+++	−	+++
Goal	Independent life within services	Normal life	?

Key:
+ An aspect that is important to the project, ranging from + (quite important) to +++ (crucial)
− An aspect that is less of a focus in a project
? An aspect that is unclear from the data in this study

Journeys, projects, narratives: important stages

However, despite these different journeys, or projects, and the different representations of mental illness that, to some extent, are implicit within them, there was also commonality, as demonstrated by the more global level of the notion of a journey through mental illness in which all clients engage. Certain moments were marked out as key within any project, within the journey through mental illness and the narrative that the client told of his or her mental health problems. For the most part, these key moments were common to clients in different locations, although the importance of different points and the way that they were constructed varied.

The beginning of a journey

Clients at all three services and in much of the newsletter data generally had very definite ideas about when the journeys in which they were engaged had begun, and why their problems had started. What clients saw as being the cause of their mental health problems, and the onset of these problems are important issues at this stage of the journey.

The causes of mental illness are not always easy to pinpoint, however, and for some clients, there was no simple reason why they had developed a mental illness.

> Jennifer talks a lot about 'my voices' or 'these voices' which she says are horrible. She says 'they don't know where they come from'.   (Winter Day Centre)

> When asked if she has any idea of causes, Christine says doesn't know if there is one, and that she doesn't know much about it. (Interview with Christine, Winter Day Centre)

However, despite this occasional absence of explanation, which in itself might be telling, most of the clients I encountered, and those who wrote in the newsletters, had complex arguments regarding what had caused their mental health problems, paralleling

Greenfeld et al.'s (1989) findings in their study of patients with a diagnosis of psychosis. Explanations were almost universally multi-factorial: clients resisted the idea that their mental health problems were caused by one thing alone, as might the general public (Räty, 1990).

> Joe talks a bit more about this combination of factors which he thinks have led to his hospitalisation, saying 'it's like the Titanic. It wasn't just the ice-berg that sunk the Titanic, it was the thickness of the metal and the rivets and all that as well.' He says he sees his experiences as like this, and the result of a combination.   (Interview with Joe, Spring Ward)

An important element of this multi-factorial model of causation is that it allows clients to remain somewhat agnostic on the question of whether mental illness has an underlying physical or social basis, as ultimately neither an internal or external model of caus- ation is entirely satisfactory (Lewis, 1995). A multi-factorial model is therefore important in a client's project and might relate to the way in which clients tend to maintain both personal strategies and a belief in medication within their journeys. It permits maintenance of a model of mental illness that emphasises the possibility of a physical foundation for mental illness, which is reliant upon trig- gers (Signpost, Pendulum) or catalysts (Chris on Spring Ward).

If mental illness has a location for the clients in my own research, for most it is in the brain. The brain was referred to far more than the 'mind' or any other possible location. How mental illness affects the brain, however, is an issue of some debate. In some cases, the exact relationship between mental illness and the brain is not entirely clear, although the connection between them is sound.

> Well, your ... your actual brain isn't sending the right messages to the rest of your body, you know, there's something wrong. It's a bit like, you know, it's a quirk of nature, something's not quite right in your brain.   (Interview with Melanie, Winter Day Centre)

More substantially, for many people the link between mental illness and the brain rests in a chemical imbalance. The number of times that this precise phrase was used by clients was striking, something also previously found in a study of the representations of mental illness held by students (Foster, 2001).

> She says that her perception of this is that it's an escape valve, and 'my brain's way of dealing with it.' 'Because it's a chemical imbalance in the brain, isn't it? That's what manic depression is.' (Interview with Kirsten, Summer Day Centre)

> Erm ... I think it's just well, in my case a chemical imbalance in the brain. My Mum, she, err, ... she went away two or three times ... and err, whether it's hereditary I don't know. (Interview with Jonathan, Winter Day Centre)

In some cases, the idea of a chemical imbalance could be even more specific. It seemed that this was an idea that was often proposed by mental health professionals, and then reiterated by clients.

> I: *So have you got any ideas about, about what causes schizophrenia? ...*
>
> MARK: *Well, I am told ... it's the wrong amount of dopamine in the brain.*
>
> (Interview with Mark, Winter Day Centre)

> I ask her about the causes of her being unwell, and she says 'I've been told, well, the professionals told my parents it is a chemical imbalance in the brain.' (Interview with Penelope, Summer Day Centre)

Serotonin was also mentioned by one client on Spring Ward and was also commonly discussed in the newsletters. This adherence to the chemical model is something upon which members of the Depression Alliance in particular focus. This sets apart their representation of depression from those found amongst the public, who seem to prefer more social models of depression (Leff, 2001). In contrast, members of the Depression Alliance were keen to highlight the physical components of depression, with less emphasis on the psychological, echoing Karp's (1992) findings in his study of a depression self-help group. The reasons behind this seem to centre on a desire to highlight the severity of the diagnosis of depression and avoid public misconceptions that align depression with general sadness.

However, most clients writing in the other newsletters, and attending the day centres and ward, were much more willing to accept that factors other than the purely chemical were implicated in their mental illness. Whatever the location and physical underpinnings of mental illness, it is rare to find an advocate for an exclusively physical model of mental illness, perhaps paralleling the tendency amongst the general public to subscribe to more 'social' models of mental ill health (Leff, 2001). Triggers or catalysts are seen as necessary to propel what might be some kind of tendency towards mental illness into a full-blown condition, something which has also been noted elsewhere (Tew, 2005b). The most popular catalyst discussed is stress. The word 'stress' was used in countless explanations, and seems to become a catch-all for life experiences, paralleling the results of Angermeyer's (1992) study of the attributions that patients diagnosed with psychosis gave for their experiences. The importance of everyday explanations for the onset of mental ill health such as 'breakdown', 'stress' and so on has also been highlighted in other studies (Wallcraft, 2005). Many clients, then, assigned the cause of their mental illness to a chemical imbalance, made apparent or exacerbated by stress.

Stress, in turn, has its antecedents: working too hard was a commonly cited cause of stress, but relationship difficulties were also frequently discussed. However, given the holistic perspective most clients take on their mental health, cause and effect cannot always be separated. Many clients mentioned relationship break-ups, a pattern commonly found in other studies (Lapsley et al., 2002), but suggested that the relationship had begun to disintegrate partly because of mental ill health, and once it had broken up, this in turn contributed to further problems. Interestingly, in this study it was almost exclusively men who spoke of relationship difficulties as contributing to their current status.

> He tells me that he's trying to put things back together as 'a while ago' he had three big things all happen to him at the same time: he had a breakdown, his marriage split up and his mother died. He says 'I went, well, not loopy, but ... .'
> (Winter Day Centre)

He says he doesn't think the marital split caused his mental health problems, but that it's exaggerated them, hence him having had such a relatively high number of admissions in the last two years. (Spring Ward)

Other causes of stress that were discussed in my study include being bullied, dealing with bereavement, financial problems, homelessness and problems with spirituality or ethnicity. Again, this role of social aspects of life acting as triggers emphasises the need for activity on the part of the client in their project and stresses the way in which a client believes that he or she is capable of doing something to help him or herself as they journey through mental illness.

However, it is important to note that many clients did not necessarily see any physical substrate to their mental illness, and this was not confined to those with more 'acute' problems. Many clients saw stress alone as being the cause of their mental illness.

LINDA: *It was stress ...*
I: *Right ...*
LINDA: *I worked under ... if I'm under stress I get ill.*
(Interview with Linda, Winter Day Centre)

I: *And did anybody tell you why you were there [at the hospital]?*
WENDY: *Yes, they did.*
I: *And what did they say?*
WENDY: *They said you've got to come in here because your brain needs a rest.*
I: *OK ... have you got any ideas what caused your brain needing to have a rest?*
WENDY: *Well, I don't know ... probably stress, overwork and over-stress.*
(Interview with Wendy, Winter Day Centre)

Some clients clearly see life events exclusively as having caused their mental illness, and do not necessarily subscribe to the idea that it results from anything more physical, or perhaps fundamental. This parallels findings in some other studies, where psychological causes are emphasised over the medical (Jones et al., 1963;

Rogers & Pilgrim, 1993), and seems to echo Herzlich's (1973) study of the representations of health held by the general public: here, many participants saw disease as being located in society, and way of life, rather than in the individual per se. It is not clear from my work, or indeed many other studies, how people who construct representations of mental illness in such a way deal with the notion that not all people who undergo stress at work or a relationship break-up become mentally ill: this topic merits further attention.

It was common for clients on Spring Ward to see a differentiation in the causation of mental illnesses, the more serious being more likely to be caused by physical predispositions, or something more '*in-built*', and the less serious, usually the conditions that they themselves believed that they had, to be more stress-related. This point will be returned to in Chapter 6, which will consider differentiation of mental illness and its relation to identity management in more detail. While this idea parallels some aspects of representations found amongst the general public (Foster, 2001) and to some extent mental health professionals (Morant, 1996), it was largely exclusive here to the clients of Spring Ward, and therefore perhaps represents an important identity management strategy for these in-patients.

Another minority position was that mental illness could be caused more directly by society in the wider sense, paralleling some anti-psychiatric ideas. This was possible in one of two ways: first, society could be responsible through its prescriptions and obsessions.

> He says that you can be born susceptible to mental illness, but out of everything, this world is the one that would make it come out.   (Interview with Rufus, Spring Ward)

Alternatively, society might create the label mental illness as an explanation for things of which it neither approves nor understands, for those whose lives follow an alternative pattern, or do not follow the predominant politics or aspirations of the day. This was, again, more prevalent in Openmind, and the more political sections of the user movement, but was also occasionally voiced on Spring Ward.

> Sarah talks about how she's had mental illness right back to primary school, as she didn't behave normally, so 'I've always

had an exclamation mark over my head' ... I ask how she'd describe 'mental illness' to someone who didn't know anything about it, and she says it's because she had behavioural problems, and this affected the way people perceived and treated her, and it was a Catch 22 situation ... I ask her what she thinks caused this, and she says just 'childish naughtiness'. She says you slip into a role when you get treated that way. (Interview with Sarah, Spring Ward)

Another issue which has provoked much debate in the mental health service user newsletters was that of voice-hearing, and whether the psychiatric profession had effectively created a mental illness out of an experience that was more common and usual than is admitted. Based on the work of Marius Romme and Sandra Escher (Romme & Escher, 1993), some sections of the user movement have focused on the situations in which people who have never come into contact with the mental health services hear voices, and how they deal with them. The suggestion is that hearing voices is more common than is recognised, and is not by definition a sinister or frightening experience, but that its current treatment in psychiatry exaggerates and over-complicates the experience. However, this view was not one that I found amongst the clients I met in the services: as will be discussed in Chapter 7, voices were discussed as alien and terrifying experiences by clients in this study, almost without exception.

In addition to making sense of the causes of their experiences, clients were also keen to pinpoint the exact onset of their mental health problems. Although there is a close relationship between cause and onset, ideas on causation do not always satisfactorily explain the actual moment when the client first experienced mental ill health. How do clients make sense of the actual moment of onset of mental health problems? When do they see their journey through mental ill health as beginning? There was an element of the client's own insight in many explanations of this: the onset was the self-defined moment of crisis, and as such it was not always clear whether a mental health professional would necessarily agree with the event pin-pointed by the client as the beginning of their journey.

On Spring Ward, in particular, it was often the case that the client's notion of when their problems had started seemed to differ from professional views. This clashing with professionals will be examined later in this chapter, when the way in which other groups' projects impinge upon the client's journey, or project, will be considered.

> He says he's sick of the fact that they blame everything on his drinking, and is angry that the doctor said he would have to be alcohol-free for six months before they could start looking at his other psychological problems. He says he drinks to cover his depression, which all started after a traumatic event. (Spring Ward)

In many cases across all three services there was an element of hindsight in the way in which clients discuss the onset of their problems. In keeping with the notion that clients construct their mental health as a journey, an ongoing project, and a narrative which changes in line with their experiences, clients often acknowledge that they now tell a story of the onset of their problems that they would not have told at that time: a process of reconsideration and reconstruction has taken place.

> He said he came to hospital as he thought it would help his parents, and now himself although he says he wouldn't have said this at the time. He says he thinks sometimes you have to go through something like this before you can say that you needed help too.   (Interview with Rufus, Spring Ward)

A common theme across all client groups was the notion of a 'breakdown'. Clients with a variety of diagnoses and histories employed the same term to describe that first occurrence of mental ill health, paralleling Reda's (1996) work on the descriptions given to the onset of mental health problems by relatives of clients.

> He asks me about being a student, and says he has eight O levels, but had his first 'breakdown' when he was in sixth form. (Winter Day Centre)

> Erm … well the very first time I went to hospital I was only in for two weeks, and I was in in L-. But I had sort of, like a

nervous breakdown ... and, erm, they ... later diagnosed me as having schizophrenia.   (Interview with Linda, Winter Day Centre)

Breakdown was also a term used in a variety of contexts in the newsletter data. It is a rather vague, catch-all term that is frequently used in everyday conversations, and as such its use is perhaps analogous with the similar catch-all term 'stress', discussed earlier: too much 'stress', the adage goes, might lead to a 'breakdown'. It might also be that the term 'breakdown' has less stigmatising connotations than, for example, the terms in which a professional might describe a schizophrenic or a hypomanic episode. However, it did not resonate with all clients, some of whom preferred a more dramatic description of the onset of their mental health problems.

Chris says he thinks there were a number of catalysts, which he lists ... But he says he had coped with these for a long time, and when I ask if it all built up, he says 'it didn't build up, it blew up'.   (Interview with Chris, Spring Ward)

Breakdown, or onset, for the clients in this study tends to lead to hospitalisation, another crucial aspect of a client's project. It should, of course, be remembered that many of the clients who participated in this and other recent studies into client understanding form part of a generation for whom hospitalisation was an inevitable, and often long-term, part of diagnosis as someone with a mental health problem. In light of the recent moves away from long-term hospitalisation (Rogers & Pilgrim, 2001), this may cease to play such an important role in clients' journeys in the future. In my own work, however, many clients referred to hospitalisation as the beginning of an acknowledgement of their problems, their recognition that they had embarked upon a journey through mental illness, and of their need to come round, get it together and so on. For many, it was the point at which their mental health problem becomes salient to themselves and others.

Despite this, for many clients, especially those at the Winter Centre, there was a vagueness surrounding that first hospitalisation. Most clients can detail when they were first admitted, and also give dates of any subsequent admissions, but many had trouble recalling the first few weeks of their first admission, an aspect also found by Lapsley et al. (2002) in their study in New Zealand. Often, clients saw this as the result of the confusion and illness that had led to their admission in the first place.

I: *So how long ago was that that you first went to Purple Ward?*
WENDY: *Errrrr ... Purple Ward was 1982.*
I: *1982 ... right. And can you remember how you felt when you first went into hospital?*
WENDY: *I didn't know where I was. I thought I was in France [laughs]*
I: *Oh OK.*
WENDY: *I didn't know where I was.*
(Interview with Wendy, Winter Day Centre)

I: *So you first went into hospital in 19 ...*
JONATHAN: *77.*
I: *1977. So can you remember what that was like when you first went into hospital?*
JONATHAN: *Erm, I can't remember the first ... couple of weeks or so.*
(Interview with Jonathan, Winter Day Centre)

Although most common amongst clients at the Winter Centre, it was not unusual to find clients whose hospitalisations had been more recent also expressing similar levels of confusion and vagueness over their admissions and mental state at that time.

S- [nursing assistant] says she remembers when Joe came in and what he said when she showed him to his room. Joe says he doesn't really remember, and thinks he was a bit confused. (Spring Ward)

While it is important not to undermine the role played by the distressing symptoms which clients might be experiencing on admission, or the role of the heavy medication that might be administered when a client is brought into hospital, especially in the case of clients who were first hospitalised some time ago, this vagueness surrounding hospital admission strengthens the idea that, for some clients, mental illness is something that takes you away from yourself and is a state that you cannot necessarily fully understand until you have come round. It is too far removed from normality and from any usual state of being.

For many people, first contact with the mental health services is a kind of epiphany. This was especially the case for clients on Spring Ward, many of whom were experiencing their first hospitalisation. The fact that a client starts using mental health services can lead to a profound self-examination, a recognition by the client that he or she needs to 'get it together', and discussion of what might be done in order to achieve this. This is something that can be particularly the case towards the end of an admission.

> He says the psychiatrist he then saw was important for him, as it was the 'day of admitting I had a problem'. He says the psychiatrist was understanding, and it was through talking to her that he realised he had a problem, but he didn't know what to do about it.   (Interview with Joe, Spring Ward)

Distress and disruption: dealing with the effects of mental ill health

Once an individual has begun to experience mental health problems, his or her journey must start to involve dealing with the way in which having that mental health problem affects his/her life. For the most part, the effects of mental health problems are characterised for clients by distress and disruption on a number of levels, paralleling two of the central themes within representations of mental illness held by the professionals in Morant's (1996) study, which centred on difference, distress and disruption.

Mental illness can cause a great deal of distress for clients of the mental health services, and this aspect should not be under-played (Repper & Perkins, 2003). For many clients, mental illness causes significant unhappiness and suffering. Hallucinations in particular are often seen as terrifying experiences, which are not forgotten (Barham & Hayward, 1991).

I: *If somebody asked you what schizophrenia was like,*
             what would you say?
MELANIE: *I'd say it was … was sheer hell, frankly [laughs]*
                    (Interview with Melanie, Winter Day Centre)

I: *If I say mental illness what does that make you think of?*
Eric: *… Erm … serious suffering …*
                    (Interview with Eric, Winter Day Centre)

This sentiment was very commonly expressed. When I told clients what I was researching, a number of them responded by telling me it was 'pretty bad', or very difficult to cope. This suffering was something that might lead, eventually, towards suicide or attempted suicide. Many clients in both the services and newsletters discussed reaching a point at which they felt they could no longer continue. Self-harm was also a frequent topic of conversation.

Mental illness is associated with a number of changes in the self, and part of a client's project within their journey through mental illness is coping with adapting to these changes, some of which are somewhat abstract, or on a more emotional level. These issues are a particular focus of material in A Single Step and Signpost. Consequences might include a loss of identity, self-esteem and a feeling of the impossibility of life. Other changes could be more concrete, for example, alterations in behaviour. Some clients discussed being irrational, or, much less commonly, feeling violent or becoming involved in crime.

Mental ill health is seen as problematic because it thwarts plans and stops you becoming what you want to be, or having the kind of life that you imagined you would have. Once embarked upon a journey, or project, in mental health, old plans and projects must often fall by the wayside. This idea was unsurprisingly more prevalent amongst longer-term clients.

I: *If you were describing your problems to someone who*
             didn't know anything about it?
WENDY: *Oh, I'd probably say, 'Oh, ermm … my life hasn't*
             turned out for the best, and plans I've made didn't come
             true, and things I wanted to do I couldn't do …'
                    (Interview with Wendy, Winter Day Centre)

However, disruption on a short-term scale was also a problematic consequence: clients on Spring Ward, for example, discussed the inconvenience of taking time off work or being away from their families. The problem of mental illness as a barrier to fulfilling goals and plans was especially obvious in Pendulum. This is perhaps particularly because clients who wrote for Pendulum often focused on the recurring nature of bipolar disorder. Indeed, the notion of recovery, which will be addressed later in this chapter, specifically involves acknowledgement of this disruptive aspect of mental illness.

Clients were acutely aware of the consequences that mental illness had for their social situations, although it must be made clear that, as argued above, a more cyclical view of the relationship between mental ill health and problems in relationships is needed: relationship breakdown could both stem from and contribute to mental health problems. However, many clients discussed the loneliness they experienced, and the problems they had in maintaining relationships once their mental health deteriorated. This was often seen as the result of other people's perceptions.

I: *So do you think people see it differently if you've been in a mental hospital? Do you think people ... ?*

DUNCAN: *Completely, yeah.*

I: *So what do you think they think if they find out-?*

DUNCAN: *I'm not sure. I mean, I've lost all my mates, you know. They all think I'm totally mental [laughs].*

(Interview with Duncan, Winter Day Centre)

That was another thing, my mental illness made me very isolated. I didn't have my mother because we'd fallen out, and I had no friends whatsoever, you know. (Interview with Scott, Summer Day Centre)

Certain social problems were seen more as resulting directly from the client and his or her problems, which might perhaps make them withdraw from society, whereas others were seen as the result of misunderstanding and prejudice on the part of other people: a wife might leave her husband, for example, when he is admitted to hospital, because she does not understand his situation. The stigma of mental ill health, as will be discussed at greater length in Chapter 6, is something which clients deal with on a daily, and concrete, basis.

Clients not only hold ideas about the effects of mental health problems on themselves, but also consider the effects on those around them, on friends and family. There seemed to be some support for the idea that one's family tend to react with more compassion than strangers, but there is variation in family reactions. Many clients spoke to me about losing contact with their relatives, and those who still had contact with their families were very thankful for this. Families were a frequent topic of conversation at all three mental health services, and clients frequently showed me photographs and took a great interest in my own family. This was despite the fact that many clients had very little or no contact with their families; this was particularly so for clients at the Winter Day Centre, where other clients often almost came to replace families.

> This [the day centre] is just like a house, a normal house, with a lot of people in it, and it's like a family. (Interview with Duncan, Winter Day Centre)

Recognition of the distress caused to relatives was also common, both in newsletters and amongst many clients at the day centres and ward as well. However, this was a major issue in some of the newsletters: Signpost is designed much more with carers of people with eating disorders in mind, and this is reflected both in the fewer column inches allotted to clients themselves and the way in which letters and articles routinely refer to clients and carers in the same phrase, the implication being that they are going through the experience together.

This introduces an interesting distinction in the ways in which effects on 'carers' or family members are represented. For some, the experience of the carer almost reflected that of the client: the carer goes through everything with the client or experiences similar sorts of things.

> He talks about two of his friends, who he says are brothers; he says that one of them was diagnosed schizophrenic a long time ago, and this 'dragged the other one down'. (Summer Day Centre)

It is almost as if, contained within these ideas about how mental illness affects family members there is a notion of contagion, long associated with representations of mental ill health (Jodelet, 1991): the friend or family member who cares for the person with mental health problems risks finding themselves in a similar situation, something which Maia de Nobrega (1999) did indeed note amongst the families of psychiatric patients in Brazil.

The alternative view, however, which is more dominant in this and other studies, is that the experience of mental illness is substantially different for carer and client (Rogers & Pilgrim, 1991). This view ties in with earlier discussion of familiarisation: can the carer ever really understand what the client is going through?

Two representations of the effects of mental illness on others then emerge: one involves the other sharing the mental illness and the client's journey, and almost experiencing it themselves as well, either by proxy or in actual fact, and the other maintains a distance between mental illness and the carer, who can never really know or understand, as the experience is too alien, too separate, too Other. These representations appear to be mirrored in the way in which user groups treat carers, already discussed in Chapter 3. For some, such as the Eating Disorders Association, carers and clients should be treated in the same way. For others, there is perhaps a need for a separate, specially designated forum for carers, one that allows them a voice without it infringing on those of the clients themselves: tension can arise in organisations that seek to represent both groups adequately (Rogers & Pilgrim, 1991).

Moving on

For many clients there is a very concrete way of following their journeys through mental illness, especially for those who have been in contact with the mental health services for longer periods: this is the story of their exact use of different kinds of mental health services and the different housing schemes in which they have lived. I believe that this is, again, a form of objectification of mental illness: some clients are able to understand their experiences with reference to the different places in which they have lived and services with which they have come into contact. This is especially the case since clients are all acutely aware of the different functions of different mental health services. At Winter Day Centre, discussion of mental health service use entailed long and very precise details of where a client had lived and for how long; some clients also maintained connections with the places in which they had lived, for example, going to Christmas parties or going to visit staff on wards. This is a way for clients to maintain an understanding of what has happened to them in the course of their mental health problems and how their lives have changed.

> And I moved from Blue Ward in the hospital, to ... err, Purple Ward, then East House, then to Wiltshire Place, and then luckily I was given a place at Surrey House ... and I stayed for ... nine years, I think it was, and I've been about ... something near on two years at, err, 200 Surrey Road, which is the satellite house, and a sort of annex almost really to Surrey House, and that's where I live at the moment. (Interview with Melanie, Winter Day Centre)

In fact, it was this extensive network of wards, hostels, group homes and flats, with which all the clients at Summer and Winter Day Centres were very familiar, that seemed to allow clients to form an often tightly knit group. Clients moved frequently, about once every two years, and shared accommodation with one another as they did.

> Mark says that he moved into one flat when Arthur [who also lived there] was in hospital, and so the staff asked Arthur if he minded Mark moving in. Mark says that Arthur had been a bit unsure, although that staff had said to him that Arthur must know Mark as he'd been around so much for so long. (Winter Day Centre)

This, of course, calls into question how far clients of the mental health services are really fully integrated into their wider communities, even though they are no longer living in more isolated hospital settings – a point made by other theorists; another participant observation study of a drop-in centre suggested that the main reason clients attended the centre was because they were denied the opportunity to participate in wider society because of the stigma surrounding their mental health problems (Hall & Cheston, 2002).

For many clients, other clients almost exclusively form their social networks.

Work schemes can also play a role in a client's journey. Having left hospital, employment can be problematic, as will be discussed below. A major complaint is that those with mental health problems fail to obtain paid work in the usual way, and often have to resort to voluntary work, or mental health service work schemes. In both the literature produced by the newsletters and conversations with clients at the day centres, more dissatisfaction than satisfaction was expressed with sheltered work schemes.

MARTIN: *I went to ... the [] Centre*
I: *Oh, OK. What's that?*
MARTIN: *... that's voluntary work ... meant to help people. And they gave me a job stamping doctors' prescription pads, which was really boring ...*
I: *[laughs]*
MARTIN: *And you used to get a pound a day, for doing it ... And I got my pound on the Monday morning, when I first started, and then they turned round and said, 'Oh, you've got to pay a pound for your dinner'.*
I: *You're joking?*
MARTIN: *So you don't get nothing*
              (Interview with Martin, Winter Day Centre)

Although it is important to recognise that these views do not come from a random sample – the clients at Winter Day Centre, for example, were often attending that day centre because they had not enjoyed any other services and were considered 'hard to engage' by professionals – these views were also echoed in the newsletter data, and have been found in other studies (Rose, 2001).

The role of medication in the journey through mental illness

Medication almost inevitably plays a part in a client's journey as part of wider mental health service use (Repper & Perkins, 2003). In general, clients in my own study believed that drugs can help you to be more in control, but that they do not replace your own efforts or activity.

> Adam, Bob and Jonathan are talking about a client that I do not know. Adam says this person has 'the wrong attitude to getting better. He once said to me that it's up to them to make me better, but it's not like that. Doctors can only do 99%, I mean 10%, you have to do the rest.' Bob and Jonathan agree; Bob says 'Medication can't control you completely. It controls you a bit, but you have to control yourself, and [acquaintance] didn't control himself.' (Winter Day Centre)

However, control and medication can be a grey area: another client at the Winter Centre talked about how clients were under control whilst taking medication, but also maintained that when he was under stress, he still lost control. It is clear that for many people, drugs fail to provide the whole answer.

This is not to deny the role of medication within a client's journey. Indeed, many newsletters and clients I spoke to were enthusiastic about the effect that medication had had on them, something echoed elsewhere (Healthcare Commission, 2004; Rose, 2001). For some clients, at least, the drugs do work.

> And as I said, when I went on the new drug clozapine it started slowly getting better, although it took maybe three or four years on the clozapine before I was fully, pretty well fully recovered, and I'm pretty good now. (Interview with Eric, Winter Day Centre)

> There is a chat about the different drugs that people are on. Joe says he doesn't want to take any, and Anna says she's read up on all of it, and although they have side effects, you get over them quickly, and the drugs do help. (Spring Ward)

Although clients recognise the side effects that some medication might have, for example, memory loss (Spring Ward), loss of sex drive (Spring Ward) and drowsiness (Summer Centre), for most clients drugs form an important part of an overall package for recovery. Similar sentiments have been expressed elsewhere: Svedberg, Backenroth-Ohsako and Lützén (2003), for example, discuss the way that clients learn to live with long-acting injections of anti-psychotic medication, coming to regard them as a 'necessary evil', but part of their recovery process.

For some, however, the drugs don't work, and this can cause much frustration. Openmind, Pendulum and A Single Step all carried articles on treatment resistance. Similarly, in this study, as in others (Healthcare Commission, 2004; Rose, 2001) clients expressed an ambivalence towards medication that should be taken seriously: for many, side effects are very worrying, and clients often feel that they are provided with insufficient information and choice in issues of medication. 'Non-compliance' with medication routines is not necessarily rooted in irrationality, but may be a very rational decision based on the problems the client has encountered with their medication (Repper & Perkins, 2003).

Other professional treatments that might be found in services could also play a part in a client's journey, some of which involve more activity on the part of the client than others. Therapy and Cognitive Behavioural Therapy (CBT) were very commonly discussed, and mostly seen in positive terms, although few people had successfully negotiated long waiting lists; Electro-Convulsive Therapy (ECT) was more controversial, with some seeing it as a dangerous and barbaric process and others as the only thing which ever helped, a polarisation also found elsewhere (Rogers et al., 1993).[1] However, within the mental health services as they stand, medication seems to be the most widely employed option. This often caused some anger amongst clients, a point that will be returned to later in this chapter, when the interaction between client and professional projects will be considered.

SCOTT: *I suppose at the end of the day I am glad there are drugs that treat mental illness.*
I: *Yeah.*
SCOTT: *'Cos paranoia, nothing gets rid of it except medication.*
I: *It's the only thing that helps?*
SCOTT: *Yeah. But there's this thing called cognitive therapy, I'm not sure about that.*
I: *Oh, right. Have you ever had cognitive therapy?*
SCOTT: *No, I haven't. I don't really know what it is.*
(Interview with Scott, Summer Day Centre)

The positive side of the journey

On reflecting on earlier parts of their journey, their current situation and their projected future, some clients believed that there were positive aspects to mental health problems, something which has been discussed elsewhere (Chadwick, 1997c; Repper & Perkins, 2003). These positive aspects can be broadly divided into three categories: the first is the notion that mental illness gives you some kind of 'extra' qualities that people without mental illness do not have. This 'extra' quality can range from something rather mystical, paralleling some anti-psychiatric ideas, such as getting closer to a truth (Openmind), or being very creative, to something more mundane, such as having company when you hear voices, or finding comfort in psychotic beliefs.

PAULA: *A lot of people, they feel very … if, I used to hear voices too, and you know, if you've been used to hearing voices for years and years, when they go, you actually miss them.*

I: *Do you?*

PAULA: *Because you've been used to … it's like having company in your head … that you've always got somebody with you.*

I: *Oh, I see*

PAULA: *And when that stops, it, erm … you can feel very lonely, because your mind sort of goes empty again. Well, not empty, but back to normal if you like.*

(Interview with Paula, Winter Day Centre)

[word association] Psychotic experience – wicked. It was a pain and joy, because I went through both. It was mostly good, and I didn't want to leave it, because I believed in it so much. It's a harsher world without it.   (Interview with Joe, Spring Ward)

It was also very common in my study to find clients who had been given a diagnosis of some sort of mania wanting to maintain the feeling of being 'high', when they were the entertainers and the proverbial life and soul of the party.

He says he doesn't want to take mood stabilisers if he'll have to take them for the rest of his life, or if they're going to suppress the highs, as he says they're what makes life OK. (Spring Ward)

This first category of positive aspects was most commonly found in the more political newsletters and on Spring Ward: it seems to be in the spirit of the Mad Pride organisation, discussed in Chapter 3, in that it examines the advantages of mental health problems, and may embrace them. It was rarely expressed elsewhere in my own study.

The second category of positive aspects of mental illness incorporates ideas that one can somehow grow as a person through experience of mental health problems, gaining a greater understanding of oneself, and perhaps even of human beings in general. This is especially common in A Single Step and less evident elsewhere. Continuing the theme of proverbs, it is summed up by the idea that 'what doesn't kill you can make you stronger'.

The third category is a broadly social one. I was repeatedly told at the day centres and ward how clients appreciated having met some good friends through the mental health services, and to some extent this sentiment was also expressed in the newsletter data: Openmind, for example, discussed the camaraderie that develops on acute wards. The importance of the mutually supportive atmosphere within the smoking rooms and lounges of mental health services cannot be underestimated and has been emphasised in other studies, such as that of Rollason et al. (2000) in Birmingham and Repper and Perkins (2003).

She says she has met some of the kindest, most lovely, sensitive and emotionally vulnerable people in hospital. (Interview with Kirsten, Summer Day Centre)

JONATHAN: *Since I've, sort of, been in the mental health system ... as I say, I've met some very nice people.*
I: *Yeah*
JONATHAN: *I've got some very good friends.*
I: *Yeah*
JONATHAN: *Probably more so than if you was outside the mental health system*

(Interview with Jonathan,
Winter Day Centre)

There is some cross-over here with elements of categories one and two, discussed above: the implication is that mental health service users might be extra sensitive or nice, and make especially good friends because of their experiences.

The future: journeying forwards

Almost all the clients to whom I spoke were optimistic about their futures, with the exception of some at Summer Day Centre, who saw their current situation in fairly negative terms and did not believe that any change was likely. However, this does not mean that clients necessarily see themselves as moving away from the mental health services in the future: the main differences between clients lay in whether they saw a future as rooted within the mental health services or outside them.

For clients at the Winter Centre, whose journeys were focused on coming and then staying round, the future was mainly constructed within the mental health services, specifically the Winter Centre itself.

I: *So I mean, where do you see things going for yourself from here, do you think you'll carry on coming to the Winter [Centre]?*

DUNCAN: *Yeah, I hope so ... not ... because I'm lazy, it's just it ... makes you relax, and not have to feel that you have to do anything. But I enjoy it just sitting and smoking and listening to music.*

I: *Yeah, sure.*

DUNCAN: *And joining in the Tutor Group, and ... you know, it's all good fun ... . I don't feel I'd be very ... sort of welcomed in the community ... I wouldn't advise relying on this service to give me a basic start to my future ...*

I: *Yeah, OK ...*

DUNCAN: *My future is here now.*

(Interview with Duncan,
Winter Day Centre)

An interesting factor at the Winter Centre was that clients used employment vocabulary when discussing their attendance at the centre: they would talk about having a day or a week off, getting paid (some clients received their benefits through the centre) and having to retire at 65. It was as if having a mental health problem and attending the centre had replaced work and precluded the possibility of getting another kind of work: going to the Centre was a job in itself. Estroff (1981) found similar results in her study of an American day centre programme. It is possible that this is an idea that the staff at the Winter Day Centre either initiated or sought to maintain: on occasions I heard members of staff telling clients that another client 'had a day off' and so forth.

Interestingly, this expectation of continued service use was despite the fact that many of the clients at the Winter Day Centre did not see themselves as currently mentally ill. Their futures were as mental health service clients but not as mentally ill people: this is an important distinction. Many clients here viewed themselves as recovered from mental ill health, although professionals would almost certainly have disagreed with this. The definition of 'recovery', as will be discussed in many places in the remainder of this book, can be something very different for clients and for professionals (Tooth, Kalyanasundaram, Glover & Momenzadah, 2003). The difficulty for clients lay in the fact that they might subsequently require further hospitalisation, something which was seen as a slip backwards in their journey. While this was acknowledged, it was something that caused some shame and embarrassment. This, again, reinforces the notion of responsibility within mental health problems: the client sees him or herself as partially responsible for any regression during the project of coming round. Another problem arises from the fact that other people, both the public and professionals, are likely to continue to regard an individual who uses mental health services as having a mental health problem and to view the idea that somebody who has recovered from mental health services may continue to use mental health services as highly unlikely: this will be discussed in greater detail later in this chapter, and in Chapter 6.

However, a future within the mental health services does not preclude a client from having his or her own plans and projects for coming round further, or for staying round. Clients at the Winter Day Centre were keen to tell me about the different aspects of the projects in which they were engaged. Most of these involved maintaining friendships, hobbies, voluntary work or education and so forth.

ERIC: *But I did do a couple of other things that time when I was bad, I stopped drinking alcohol ... Smoking, well I gave up a year ago when I was here.*

I: *... **So you think that giving up smoking and giving up alcohol has helped as well as the clozapine?***

ERIC: *It has, yeah. Particularly the alcohol. Because, you know what happens, it actually affects the brain quite strongly. So if you're mentally ill and drink a lot of alcohol it's even worse, you know ...*

(Interview with Eric, Winter Day Centre)

This is not to imply, however, that all clients at the Winter Centre felt the same: for some, moving away from the mental health services was the ultimate goal.

> Adam says he's taking things very slowly, but he'd like to have a council house with a little garden, and live there and maybe have another family. He keeps saying he just wants to be 'you know, normal'. He says he'd put all his money into it. He says he'd like a job in the future. (Winter Day Centre)

The distinction between clients who saw their future as within the services and those who saw their future outside services was obvious on one occasion in particular in my study, when discussion centred on what clients would do if they won the lottery. Bob's dreams still maintain his position within the day centre; Tim's do not seem to.

> I talk to Bob and Tim about the lottery syndicate. We talk about what we'd do if we won. Bob's plans all centre around the Winter Centre and services: he says he'd buy two vans and drivers for the Winter Centre, and would buy hospitals and things. Tim says he would buy a £250,000 house and live in it. He also talks about the places he'd travel to: Austria, Switzerland, Italy, Canada. (Winter Day Centre)

For the majority of clients on Spring Ward, a move away from both mental illness and from the role of mental health service user was seen as perfectly possible, assuming that they managed to get it together properly, and then to keep it together: their journeys through mental illness, it seems, were envisaged as being more short-lived than clients at the Winter Day Centre.

> I ask how he sees the future, and he says he sees himself being 100% better, and if he needs to take medication so long as it does its job and doesn't have side effects, he'll be happy. (Interview with Chris, Spring Ward)

The mental health services might continue to play some kind of role in the client's future: a client might, for example, continue to take medication, as Chris accepts above, or even require further hospitalisation if the client really wants to ensure that he or she 'gets it together' properly.

> We walk past the building work [new wards were being built on the hospital site], and all three of the clients I am with say that they won't be back on Spring Ward, and therefore won't see the new ward. Matthew qualifies that, and says he won't be back for drinking, and Rufus and Anna both say they suppose they might be back at some point. (Spring Ward)

In the main, clients here believed that they could return to any former job, house, life and so on, but made particular mention of the activity needed on their part if they were to achieve the kinds of futures they wanted.

> Joe says that the ward is sorting out his medical problems but not his psychological ones. I ask what can sort these out, and he says 'myself'. He says he also thinks he needs counselling, but there is such a long waiting list. (Spring Ward)

For clients at Summer Day Centre, the future was mixed. For some, the future was fairly bleak, as they saw themselves as having stagnated somewhat, and having stopped moving forwards in their journeys.

> Maria talks about other friends of hers moving on, but says she just feels like she's standing still. (Summer Day Centre)

> Paul sighs, and says to Richard 'look what we've come to, have we come to this?' and Richard doesn't really say much in reply. (Summer Day Centre)

In addition, for some, the future was firmly within the mental health services, and they accepted this role indefinitely. Here, once more, the issue of what a client would do if they obtained a lot of money framed a discussion of the future.

> Scott talks about what he'd do if he were rich. He says he would buy his own place, but he'd still come to the day centre, and says he thinks part of the problem is that he just can't look after himself properly anymore.   (Summer Day Centre)

Others, however, saw themselves as capable of moving away from the mental health services and the role of mental health service user, and of establishing a life elsewhere in the community, albeit with the aid of other services.

> Simon says he's also found out about a place where you can do NVQ's[2] in different things, and that it's for the long term unemployed and also people who are 'under mental health'. ... He says he's thinking long term, but he's going to take it quite slowly. He says in the long term he'd like to get back to work, maybe in something like painting and decorating. (Summer Day Centre)

Recovery and cure

All of the above discussion regarding the future of clients' journeys contains notions of recovery and cure. Within the mental health services, and especially the user movement, there is considerable discussion over the appropriateness of the concept of 'curing' mental health problems (see Tew [2005b] for a discussion of this). Many sections of the movement prefer the idea of recovery. The terms have important semantic differences. The notion of cure was, almost without exception, something passive within my own study, whereas, in contrast, the notion of recovery was much more active and involved the client, and what he or she does, to a much greater extent. Curing is the domain of medical professionals, who heal or make better; recovery is more the domain of the client, and is a process of working towards mental health: it is about seeing beyond problems, but not necessarily getting rid of them completely (Repper & Perkins, 2003). The distinction is striking, and the discussion of the differences in the two concepts symptomatic of a mental health system and user movement which is undergoing a profound change in philosophy.

The mental health service user movement goes to great lengths to define what is meant by recovery: there is recognition that the term has multiple meanings.

> I consider myself to be fully recovered. Recovery for me is being able to look at what has happened to me in my life, face it and then deal with it. Recovery to me isn't getting rid of the symptoms of the illness. (Openmind, 105)

> There is little recognition in current service models that recovery from severe mental health problems is possible. In the US, 'recovery' has been suggested as a guiding vision for service users and mental health workers. 'Recovery' is described as a deeply personal, unique process of changing one's attitudes, values, goals, skills and/or roles. (Pendulum 16(1))

As this quotation shows, there is a feeling within certain sections of the user movement, and indeed amongst some professionals, that the current system of British mental health services fails to sufficiently incorporate the concept of recovery (Bracken & Thomas, 2005), although there are signs that, at least in principle, this might be changing, with both the Department of Health and the National Institute for Mental Health in England making recent reference to recovery (Wallcraft, 2005).[3]

Much of this relates to the issue of who has control in mental health issues, the client or the professional (Tooth et al., 2003): this theme will be returned to on numerous occasions in the remaining chapters. As Wallcraft (2005) and Repper and Perkins (2003) point out, taking control of one's life is an important element in the complex and often idiosyncratic definition of recovery. The role of the individual in developing their own strategies for recovery, and the way that professionals fail to acknowledge, and hinder this process, is discussed forcefully by Coleman (1999), who draws on his own experiences to support the notion that recovery is an 'alien concept' within the British mental health services. Similar arguments are made by Lapsley et al. (2002), who studied stories of recovery in New Zealand: they divide the journey of recovery into three stages – glimpses of recovery, turning point and the road to recovery. Different aspects, including research, and support from others, help with this journey, which leads to a recovery of hope, self-esteem, relationships, agency and a transition of identity. Comparable themes regarding what helps in recovery also emerge in Onken, Dumont, Ridgway, Dornan and Ralph's (2002) study of 115 American clients: this study also examines what hinders, citing, among other things, problems within the formal mental health service system, lack of resources for client groups and material poverty.

Although the notion of recovery seems more in-keeping with that of the active journey through mental health problems discussed here, not all clients within my own study reject the concept of cure outright. For some members of Depression Alliance, for example, the curability of depression is a major issue, in-keeping with the organisation's more medically-based stance. For example, there was a discussion of the need for governments and business to provide funding to research the cures for depression to the same level as research into cures for cancer. The implications of the notion of seeking a cure for depression in the same way as professionals search for a cure for cancer are striking: not only does it reinforce the idea of mental illness as analogous to physical illness, but it re-introduces the notion of a passive client, or perhaps even 'patient'. However, while this certainly fits in with much of A Single Step's faith in drug treatments, it would be wrong to assume that the notion of recovery is absent from all material within this newsletter. Indeed, for many clients who contribute to A Single Step, as for the majority of clients I met at the day centres and wards, a mixture of recovery and cure is needed in the project of overcoming mental illness. This mixture might be highly personal (Lapsley et al., 2002) and contain different kinds of personal strategies, professional treatments and, to some extent, luck.

A minority of clients in my study felt that their journeys through mental illness would last indefinitely, as they believed their mental health problem to be a permanent and continuous condition, with little chance of reprieve. Again, rather than being something that is associated with conditions that might be labelled psychosis, which have been seen by the public (Foster, 2001) and professionals (Morant, 1996) as more permanent, and

represented as more controllable than curable, this is a representation which is seemingly found more frequently in Signpost and
A Single Step than elsewhere, although some members of MDF
voiced similar opinions in the Pendulum debate on recovery. From
this perspective, once you have a mental illness you will always
have that mental illness, and it will be obvious to yourself and to
others. For some clients, the situation seemed particularly bleak,
and recovery seemed a very distant possibility, whatever kinds of
treatment or self-help might be involved.

> She says she doesn't really know what the point is, as she says
> once you've said what your problem is there isn't much more
> they can do, and it's not as if the doctor can wave a magic
> wand.   (Summer Day Centre)

> Paul talks about his planned move to another area, and a
> different day centre, and says to Mary, 'It doesn't make any
> difference, though, I could move to Australia and I'd still have
> my problems'.   (Summer Day Centre)

However, it can also be that a condition is seen as permanent but
only known to the person who has experienced it. Indeed, other
people might be convinced that the client has recovered, and the
client might play along with this, while secretly aware of the reality
of their situation. This view, frequently espoused in Signpost, was
largely exclusive to people with eating disorders, although some
clients talked about hiding the fact that they heard voices, or held
beliefs that professionals saw as delusional. The inverse of this situation is, however, generally more common, that is, the client, or
former client, believes himself or herself to be recovered but feels
that others, whether public or professionals, fail to appreciate this
and continue to regard them as mentally ill.

An alternative way of constructing mental illness is that it
might be recurrent, but not permanent. A client might suffer
from 'episodes', but this does not mean that they are ill all the
time. This was a particularly popular position for clients at the
Winter Day Centre, and for people writing in Pendulum. As
already mentioned, most clients I met at Winter Day Centre saw
themselves as well, and recovered, despite the fact that they were
using the service as often as daily. For most, when you were out
of hospital, attending the day centre and succeeding in your

project of staying round, you considered yourself, and should be considered by others, to be well.

ERIC: *I'm really, being frank with you, since I've been well, for the last six months, you know …*

I: **Uh-huh**

ERIC: *I've been doing more than I've done since … pretty well since before I was ill, basically.*
(Interview with Eric, Winter Day Centre)

JASON: *I've, I've been all right mentally for about ten years now.*
(Interview with Jason, Winter Day Centre)

However, clients acknowledged that becoming ill or unwell again was a possibility, and that if this happened they would be readmitted to hospital and could be considered patients again. Here Paula and I are discussing what people who attend the day centre should be called (e.g. clients or patients): Paula says she prefers the term 'resident'.

I: *So you said you think you're more a resident here than a patient?*

PAULA: *Yeah. …*

I: *OK, so in hospital are people residents or patients?*

PAULA: *They're patients.*

I: *Right, so they're different?*

PAULA: *Yeah.*

I: *So -*

PAULA: *They've got an illness.*
(Interview with Paula, Winter Day Centre)

A similar distinction is made on occasions in Pendulum with regard to manic depression. Although these were the most common locations in which this kind of representation could be found, it was also sometimes evident in literature on depression, eating disorders and at Spring Ward and Summer Day Centre.

The importance of luck

A journey, however, does not rely entirely on the client and his/her use of services, medication and own activity: luck may also play a role in the process. This is illustrated well in this extract from an interview I conducted with Mark at Winter Day Centre, and is a story that Mark told when I asked if he had anything more to add.

MARK: *There's one chap in [Ward] when I was there, very disturbed, had been there for a number of years, and he was on that particular medication at night, and Dr M- put a line through the lot, and all he put was 600 mg chlorpromazine every night. And at this point [patient] was so far gone, it was like water off a duck's back to him.*

I: *So is that a big dosage of chlorpromazine?*

MARK: *Yeah, yeah.*

I: *So what does that sort of dosage do?*

MARK: *Lethargic, calms you down. Can make you very sleepy, but [patient] was so far gone that, you see, he wasn't responding. He first came in in 1980 when I was there. And the O[ccupational] T[herapist] said to me 'Have a look at [patient], you were in that state when you came in, you were very far gone'. And whereas I got better ... he never did.*

I: *Right*

MARK: *So I was the fortunate one.*

I: *So is he still in [Ward]?*

MARK: *He's still in [hospital] somewhere. [inaudible] he never got out.*

(Interview with Mark, Winter Day Centre)

Other representational projects

Within social representations theory, and especially explicit within Bauer and Gaskell's (1999) concept of projects within representation, is the possibility for consideration of the way in which the representations and projects of different groups come into contact with one another, and the consequences of such co-existence of different understandings (Foster, 2003). This allows for a consideration of the power relations at play within a particular context and the ways in which representations might interact and clash with one another, something which is particularly useful in a field such as mental health, where groups with differing power, and different interests, come into regular contact with one another.

In the next section of this chapter I will focus on the mutual influence between clients and two other groups – the general public and mental health professionals. The representations of the first group, the general public, clearly have an effect on clients of the mental health services, an effect that can, as I will show, be far-reaching. However, they do not have such an immediate, day-to-day impact as the representations held by mental health professionals. Clients come into contact with these on a very regular basis, and they can have very significant effects on clients' lives and on the possibilities that clients have for journeying through mental illness in the way in which they feel is most appropriate for them. These power issues will be examined in this section in more detail.

The public and clients' journeys through mental illness

In all the services that participated in my own study and in all the newsletter data, clients saw public representations of mental illness as very negative. Clients felt that the general public saw the mentally ill as dangerous, frightening and criminal, elements that are indeed often central within public representations of mental illness (Nunnally, 1961; Jodelet, 1991). The stigma associated with mental ill health has long been a focus of research (e.g. Goffman, 1968). Farina (1981) has highlighted the way in which clients fear public reaction, to the extent that they will interpret others' reactions towards them as negative if they believe that stigmatising information has been revealed, even when this is not actually the case.

> Sarah says that she thinks that the portrayal of the mentally ill is always that they are threatening, and that they are always associated with criminals ... . She says that there is always the association of crime and mental illness, as if people need that as an explanation for people having done awful things. She says people with mental illness are much more likely to die than to kill.   (Spring Ward)

There is a great sense of frustration surrounding the issue of public representation of mental illness for clients of the mental health services, a feeling that the public do not understand, and that the ideas that they have are unfair and ill-informed.

> And the sad thing about it was, that with the telly and the news and that, they give you the impression that schizophrenics are violent ... but if they're treated for it, they're OK.   (Interview with Mark, Winter Day Centre)

> She doesn't like the term 'mental illness' because 'ignorant people think of schizophrenics who chop people up and we all get tarred with the same brush. People think we should all be locked up'. This really annoys her.
> She says on her last admission she told everyone she doesn't think it should be called a psychiatric hospital, but 'an emotional rehabilitation centre'. She says people lump it all together and think of maniacs ... 'when people haven't been to a psychiatric ward they think we're all climbing the walls or in padded cells and strait jackets, that we're all screaming'.   (Interview with Kirsten, Summer Day Centre)

This last quotation is particularly interesting in that it accuses the public of failing to differentiate sufficiently within mental illness, and seeing all those with mental health problems in the same negative terms. This point will be returned to in Chapter 6.

For some clients, the fact that the public hold negative representations of mental illness and people with mental health problems is unfortunate, yet understandable. Many clients used their own ideas before diagnosis as a point of reference.

JONATHAN: *I was getting very angry. Because I thought I was in hospital ... because it has got stigma, you know ...*
I: *Right, yeah.*
JONATHAN: *I mean, I felt the same as everybody else – we used to call it the loony bin*
> (Interview with Jonathan, Winter Day Centre)

The problems associated with the negative representations that the public have of mental illness, and people diagnosed with it, are far-reaching. Clients in my study believed that the public's representations of mental ill health lead them to engage in discrimination and avoidance, and many clients also had stories detailing problems that they had encountered with members of the public.

MARK: *I was talking to this AA [Automobile Association] man when [Community Psychiatric Nurse]'s car broke down a few weeks ago ... and we were waiting at the garage to sort the car out, and I told him I'm schizophrenic, and he kind of jumped back ... he thought, he naturally assumed I was going to be violent.*

I: *Right, yeah*

MARK: *And he said, 'You look all right to me'. And I said well, as long as you take the medication you're OK, you're under control.*

I: **So how does that make you feel, when people sort of jump back? When you tell them?**

MARK: *Well, it's a bit unnerving, really. It's not ... people don't understand.*

(Interview with Mark, Winter Day Centre)

At Spring Ward clients would often use their ideas about public representations of mental illness as devices for humour or mockery, sometimes of themselves. Clients were, in the main, acutely aware of the way in which the hospital was viewed, referring to it as the 'loony bin', the 'house on the hill' and so on.

At some point during the morning, a siren [fire alarm?] goes off for a while, and Richard laughs and says it's someone who's got out, and that will worry the neighbours.   (Spring Ward)

The role that clients saw the media as playing in influencing and sustaining public representation is somewhat ambiguous. For the majority of the newsletters surveyed here, especially those that take a more political stance on mental health issues, the media is a foe, in that it persists in promoting demonised representations of people with mental health problems, which can have unpleasant consequences for clients, a view supported by some psychiatrists (Byrne, 1997) and by many research studies in the area (Foster, 2006a; Philo et al., 1996).

I: *[word association] Mental illness?*
MARY: *'Stigma. There's a lot of bad press, like with schizophrenia.'*
                (Interview with Mary, Winter Day Centre)

> Gail says she was really annoyed that the only one of Harold
> Shipman's[4] victims who had her diagnosis printed in the media
> was the one with mental illness, as if the fact that she had manic
> depression meant that she had asked for it, or it had been her
> fault.   (Spring Ward)

There is often considerable outrage at the way in which the media
deals with mental health problems, and many of the newsletters
discuss ongoing campaigns that encourage better treatment of
mental health within the media. Mental Health Media, which
grew out of the Mental Health Film Council founded in 1963,
has also played a crucial role in campaigning and providing a wide
range of information regarding mental health issues and the
media. It also organises the annual Mental Health Media Awards,
at which examples of sensitive and positive media treatment of
mental health issues are recognised.

Increasingly, however, as shown by the Mental Health Media
Awards, the media is also viewed as a potential ally to the mental
health service user movement and as a tool that should be used in
the campaign to provide information and to change opinions
(Anderson, 2003). In my study, newsletters therefore discussed
media coverage of appeals, articles that had appeared in the press
offering advice or tips on dealing with mental health problems,
and might appeal for clients to act as 'case studies' in media discussion of mental health problems. Indeed, both Depression
Alliance and the Hearing Voices Network were established in the
first place in direct response to television programmes. In addition, television documentaries are often credited with instigating
reform of mental health policy: in 1981, a documentary entitled
The Silent Minority, which highlighted abuses within two psychiatric hospitals, provoked public outrage and is regarded as having
contributed to the ideological shift towards care in the community. The relationship between mental health organisations and
the media is therefore complex: the media is seen both as contributing to the problem and to its solution. Within the services

themselves, however, all the clients with whom I spoke saw the media as more problematic than beneficial.

Clients of mental health services also believe that the public's representations of mental illness have significant consequences for them, often preventing clients from journeying through mental ill health in the way in which they would like. Clients in this study seemed to find little evidence of what Crocetti et al. (1974) claim is an increasing tolerance towards the mentally ill on the part of the public, and contrary to Weinstein's (1983) findings, seem very much affected by the way in which other people label them. There was more support for the recent suggestion (Office for National Statistics, 2003) that public attitudes towards people with mental health problems remain negative, and indeed are perhaps even worse now than in the late 1990s.

> Karen says that once you have been given the label of mental health problems, it affects everything. Penelope says she thinks it's like rubbing salt into the wound, and everyone else agrees.
> (Summer Day Centre)

Public representations of mental illness are seen as particularly relevant in issues of employment.

MARTIN: *Yeah, I'd like to have another job, you know. It's just getting people to accept me for what, after what I've been through.*

I: *Right, is that difficult?*

MARTIN: *Yeah ... most [jobs] I've been for ... I went to [factory], erm ... at the [location], and he read my form, and that, and he said, 'We don't employ people like you'. I just walked out.*

I: *Really?*

MARTIN: *I thought, you nasty, miserable, little git.*
(Interview with Martin, Winter Day Centre)

> Paul says that it doesn't matter how many qualifications you have, but if you've used mental health services, you can't get a job. He says there is a lot of stigma attached to it. (Summer Day Centre)

This is reflected in wider data on mental health and unemployment: government figures suggest that 71 per cent of those who experience a mental health problem are unemployed and reliant upon benefits (Office for National Statistics, 1999). Employment is a particular issue of campaign for the service user movement, with some organisations working hard to promote good practice with regard to mental health issues at work, funding phone-lines to deal with calls relating to problems in the workplace.

This indirect consequence of using mental health services, through public representation and discrimination, leads to issues of the more material effects of mental illness, again affecting a client's journey through mental illness very significantly. Many clients discussed how, as a result of a complex mixture of factors, people with mental health problems are very poorly off in terms of housing, employment and financial issues. A consequence of mental health problems might be a reliance on benefits, especially if it is impossible for the client to find long-term paid employment. Benefits were a favourite topic of conversation, both in newsletters and at the day centres and ward. Staff and volunteers at the services often helped clients with claim forms, and financial problems were never far from the surface in conversation.

> Finances are also discussed; Bob tells me 'something you might be interested in' is that all the users get different amounts of money, depending on what sort of housing they live in.   (Winter Day Centre)

Homelessness and housing problems are also a large part of the reality for those with mental health problems. A report by the Social Exclusion Unit claims that half of the rough sleepers in the United Kingdom have mental health problems (Social Exclusion Unit, 1998), and certainly many clients in my study had been homeless at some point. Often, they discussed this in a surprisingly matter-of-fact manner. However, the issue of homelessness and mental ill health cannot be understood in a causal, linear fashion, and there are many issues at play within the relationship between the two.

The numerous ways that such failings in material needs affect the client's process of recovery have been highlighted by other theorists (Onken et al., 2002): clearly, a client might have particular ideas regarding what is likely to help her in her journey through mental ill health, but if one of these strategies might involve having a job and finding suitable accommodation, when she is stopped from doing either for a variety of reasons, she will be forced to change her ideas, and journey.

Mental health professionals and clients' journeys through mental illness

Just as clients have ideas about public understanding of mental health problems, so too do they have ideas regarding professional representations of mental health problems.

Within my own study, two strands of thought regarding professional representations could be discerned. The first position advocates the acceptance, support and maintenance of professional ideas. Many of the clients in this study did not challenge professional representations of mental ill health, and accepted them as matters of fact.

> I ask her about the causes of her being unwell, and she says 'I've been told, well, the professionals told my parents it is a chemical imbalance in the brain.' She says she thinks this is a good explanation, as if it was more complicated, she wouldn't be able to grasp it.   (Interview with Penelope, Winter Day Centre)

Similarly, some newsletters, for example, Signpost and, in particular, A Single Step incorporated professional views in the form of commissioned articles. A Single Step, in fact, was funded by Priory Healthcare, a company that runs a number of private hospitals, during the period of this research. It was clear that these newsletters sought to perpetuate professional representations on some level, although the material produced by clients within them did not always agree. For example, clients' letters sometimes advocated various kinds of alternative or complementary treatments, or reduction in medication. Such letters always prompted an editorial postscript along these lines:

> Please note that you should never change or alter your medication, or start to take any other preparation or herbal

remedy, without first consulting your GP.   (A Single Step, 2000(3))

A Single Step appears to seek to establish an alliance with professionals, for example, in launching an annual award for the general practitioner who deals best with depression, but the hierarchy of client-professional relations is clearly maintained.

This is not the case in the other newsletters, or in all services. Openmind, in fact, includes a high proportion of contributions by mental health professionals, but these tend to come from the more radical sections of the profession, those who deal in 'post-psychiatry', for example (see Chapter 8 for a more comprehensive discussion of post-psychiatry). Indeed, Openmind in particular mocks many aspects of more mainstream professional representations and relations between clients and professionals: this is particularly evident in some of its cartoons.

If professional representations were challenged by clients in my study, it was often on the basis that they incorporate elements of misunderstanding, of mistake and an over-emphasis on medication. Misunderstanding has already been mentioned briefly: many clients feel that professionals fail to understand what they are going through, what they are saying or what they are attempting to do. This misunderstanding may stem from a general ignorance, or from an inevitable lack of comprehension if the client's experience is seen as too far removed from that of the professional, as discussed in Chapter 4.

> She says in her last admission she said to her consultant ... 'you may have read all the books, got all the qualifications, but you are not the one who's living through it. They need to really listen to what their patients need'.   (Interview, Summer Day Centre)

Mistakes are often an integral part of clients' representations of professionals and professional understanding. This includes issues pertaining to diagnosis, which, clients recognised, was neither foolproof nor stable. Clients also form their own ideas regarding their diagnosis and might see those of the professional as erroneous.

> He says he's on 24 hour obs [observation] because they're worried that he'll go really low again, but he says he won't, as

it's just what he's like, and now he's gone up he'll dip a little and get a bit weepy, but he won't dip right down again, as it's normal for him. (Spring Ward)

Lastly, the most frequent complaint from clients regarding mental health professionals centred on the importance they assigned to medication, often at the expense of other forms of treatment and care. This was common in all the services I visited and all the newsletter data: medication is viewed with ambivalence by almost all clients, and the fact that psychiatrists in particular are sometimes seen as dismissing concerns that clients express is a source of much frustration. This is supported by a great deal of work conducted by the mental health service user movements (Pilgrim, 2005; Rogers et al., 1993; Rose, 2001) and by other bodies (Healthcare Commission, 2004). In my own study, professionals were seen by clients as having an almost blind faith in medication that might make them ignore other avenues.

MARK: *And, erm, I went to [] Hospital in '79 ... and I wasn't responding to medication because the thing was ... I was tipping the medication down the toilet ... I thought they were trying to kill me with it.*
I: *Right, OK*
MARK: *And the doctor who was treating me at the time said 'he's not responding to the medication, so he's not schizophrenic. He's got an adolescent illness that he'll grow out of.'*
(Interview with Mark, Winter Day Centre)

He says he recognises now that the primary function of the ward is medical, not psychological. (Spring Ward)

Even while accepting that medication helps them, many clients express a desire to decrease their dosage, or try to live without medication, an idea that professionals tend not to support.

He says that he had to go to the hospital yesterday, as he wanted to stop taking his medication, but his consultant said that all patients want to stop taking their medication ... He says he doesn't fancy having a 'life sentence' of medication. (Summer Day Centre)

This, again, supports the notion that client representations of mental ill health rest on more social, interpersonal issues than those of professionals: like the general public (Leff, 2001), clients might see medication as less useful than other forms of treatment, and mistrust what they see as professional over-reliance on it.

Clients are also aware that professional representations lead to particular courses of action and agendas – what might be termed professional projects. This next section will deal with the ways in which client projects, or journeys through mental illness, and professional projects and agendas come into contact with one another, and interact. This interaction was often most evident in the kinds of service the professional provides, and whether this coincides with what a client seeks from a service. Much of this discussion will be based on a consideration of power structures within the mental health services.

For many clients, although the mental health services play a continuing role in their journeys, this is not always in a helpful capacity. Clients were especially keen to give their views on the services which they were using and had used: in fact, it was often the case that, when I introduced myself and my research study, clients would spontaneously start to discuss their views on the mental health services, rather than on more specific aspects of mental health problems. It is evident from these views how far client and professional ideas and projects coincide, or otherwise.

> When I say I'm looking at service users' ideas about mental health and mental health problems ... Joe interprets the question as one about services, and says when he was in hospital twenty years ago, it was very different. Liz agrees. Joe says it's much more relaxed now, and the staff are more relaxed, and less regimented. He says that twenty years ago, there wouldn't have been china cups, even though people weren't violent. Matthew says he was surprised there were ovens and things here on the ward. Liz says the staff are much better with them. (Spring Ward)

In general, clients emphasised personal relationships with particular professionals in discussions about what made a mental health service helpful, rather than more general aspects of wider service culture and philosophy. Clients at all services, and in all newsletters, discussed the importance of really being listened to by staff, especially consultants: many felt that consultants did not listen properly, or dedicate sufficient time to their clients, instead wanting to see a client for two minutes and then be rid of him or her. These results are also reflected elsewhere (Healthcare Commission, 2004; Repper & Perkins, 2003); in particular, it has been found that psychiatrists are particularly unwilling to engage with clients when they want to discuss the content of beliefs which are regarded as part of psychotic illness by professionals (McCabe, Heath, Burns & Priebe, 2002). My own study would support the idea that, rather than seeing engagement with such ideas as unhelpful, it would lead to a more satisfactory consultation, and limit interactional tension between professional and client (McCabe et al., 2002).

Poor communication between staff and clients was a point of some contention at both Spring Ward and Summer Day Centre, and in the newsletters. There was a real sense in this study that the majority of clients wanted to be involved in the process of their treatment, as part of their wider journey through mental health problems, and to negotiate with staff, but that their attempts to do this were often thwarted, an aspect that has also been noted in other studies (Tooth et al., 2003). A useful example of this comes from Spring Ward, where some clients were able to get 'PRN'[5] medication if they felt they needed it.

Chris says that the other day he felt bad, so decided to go and do some painting to calm himself down, thinking he would resort to PRN if that didn't help, but that when he decided he did need PRN he was told it wasn't available for him anymore, and the decision had been taken without consulting him. (Spring Ward)

Clients also often discussed their need to talk, and to discuss their own views, but felt that the focus of much mental health treatment was on drugs, not on talking. This was particularly the case on Spring Ward and in the newsletters, but could also be found elsewhere.

I don't believe the hospital caters enough for people to come outside ... . Because they want to fill them with drugs, and chlorpromazine and drugs that they're not even sure work. (Interview with Duncan, Winter Day Centre)

He says he knows someone who is a psychiatric nurse who now does her own research, as she can't work at the hospital as she thinks there is too much emphasis on drug treatments at the expense of talking. Al seems to agree: he says that everyone has problems, and if you give people lots of drugs, in the long term it doesn't address the issues.   (Spring Ward)

Another problem in the relationship between professionals and clients arises from a feeling of a lack of continuity of care: due to staff changes it is often hard for clients to develop and maintain a productive relationship with professionals, something that was seen as a crucial part of treatment by clients, especially as this could lead to deeper and more productive conversations. Again, this has been reported in many other studies (e.g. Healthcare Commission, 2004)

I: *Right ... how about nurses?*
MELANIE: *They come and go, at the moment, I find. It's just ... sad that they have to go, I suppose.*
                (Interview with Melanie, Winter Day Centre)

Al says he's been dealing with one doctor the whole way through, and then another doctor on the ward round started delving into his personal life.   (Spring Ward)

All of these aspects again point to clients holding more psychologically based, interpersonal representations of mental illness, and what might help with mental health problems, than is currently appreciated in some sections of the mental health services.

Positive and negative aspects of the philosophy of the mental health services were largely discussed in Openmind, and occasionally in Pendulum, although as can be seen from some of the above discussion, they were often either implicit or explicit topics of conversation at the mental health services themselves. The most common complaint within the newsletters was that the mental health services, in their current format, fail to allow clients to take control of their lives and mental health. It is possible to see reflections of this in the way in which the positive and negative aspects of mental health services were construed by the clients in this study. Opportunities for negotiation, for constructive talk, for participation in the process of treatment were welcomed; aspects of the services that took away a client's opportunity to speak out, to plan their own recovery or failed to support them in what they saw as important within that process of recovery were seen as detrimental.

A closer discussion of the interaction between client and professional representations in each of the three services in my study will highlight the ways in which clients' journeys are supported or thwarted by professional agendas.

In general, professionals' aims and objectives at the Winter Centre did not seem to clash excessively with those of the clients. The relationship between client and professional agendas was more one of comfortable influence. I believe that this was because the professionals here recognised that clients had their own plans and ideas, and worked in a very subtle way to influence them, something which the staff on occasion acknowledged to me was part of the ethos of the centre.

PAULA: *And I like it a lot here. It's good. The staff are all nice.*
I: *Yeah. So what didn't you like about the [another drop-in centre]?*
PAULA: *I don't know ... there was ... here they don't tell you what to do. They ask you. There you're sort of compelled to do things.*
I: *Oh, I see.*
PAULA: *And I didn't like that.*
                                        (Interview with Paula, Winter Day Centre)

BOB: *... but nurses, students, the O[ccupational] T[herapist]s, they're just wonderful, really. There's no harassment, and you get with people, like ... because there's no harassment with the nurses, there's no harassment with the people.*
I: *Right, I see*
BOB: *It rubs off on them ... .*
                                        (Interview with Bob, Winter Day Centre)

The staff at the Winter Centre were generally seen as extremely helpful and approachable, and the ethos of the Winter Day Centre was something that was very much appreciated by the clients. Indeed, it was this that many clients claimed had led them to stay at this service rather than move elsewhere. Again, the important issue for clients seemed to be that they were treated as equals by the staff, who refrained from telling them what to do, and instead invited them to do things if they wanted to.

In some ways, many clients seemed to regard themselves as members of the same in-group as staff – that of people at the day centre – all pulling together, albeit occasionally mockingly.

> Alfred is talking to a new client, and introduces him to the Manager, saying 'He's the head patient around here'. (Winter Day Centre)

This was especially obvious in the ways clients reacted when 'management', other professionals from the Hospital Trust came to visit the centre. 'Management' were the out-group; staff and clients at the centre were the in-group.

> Bob says he's waiting for 'management' to come: they're coming for a visit, and he's going to show them round. He says we don't know who's coming until they arrive. Another client sits down and starts to amass a pile of cigarette butts to smoke: Bob asks me if 'we could stop him doing it today, as it's the party, and as management are coming.' (Winter Day Centre)

Although clients did not discuss it, to an outsider such as myself elements of the structure and routine of the day centre did continue to maintain a distinction between clients and staff: identification badges were only worn on more formal occasions, and staff tended to dress casually; however, staff never wore jeans, and the Manager and Deputy Manager of the centre both consistently wore black trousers and white shirts. Staff were noticeable in that they carried nothing but sets of keys (also noted elsewhere e.g. Clark [1996]; Gittins [1998]), whereas clients carried bags with them. In general, space in the centre was not as segregated as on Spring Ward and Summer Centre, although the staff did have access to a locked staff room in which client notes were kept, and tended to use the toilets on the top floor, whereas clients used the ones nearest the drop-in facilities. However, staff spent long periods in the other areas with the clients, something which did not happen to the same extent in Spring Ward or Summer Day Centre. Despite this, the old power structures of the hospital were sometimes still discernible: clients would sometimes call the staff 'Nurse', instead of using their first name; a farewell card given to me by the clients was signed by 'All those *on* the Winter', as one might be 'on' a ward; on fire procedure notices, although most references to 'Patients' had been replaced by stickers that said 'Persons', these had occasionally peeled off. Representations can live on in institutions and practices long after principles have theoretically changed.

There was a very different relationship between clients and consultants, who tended to visit the Winter Day Centre once a week, and were seen much more as barriers to the plans and projects that the clients had. This distinction between positive attitudes towards nurses, and more negative ones towards consultants has been noted in other studies (Raphaël, 1977).

I: *Consultants?*
MARY: *Nervous about speaking to them. It's a little bit us/them, you know.*
(Interview with Mary, Winter Day Centre)

Often, this manifested itself in clients' interpretations of consultants' unwillingness to talk to clients for as long as the clients wanted to talk, or in the arrangements they made for clients' hospitalisations, or moves from one house to another.

I: *And so what do you think of when you think of consultants*
MARK: *Erm ... good people but you have to watch them. [Laughs]*
I: *Why do you have to watch them?*
MARK: *Because they will put you in hospital.*
(Interview with Mark, Winter Day Centre)

I: *OK. How about consultants?*
X: *They'll talk to you for two and a half minutes.*
(Interview, Winter Day Centre)

Although not as obvious as on Spring Ward, clients would also engage in a little subversive humour that mocked the power relations between themselves and the consultants, showing their awareness of the system.

> Paula says she thinks her daughter has got a boyfriend, a boy she's at school with. Paula giggles and says 'Do I hear [wedding] bells?', and Larry says 'Don't say that, dear, the doctor will put you on clozapine,' and lots of people laugh. (Winter Day Centre)

On Spring Ward, power relations were far more evident than at Winter Centre, but the same division between nurses and consultants was apparent. Overall, clients expressed appreciation for what the nurses did, and many sent thank you cards to the ward after their discharge. During their admissions, however, most of the frustrations surrounding the nursing staff centred on a lack of time or excessive focus on medication at the expense of other kinds of care.

> I ask Chris what things are unhelpful, and he says that 'in here' it's people saying that they will do something and then it not happening, or listening without understanding. He says sometimes in here he feels like a child crying for its bottle. (Interview with Chris, Spring Ward)

However, opportunities to talk were welcomed. In line with current practice, Spring Ward operated a primary nurse system, through which clients were assigned a particular nurse to talk to on request, on a one-to-one basis. This was very popular, and many clients discussed how much it helped them.

In contrast to Winter Centre, however, clients saw nurses as being higher up the hierarchy, and more powerful, than they were.

> Julian decides in conjunction with Mary [nurse] that he'll come back [from leave] on Monday for the ward round, and they joke about 'being as one on this'. Mary says something like 'we've got so much in common' and Julian says yes, but she's his superior. She says she's not, and Julian says 'You are – you've got all the power'. (Spring Ward)

Again, physical distinctions were maintained between staff and patients which seemed to reinforce these power relations. Staff wore smart casual clothes, and their hospital badges, and this was not lost on all the clients.

> One of the nurses comes in to do the bedboard,[6] and Mandy says after she leaves, 'They crack me up, with their little black trousers'.   (Spring Ward)

Similarly, space was used very differently by clients and by nurses. Some of the rooms used by staff were locked, and in those that were not, such as the Ward Office and the Staff Room, clients tended to stand on the threshold rather than entering the room. Likewise, most clients spent their time in the smoking room, and it was rare for staff to spend much time here: some staff members, usually the younger, newer nursing assistants would occasionally sit in the smoking room, although only clients would smoke here. Even when staff were engaged in 24-hour observation of a client who was in the smoking room, they would often sit on a stool outside the smoking room rather than coming in. The lounge, where the television was located, and the garden area were more neutral territories, and were used by clients and staff alike. On Spring Ward, staff had their own toilet which was kept locked.[7]

Clients expressed much of their dissatisfaction with the ward by referring to the Ken Kesey novel set on a psychiatric ward (also made into a film starring Jack Nicholson) 'One Flew Over the Cuckoo's Nest', which provided clients with a convenient short-hand, and an important symbolic resource in the act of meaning-making (Zittoun, Duveen, Gillespie, Ivinson & Psaltis, 2003).

> Chris says he hasn't slept for a few nights, and he hopes that 'Nurse Ratched' isn't on tonight. Alan laughs, and I ask who he thinks is like Nurse Ratched, and Chris says it could have been any of the three who were on last night.   (Spring Ward)

The abuses of power described within this book are particularly explicit, again emphasising how aware of power differentials clients on Spring Ward were.

> Michelle is laughing at how much Joe said in the community meeting, and Rufus comes in and tells Joe that they're all going to be kept in longer now because of the things he said.

> People start to talk about 'One flew over the cuckoo's nest', and say that Joe will be taken away and 'seen to' if he carries on like this. (Spring Ward)

Consultant psychiatrists were regarded separately from the nurses once again. It is possible that the different ways in which clients saw consultants and nurses at Winter Centre and on Spring Ward are symptomatic of tensions that exist between these two professional groups already (Robertson, 1996), as it has been claimed they differ significantly in their professional cultures (Serino, 1987). Consultants were seen as the ones with the ultimate power, and indeed were, in that they were the ones who put clients on section, or threatened to do so. There was considerable recognition of the problems of power within the psychiatrist/client relationship.

> Richard says the ward round is a bit like the inquisition. Later, Ben likens it to being sent to see the Headmaster. (Spring Ward)

The material manifestations of differences in power were often discussed by clients: there was talk of the 'regal' high-backed chairs in which the consultants often chose to sit during interviews or in ward round meetings; clients joked that they would be diagnosed with delusions of grandeur if they parked in the staff car-park and so on.

> He says that a member of his family is a psychologist. Then he says 'Keep it in the family, we just go in through different doors' and everyone laughs. (Spring Ward)

The power relations, and distinctions between clients and staff, then, were something which provided fertile ground for humour and mockery on Spring Ward.

> Julia [nursing assistant] gets up from a stool outside the bathroom, where she is waiting for someone who is on 24 hour obs [observation]. Rufus is hanging around, as he wants to see the doctor, and at one point he sits on the stool vacated by Julia. When Ellen [staff nurse] asks Julia to make her a cup of tea,

Rufus says 'Make me one too, Jules, I can't do it as I'm doing obs,' and the nurses all laugh. (Spring Ward)

However, the long-term consequences of professional representational projects were most obvious on Spring Ward, especially in issues of definition and of section. Definition of the normal and abnormal was a particular issue of concern for many of the clients I met on Spring Ward who had been given any diagnosis of mania. For them, elements seen by a professional as abnormal and symptomatic of a problem were often normal *for them* and a part of their personality. They were not something that clients necessarily saw as problematic or wanted altering with mood stabilisers.

She says that she thinks that some of her personality has been taken away since she was labelled and put on medication: she says she thinks her mania is part of her personality and she thinks that Rufus is probably the same. She says that the drugs level you out, but they stop your personality coming out too. (Spring Ward)

Aside from definition, the other arena in which professional representations have more weight and significant consequences is the sectioning of clients. On Spring Ward, in particular, sectioning was a frequent topic of conversation, largely as it was more immediately relevant, given that clients were sectioned, on section, appealing their section and being taken off section while I was there. For some, sectioning was a clear exercise in power relations.

Al [discussing another patient who has just been sectioned] says it's because he challenged those in power. The other patients seem to think it's more a question of his being ill. (Spring Ward)

The ability to section clients places psychiatrists firmly at the top of the hierarchy in mental health, something of which clients in all locations were acutely aware.

I: *How about psychiatrists, or consultants?*
SCOTT: ... errrr ... *officials, authority.*
I: *Why do you think you say that?*

SCOTT: ... ... *because they're the ultimate authority, aren't they? And they have the power to put you, I've never been under a section, but they have the authority to put you under a section.*

(Interview with Scott, Summer Day Centre)

However, the distinction between being on section and being a voluntary patient is not always clear-cut. Voluntary patients, those who have been admitted for treatment with their consent, might feel that the threat of section is used to keep them in check.

> Rufus comes in and tells us he's off section but is here as an informal patient. He's very happy. He hugs Anna, and she says 'so what happens if you try to leave?' and he says he'll be put back on section, but he's really pleased.   (Spring Ward)

> Al has been in with his doctor, and has asked if he can go out. His doctor has said he isn't well enough, and so Al asked if he is on section, and his doctor said no, but Al says he knows that if he tries to go, that means they'll section him.   (Spring Ward)

'Voluntary', then, can become something of a euphemism within the mental health services.

> He says he was admitted voluntarily on [date] and when I ask how that happened, he said the police and a psychiatrist were involved, so 'as voluntary as you can get without using the word as a contradiction'. (Interview with Rufus, Spring Ward)

Interestingly, however, despite their relative powerlessness in the situation, clients would often talk about 'my section', thereby taking possession of that over which, in actual fact, they had little control.

Clients at Summer Day Centre were also engaged in a struggle for power, both with the staff at the centre, and with consultants. With staff, the struggle centred on what some clients wanted from the centre and what the staff were providing. Given that during this part of the study I spent more time in the drop-in facility, it is perhaps unsurprising that the clients I spoke to saw this as the most valuable part of the centre, although it was not regarded as such by the staff. Many clients came to the day centre to attend group activities, and did not use the drop-in at all.

> Paul then starts talking to me about some of the problems with the centre. He says sometimes you come in and plan to talk to your keyworker about something, but then they're too busy, or they're off sick, so you don't achieve what you set out to do in the first place. He says this can lead to angry outbursts. He says that today the staff have been in a meeting since the centre opened, and they should be out at 10:30 and come and say hello, but instead they're still in the meeting. He and Keith talk about them being short staffed. He says often you want to talk to someone and just don't manage to. They say that sometimes there are staff just sitting in the staff room not doing anything. (Summer Day Centre)

This last point has been made by several user-led studies (e.g. Rose, 2001). Similarly the distinction between staff and clients was maintained in some subtle ways: staff wore casual clothes and their ID badges, although the latter was at the request of the clients. Space was also used differently: clients would rarely enter the staff room, which was kept locked, and although staff did sit in the drop-in, they did so at designated times, and casual use of the area was less apparent. The clients also had a 'user room' in the basement which was a staff-free zone, although during the summer months clients tended to avoid it, as it was rather dark and dingy, and preferred to sit outside to smoke.

The problem of thwarted projects was also apparent in some interactions with consultants.

> 'I often think they don't listen; I sometimes feel like tearing my hair out.' She says that they 'need to learn to listen more, as they're all wrapped up ... They need to really listen to what their patients need.' (Interview, Summer Day Centre)

I: *How about if I say consultants? Or psychiatrists, what does that make you think?*
Y: *Well ... I sometimes wonder ... whether he listens to me.*
(Interview, Summer Day Centre)

At Summer Day Centre I observed less humorous subversion of the power relations between staff and clients, and more overt challenging, and despondency.

> D- [nurse] comes in at 1:30 pm to see if anyone else is waiting to join the café group, and Scott, who has come back in and been sitting with his eyes closed by the radio, says he'll come. At that point D- says there might not be room, as they already have eight people and only one member of staff. He asks if Laura wants to go, and she says she does. Scott says it doesn't matter, as he's already been into town once today, and Laura should go. She does. William challenges D- and asks why there is a limit on the people who can go, and is it 'more cuts?' (Summer Day Centre)

While many clients talked about their appreciation of staff at the centre, Summer Day Centre was the only location at which similar amounts of ambivalence were expressed towards day centre staff as to consultants.

Summary and conclusions

In this chapter I have argued that clients of the mental health services are engaged in particular journeys with regard to their mental health and that they employ representations accordingly within these. These journeys vary according to the particular context in which they evolve, and provide clients with a way of objectifying mental illness, of understanding it and orientating themselves towards it.

However, the idea of the journey operates at two levels, the specific and the global. At the specific level, context is crucial in shaping the client's journey, as the client draws on elements from his or her own and others' experiences, and is influenced by the staff and institutional elements of the service: the way that clients at the Winter Centre conceptualise their journey in terms of 'coming round', clients at Spring Ward use the idea of 'getting it together', and clients at Summer Centre engage in journeys that centre on the notion of 'keeping going' expresses this well. However, there is also commonality between the different journeys in which clients in different contexts engage. As such, the more specific journeys in which clients engage in the services relate to the global level, that of the wider journey through mental illness of all clients of the mental health services, discussed within the mental health service user movement, and within many other studies.

As such, mental illness comes to be linked inextricably with the experience of mental health and mental health problems, and takes on a linear, narrative structure; the idea of a journey, or project, binds elements from the client's past and present, and encourages projection forward into the future anticipated by the client.

However, clients also come into contact with other representations, projects and agendas, for example, those of the general public and of staff at the services, which can either support or thwart the journeys of the clients themselves. In particular the representations and agendas of mental health professionals can have far-reaching consequences. While this imbalance of power between patient/client and doctor/psychiatrist is certainly not unique in the health services,[8] the notion of lack of insight in mental health problems and a long history of subjugating client understandings are added complications.

The idea of a journey through mental illness, then, provides clients with a framework within which to deal with aspects of mental health and illness. One important aspect with which clients inevitably deal is their own identity: representations and ideas play an important role in the negotiation of identity, and it is to this topic that the next chapter will turn.

6 Labelled, spoiled, negotiated and rejected: issues of identity

Introduction

In light of the stigma associated with mental health problems, an enduring question in the social sciences has been how being diagnosed with a mental health problem affects an individual's identity and sense of self. Goffman's (1961; 1968) consideration of the moral career of the mental patient, and subsequent attempts to deal with a stigmatised identity, and Scheff's (1966) adaptation of labelling theory have been particularly influential in attempting to answer this question. In this chapter, I intend to re-examine these important theories, in light of data from my own research, and other recent studies, considering how a client of the mental health services maintains and constructs his or her identity in the face of the negative representations found amongst the public. How far can the developing alternative representations of mental ill health discussed in the previous chapters protect a client from the stigma associated with mental illness in other representations, and how much identity work is needed to sustain a positive identity under such circumstances?

Representations and identities: a complex relationship

Since it has been argued that social representations create and maintain identities (Duveen & Lloyd, 1986; Duveen, 2001), so it follows that the representations, projects and narrative strategies highlighted in preceding chapters play a crucial part in identity processes. Moreover, they have an important ontogenetic role: engaging in a particular journey is likely to lead to the establishment and maintenance of a particular identity (Foster, 2003).

However, the relationship between identity and representation is unlikely to be uniformly close in every situation. When the object of representation is particularly, and personally, salient for the individual, identity, and the project in which an individual engages in in relation to that representation, will be substantially intertwined and, to some extent, interdependent. This is even more likely when there is potential conflict surrounding the object of representation, such that the identity of the individual might be threatened in some way. Mental health service clients are clearly in such a position: negative representations of mental illness, and what it is to be mentally ill, abound amongst the general public, as discussed in Chapters 2 and 5. Any representation on the part of a mental health service client must therefore involve significant amounts of identity work, whether in the form of acceptance of public representations, and their consequences, or of rejection and redefinition.

I would also maintain that a holistic, circular view of the relationship between a client's journey through mental illness and identity is, in this case, more appropriate. Certainly, representations and the journey through mental illness create and sustain identities; however, in the case of the mental health service client, a particular project, or journey, may be embarked upon precisely because the client wishes to maintain elements of their pre-service use identity, created through other representations. In the case of the clients in this study, it is clear that identity work is not only influenced by the client's journey but also influences that journey: coming round, getting it together and keeping going all establish identities for the client as more or less active in their mental health, more or less responsible and so on, and as these identities become established, they consolidate the particular strategies involved in those journeys.

Spoiled or labelled

Two major sociological theories have been proposed that purport to deal directly with the identity work of people who have mental health problems: labelling theory (Scheff, 1966) and techniques of managing spoiled identity (Goffman, 1961; 1968). These theories have had a significant impact on work on mental health service user understanding, as the volume of work devoted to the discussion of Scheff and the recent increase in work on 'stigma' (Link & Phelan, 2001) testify. Indeed, Scheff and Goffman's works are still referred to as being amongst the most scholarly contributions to medical sociology (Cook & Wright, 1995). Consequently, this chapter will begin by reassessing these theories, before moving on to suggest that although elements of these ideas do have continued relevance in some cases, both at an individual and a collective level, strategies of identity management seem to go much further than they suggest. A mental health service client's identity is not automatically spoiled or negated, rather it is negotiated and re-negotiated through complex processes involving many others, and takes place within the context of representations and the journey through mental illness in which the client engages.

Labelling theory

As highlighted in Chapter 2, Scheff (1966) proposed a theory of labelling within mental health, the main components of which were social role and societal reaction, which has had a continuing impact in the sociology of health and illness (Busfield, 2000). Drawing on Becker's (1963) theory of deviance, and not necessarily rejecting other psychiatric or psychological notions,[1] Scheff proposed that psychiatric symptoms should be considered violations of social norms; not all rule-breaking, however, is labelled as mental illness, in that most is 'denied', and of limited, short-term significance. Whether such rule-breaking is labelled as a mental illness or not depends on a variety of factors, including the characteristics of the rule-breaking, the rule-breaker and those around him/her. If rule-breaking is labelled mental illness, the individual concerned is then subject to a societal reaction that stabilises this residual rule-breaking, and he or she subsequently begins to maintain the expected social role. The patient is rewarded by staff and other patients in the mental health services for playing the role of mental health patient, and punished, for example, in the form of discrimination, if he or she attempts to adopt any another role.

As previously mentioned in Chapter 2, Scheff's theory has provoked a significant amount of criticism, often for the role it assigns to society within the process of mental ill health. Although certainly not without its problems, I maintain that Scheff's theory still has some relevance to clients' identity construction.

First, clients in my own study often demonstrated an awareness of the notion of 'labels': aspects of Scheff's work, and other socio-logical theories of labelling (e.g. Becker, 1963) seem to have passed into common-sense knowledge. Much of this might result from associations with anti-psychiatry, which provoked public interest and debate in the 1960's and 1970's (see Laing [1994] for an interesting discussion of this): in particular, labelling is dis-cussed with some frequency in mental health service newsletters, especially those which seek to challenge the psychiatric status quo. Clients in the mental health services also made some reference to the notion.

> Rufus ... comes into the smoking room excitedly having seen his psychiatrist, and says 'I've got a label ... I'm hypo-' and then the phone rings and he goes off to answer it. Anna keeps saying 'Oh, what's his label?' and tells me about hers.   (Spring Ward)

An aspect of Scheff's (1966) theory which, I believe, remains par-ticularly relevant, despite criticisms to the contrary, is that of the role of wider society in the creation and maintenance of mental illness, and the mentally ill role. The significant effects of being considered mentally ill by others on employment prospects, financial situation, relationships and so forth, have already been discussed in Chapter 5. There was considerable feeling amongst clients that these problems were the consequences of other people's ideas, not anything inherent within themselves, something which has been mirrored in many other studies of client understanding (e.g. Rogers et al. [1993]).

> Michelle says one of her GP's [General Practitioner] visited her the other week and said she was very different when she's on medication than when she's not. She said that the difference is because of other people's attitudes, which she says change according to whether she says she's medicated or not. (Interview with Michelle, Spring Ward)

She says that once you have been given the label of mental
health problems, it affects everything. (Summer Day Centre)

This study, and others like it, provide substantial evidence for the
continuing role of society in forcing the mental health service
client to maintain their role as 'mentally ill person', by refusing to
recognise that a condition might be more transient, acknowledge
recovery, or by precluding other possibilities for the client in
terms of housing, social life, employment and so on. This seems
especially true for clients who have been using mental health services
for longer periods.

However, more recent work suggests that other aspects of
Scheff's (1966) theory are rather more out-dated, or less relevant
to today's mental health service clients. Scheff (1966) asserts, for
example, that patients will be rewarded for behaviour in-keeping
with the mental health service user role by staff and other
patients. This might be partially the case within certain contexts:
staff usually expect clients to continue attending the day centre,
for example, and recent work suggests that, despite guidelines,
professionals might not always encourage clients to play an active
role in their own care planning (Healthcare Commission, 2004),
and instead anticipate a more traditionally passive role for the
patient. However, in other circumstances professionals, and
certainly other clients might not encourage the client to maintain
the service user role. The shift in mental health services from
long-term institutional care towards short-term acute wards and
community-based services means, for example, that staff on acute
wards are focused on patients reaching the stage at which they can be
discharged back into the community, albeit with differing levels of
mental health support. Similarly, other clients are often actively
involved in encouraging and enabling the client to move away
from the 'mental health service user' role: the self-management
programmes led by sections of the mental health service user
movement and supported by some professionals (Repper &
Perkins, 2003) are a prime example of this, but it was also a feature
of interaction between clients in this study on a smaller scale.

However, this should not imply that staff on the ward do not
encourage the client to adopt the role of 'patient' while they are in
the hospital, and clients are expected follow the rules and routines
of the ward, and can be sanctioned, even with threatened or

actual sectioning, if they step too far outside these. Similarly, on discharge clients are expected to take their medication and keep outpatient appointments: perhaps there is a 'client role' that is the modern-day equivalent of Scheff's patient behaviour.

Another ongoing problem is Scheff's (1966) designation of symptoms, or 'symptom behaviours', as rule-breaking or infringement of social norms. While some clients report coming into contact with the mental health services as a result of abnormal behaviour, for example, expressing beliefs that friends and family found bizarre, this is not exclusively the case. Many clients also report having kept their symptoms a secret, fearing them and the conclusions that doctors might reach on their basis.

Although Scheff (1966) maintains that he places more emphasis on the diversity of reasons behind rule-breaking and examines it as a more involuntary process than Szasz (1961) does, there is still the problem that labelling the symptoms that clients have experienced as violations of social norms does risk belittling the very real suffering that mental health problems can cause. It is crucial not to deny the distress and chaos that symptoms of mental ill health can bring to the client and to those around them: to label them rule-breaking risks under-playing this factor. However, Scheff's discussion of the way that patients might also, on occasions, voluntarily act in the way that they are expected to continues to have limited relevance: this is something that Estroff (1981) found in her ethnographic work with clients in an American community programme, and in my own study was occasionally true of clients on Spring Ward, albeit often in a somewhat tongue-in-cheek fashion.

> Matthew jokes that he's planning on going shoplifting at the local supermarket, as he'd never get sent to prison, as he's a psychiatric patient. Al says that's right, and whatever you do now you'd always end up back in here [psychiatric hospital]. Matthew says he's going to nick a pair of hospital pyjamas when he goes home and put them on if the television licence people come round and make out he's mad. (Spring Ward)

Ultimately, the most fundamental problem with Scheff's labelling theory is his conviction that all individuals within a society are capable of 'playing' the mental health service user role, as it is something with which we become familiar from childhood, through television and other forms of media. While research cited in Chapter 2 demonstrates how society does indeed draw on media images of mental illness in this way, and also provides support for Scheff's notion that these stereotypes are continually reinforced in interaction, this would surely imply a stability of representations of mental illness across different groups, and that mental health service users would therefore hold the same representations of themselves as the general public, and behave in ways that correspond with public expectations. The data from this, and other studies, do not support such an assertion.

Instead, there would appear to be a large discrepancy between public representations of people with mental health problems and the representations held by clients of the mental health services. Clients in this study seemed very aware of the role that the public might expect them, as users of mental health services, to take, and felt that this was neither a role that they were prepared to accept, nor that it was justified.

> Richard tells a story about when he was on the ward at the main hospital site, and how there was nothing to do at the weekend, and so one Sunday he was taking a walk around the car park, and was approached by a security guard, who didn't believe he was just walking. Richard told him he was a patient on one of the wards, and told him which one. The security guard asked what that was for, and Richard said 'psychiatric'. He says the guard jumped back and said 'All right, mate,' and left him alone. (Spring Ward)

Public representations of mental illness are, as shown in Chapter 2, clearly centred on ideas of violence, unpredictability and social deviance. These representations have been shown to be maintained and propagated by the mainstream media (Wahl, 1995; Rose, 1998; Philo et al., 1996). If Scheff's (1966) theory were correct, mental health service users would therefore see themselves in similar terms, and behave accordingly. Throughout this study, and others, clients were anxious to point out that their reality was very different from this: violence, crime and social deviance were generally not part of their lives.

Some elements of labelling theory, then, seem to have continuing relevance, namely the consideration of society's role in keeping a client in the role of mental health services user. Overall, however, it provides an inadequate perspective from which to consider the effects of being a client of the mental health services on an individual and on the identity work in which the individual is engaged.

Spoiled identity

How far can Goffman's (1961; 1968) ideas on the management of spoiled identity provide a more comprehensive account? The notion of stigma is crucial to Goffman's (1968) work, and this too is a term that has clearly passed into common-sense understanding and is a preoccupation for clients (Byrne, 1997), even if some theorists argue that there has been a decline in academic interest in the subject (Hayward & Bright, 1997). All the newsletters examined in my own study referred to the stigma of mental health problems in broad terms, although clients at the three services discussed stigma almost exclusively in relation to the psychiatric hospital, not in terms of mental health problems per se. Clients in the services in this study generally referred directly to stigma more frequently than they did labelling.

I: *[word association] [Hospital]*
JOE: *'concern ... because of the stigma attached to the hospital in the city. Naivety.' Not many people know he's here, and people have very different ideas about the hospital, and mental illness from what it is.*

(Interview with Joe, Spring Ward)

Goffman's (1961) work also centres on the 'moral career' of the mental patient. It is during the ex-patient phase of the career that the individual is called upon to manage his or her stigmatised, and discreditable, identity. Goffman (1968) pays particular attention to the management of a variety of 'spoiled' identities, from those that are visible and obvious, and therefore more likely to be discredited, to the more invisible and less obvious, that are consequently more likely to be discreditable. He makes frequent reference to the mental health patient, and many of his points remain useful. Some aspects of his work, however, seem problematic in today's context.

Goffman (1968) discusses different ways in which an individual might respond to being in possession of a stigmatised identity. Some of these, such as direct attempts to correct the stigma, are less relevant in the case of mental health problems. Others, however, seem more pertinent: for example, Goffman (1968) discusses the possibility of establishing an unconventional interpretation of the situation. Some stigmatised individuals might therefore interpret their status as a blessing, which would be in-keeping with some of the ideas expressed in Chapter 5 on positive aspects of mental illness.

In addition, and interestingly, Goffman discusses how those with discreditable identities might 'stratify' others with similar stigmatised identities, seeing their own stigma as less serious. I found some evidence of this, as some clients differentiated between different types of mental health client, especially on Spring Ward.

> Anna talks about the patients up at Purple Ward, and says there is a lot more 'dribbling' and she thinks they're on much more medication. She says she doesn't think it's acute over there, and Mandy says no, it's long term.   (Spring Ward)

This will be discussed in more detail later in this chapter.

In line with much of his other work (e.g. Goffman [1959b]) Goffman also focuses on face-to-face interaction and the range of possibilities available to a stigmatised individual within it. One of these is the avoidance of contact with 'normals' for fear of uncertainty and tension in interaction. A lack of contact with the wider community might characterise the interaction patterns of some clients in this study, but a fear of discomfort in interaction or revelation of a stigmatised status were not the only motivating factors in this decision. For many clients, panic attacks and anxiety meant that any kind of interaction was difficult outside their normal routines. For others, limited possibilities of social interaction owe more to discriminatory practices on the part of the general public than to a personal choice (a point noted elsewhere e.g. Repper & Perkins [2003]), or to them feeling somewhat constrained by the possibilities afforded to them within 'care in the community'.

PAULA: *Can I just say that sometimes, and I don't mean to sound horrible, but sometimes I think I don't belong here because I'm too well.*

I: *Right*

PAULA: *I mean, I like everybody here, don't get me wrong, but I don't think, really, that I belong here.*

I: *OK*

PAULA: *And I do come because it gets me out, and because I have to.*

I: *Yeah*

PAULA: *But really I don't ... you know, I feel like I'm missing out, being in the community.*

I: *Yeah*

PAULA: *That I'm here. I mean, all my time is spent here. And I need to mix with, I don't mean normal people, but people that haven't got a mental illness.*

I: *Right, so you'd say ...*

PAULA: *Just everyday people.*

(Interview with Paula, Winter Day Centre)

If the discreditable individual does engage in interaction with others, Goffman claims that he or she may undertake strategies of information control, in an attempt to 'pass' as a member of the non-stigmatised group. Some clients did appear to engage in such strategies, especially concealment of experiences of the mental health services.

Richard talks about his concerns over bank nursing assistants,[2] and says that he supposes that they don't get access to the notes, but they are in hand-overs,[3] he imagines, so they must get to know some things. He says he thinks you could end up in a bar in town talking to a woman and one of the nursing assistants might see you and tell the woman you'd been in the hospital. Then he says maybe he's just being paranoid, but, growing up in [town] you are aware of the stigma that surrounds [hospital], and a lot of people hide the fact that they sometimes go into the hospital.   (Spring Ward)

It is important to note, however, that for some clients information control does not appear to be such an issue: some clients in this study sought to introduce themselves at the outset with their diagnosis. However, this is likely to be because clients did not feel that they needed to engage in information control on these occasions, which occurred in mental health services or in the newsletters, where a readership of similarly potentially 'stigmatised' individuals could be assumed. It is also possible that I was seen by some clients as an ally, one of Goffman's 'wise', or within a medical staff context that encouraged such admissions.

> Mark is keen to place me, and introduces himself as 'I'm Mark. I've got schizophrenia.'   (Winter Day Centre)

Other clients, or former clients of the mental health services, might also seek to publicise their identity as a survivor of the mental health services in a more political way. The Mad Pride movement, and those associated with similar groups, provide a good example of this: introducing oneself as 'Mad' represents an important challenge to the general public's and professionals' representations about what constitutes mental ill health and an attempt to reclaim and redefine a stigmatised identity. This will be discussed in greater depth later in this chapter.

Goffman also focuses on the issue of personal and social identities. While not wishing to subscribe to the notion that personal and social identities can be conceived of separately, or even as part of a continuum, there are clearly aspects of our identity that are more personal than others. For example, to be somebody's husband or somebody's mother, while still clearly part of a wider social construction of roles, norms and representations, is a more personal part of an identity than being a user of mental health services, and therefore part of the wider group of mental health service users. Goffman (1968) suggests that interaction between 'stigmatised' and 'normal' individuals might be easier if transferred from the more social ('I am a mental health service user and you are a "normal"') to the more personal plane ('I am Jane and you are John'), although he states that there is evidence that this is often not the case. For the clients in this project, however, much identity work centred on more personal aspects of identity: clients often focussed on defining themselves in terms of their families and personal achievements. Clients at all three services would talk at length about their families, even in cases where they may not have had contact with them for some time. Showing each other, and me, photographs of their families was also very important to clients, as was finding out about my own family.

Along these lines clients might also emphasise their other achievements and experiences, such as education, employment and so on, demonstrating that it was not possible to define them purely as mental health service users, but was also important to recognise their achievements in other areas. This idea is supported by Lally (1989) who claims that an important strategy for hospitalised patients might be the de-emphasis of so-called incompetent aspects of the self and the emphasis of 'competent' ones.

SCOTT: *I mean, I'm not going to go to the [Work] Project and do woodwork, work from 9 till 4. I mean, they expect you to work hard for virtually nothing, when I used to have a good job with the university, I'm not going to do that, you know.*

(Interview with Scott, Summer Day Centre)

Goffman also suggests that the stigmatised individual will feel a sense of ambivalence towards the self. Indeed, his work is founded upon the notion that the mental health services client will feel that their identity is compromised. This, like Scheff (1966), would seem to imply that clients of the mental health services subscribe to similar representations of mental ill health as the general public, something which my own study has not found. Certainly, clients did express ambivalence towards themselves in some ways, often using humour to do so. This was especially the case in Spring Ward, where clients might see their admission, or re-admission, to hospital as a failure on their part, a failure to successfully take control of their lives and their experiences. However, this does not mean that clients saw their mental health problems in a similar light as the general public. Ambivalence to the self, for example, did not stem from feeling oneself to be violent and unpredictable, in line with public representations. Rather, it seemed to stem from feeling responsible for failing within one's journey through mental illness.

She says that last time she was only out of hospital four weeks, which was 'pretty pathetic'. She uses the term pathetic a couple more times in her descriptions of her experiences. (Spring Ward)

Goffman's theories of stigma and of the moral career of the mental patient still have some relevance today. However, I believe that the strategies of identity work in which clients are engaged go beyond passing, or unconventional interpretation, and are more complex than Goffman's work on asylums and stigma might imply.

Recent work on stigma and labelling

As mentioned in Chapter 2, many aspects of these theories have come in for heavy criticism: in particular, Scheff's failure to research any clients' perspectives is a particular problem. However, other theorists have focused on the differing roles of society and individual in the process of labelling: Lally (1989) claims that it is self-labelling that is the key issue in determining a client's understanding and success in the mental health services and that labelling by others is relatively unimportant. He describes a process of 'engulfment' of identity by the label 'mentally ill person' that comes from within, rather than from society. Link (1987) states that it may be the very expectation of rejection by the rest of society that leads to the mental health service user feeling stigmatised, and Quadagno and Antonio (1975) go as far as to say that labelling theory presents an 'over-socialised conception of man'. Taken to their extremes, these arguments can seem somewhat victim-blaming in their refusal to examine the role that society might play in stigma and labelling. It could also be argued that this particular branch of the literature over-emphasises the split between internal and societal influences: after all, expectations of rejection by society are likely to stem from an awareness of society's negative conceptions of mental ill health, and it is hard to see how the individual's self-concept can remain so independent of the society in which he or she lives.

Although there are clearly some problems with parts of theories of labelling and stigma as they were originally conceptualised, it has been argued that it is premature to dismiss them (Link,

Cullen, Struening, Shrout & Dohrenwend, 1989). Perhaps the answer is to incorporate some elements of the role of the reaction of the individual concerned to the stigma. Link et al. (1989) suggest that we need to consider the stigmatising societal conceptions of mental illness that are learned through socialisation; if a person is labelled, such conceptions become relevant. This might then lead directly to negative consequences for the individual's self-esteem, social network and so on, or this might be mediated by the individual's response to being labelled (e.g. secrecy, withdrawal, education). Unarguably, the negative consequences suffered by the individual lead to vulnerability to new disorders or repeat episodes of existing disorders. Similarly, other recent work on stigma has attempted to develop a distinction between felt and enacted stigma (Gray, 2002; Scambler, 1998), with felt stigma being internal, self-stigmatisation on the part of the individual, and enacted stigma being the external discrimination that the individual might experience within society.

Such an approach begins to address one of the main problems with some work using theories of stigma and labelling, Scheff and Goffman included, in that it presents an overly passive portrayal of the individual as a helpless victim (Link & Phelan, 2001). Link and Phelan (2001) claim that there are, of course, numerous examples of resistance which call this into question; however, the fact that strategies of avoidance are necessary does, of course, demonstrate the fact that stigma exists in the first place. An important point has been made by Oyserman and Swim (2001): we need to take an insider's perspective if we are to truly understand the experience of those who we might consider to have a stigmatised identity. As they point out, 'an insider's perspective acknowledges that stigmatised groups are not simply victims or passive recipients of stereotyping, but rather actively attempt to construct a buffering life space' (Oyserman & Swim, 2001, p. 1). In other words, if we are not members of the stigmatised group ourselves, we need to talk to that group about their experiences and understandings, rather than assuming they are the holders of an automatically labelled or spoiled identity.

Several studies that attempt to examine client's feelings about stigma suggest that alternative conceptions and reactions are indeed possible, or even probable. For example, Prior (1995) examines the case notes of an individual who has used psychiatric services for nearly forty years, but maintains a strong sense of personal non-stigmatised identity and social networks outside the mental health services. For this individual, it is through not mixing with other patients that this positive identity can be maintained, whereas for many others it is precisely through social action and interaction with other clients and former clients that new non-stigmatised identities can be developed and negotiated. An ethnographic study of Canadian ex-psychiatric patients (Herman & Musolf, 1998) found just this: participants engaged in a variety of strategies to reject and resist the identities that society aimed to impose upon them, both in the form of expressive rituals (including anti-deferential rituals and self-harm) and instrumental action (engaging in activist groups, refusing to participate in services and so on).

A study of stigma and people with schizophrenia in Greece has suggested that negative social comparison is not automatic: indeed, to assume that diagnosis with schizophrenia involves developing a stigmatised identity ignores the fact that our identities are multi-faceted, and so multiple comparisons are available to each of us (Finlay, Dinos & Lyons, 2001). Similarly, Corrigan and Watson (2002) argue that client's reaction to the stigma associated with mental ill health might depend on the parameters of the situation: reaction may depend on a number of factors, including the salience of mental illness, negative action by others, perceived legitimacy, group identification and so on, and lead on some occasions to a loss of self-esteem, on others to an energised and righteous anger, and on others to no reaction apart from to ignore it.

Identity work involves an ongoing definition of the self in relation to many elements and to many others: as theorists such as Mead (1977) have pointed out, we come to know ourselves through appreciating how we appear to others and becoming an object to ourselves. It is no coincidence that many theorists adopt a linear, narrative definition of identity (e.g. Weinreich, 1983). An identity is often seen as a work-in-progress (Hall, 1991), dependent upon relationships and experiences in the past, and with the potential to be influenced by those in the future. This ongoing process of identity negotiation and formation in relation to others and within specific journeys within mental health deserves closer attention.

Identifying yourself

This section will focus on the ways in which identity is communally established by clients of the mental health services and how clients involve each other, staff and others in this ongoing process.

Other clients are crucial for the construction of identity: two processes in particular are implicated in this, unification and differentiation.

In seeing all mental health problems as comparable, clients can make sense of their own experiences with reference to those of many others. For some, any condition that can be seen as mental illness leads to a commonality between service users, something which they share whatever the specificities of problems or experiences.

MELANIE: *I mean I can't understand that we all have the same symptoms. Which, I don't understand mental health at all … I mean, how it actually works or anything, but … I mean, we are all here for a reason, and that's because we are mentally ill.*

I: *Yeah*

MELANIE: *Schizophrenics, manic-depressives … psy-, you know, you get into psychotics. Psychotic people …*

(Interview with Melanie, Winter Day Centre)

For many, the mental health service user movement provides a forum for the creation and maintenance of identities and for a unification of clients within this process, challenging stigma in the process (Gray, 2002). Again, for some, there is a commonality between all mental illness: anyone who has ever experienced any kind of mental health problem, and used the mental health services, can, and should, be considered a group, especially for political purposes.

For others, there is an identification with all other clients who have similar problems and experiences to themselves: for example, MDF and Depression Alliance are organised with the intention that people with diagnoses of, in this case, bipolar disorder and depression respectively have a forum for discussion of their experiences, and shared negotiation of their identities.

Many of the service user movement newsletters devote sections to discussion of 'positive stories', of overcoming mental health problems and so on. I believe that here clients begin to make sense of their experiences, and of themselves, through the stories of others. Clients negotiate and employ representations, and embark upon and engage in particular journeys through mental illness in order to create and sustain their own identity as users of the mental health services, as people with similar experiences. This process was not confined to newsletter data: clients at the different services would compare experiences and stories, and negotiate meanings communally around these shared identities and experiences.

> Anna seems pleased to see Helen, and they have a good chat. They compare their past and recent experiences and progress ... Anna says Helen has had a 'manic episode, that's right, isn't it?' Rufus is there and gets very excited about the possibility of Helen sharing his experiences. He says that they are both just naturally 'up there' people. (Spring Ward)

However, not all mental health service users employ unification exclusively when defining their own identities in relation to other clients. Differentiation of mental illness and of mental health service clients was also a very important strategy through which clients defined themselves. For some clients it was important to make a distinction between themselves and other categories of client, as already briefly mentioned above.

Clients might differentiate between themselves and other clients using the same service as them. Often the implication of such a differentiation is that the client believes others within the particular service to be more mentally ill than him or herself, or to be mentally ill in the first place when he or she is not.

> He says he only comes in once a fortnight for his injection, as he doesn't like it here. I say something like 'that's a shame', and he says it's not, it's because here all the people are unwell and he's well. He likes to do things, and can't just sit in a chair all day. (Winter Day Centre)

There might be an element of mockery of the other clients involved in such a process of differentiation: in some cases the client might align themselves more closely with members of staff, or even with me as a researcher, than with the other clients.

He talks about the day-trip and asks if I'll be going. I say I hope to, and ask if he is, and he rolls his eyes as he looks at the list of people who've signed up, and just says 'One flew over the cuckoo's nest'.   (Summer Day Centre)

For clients on Spring Ward, in particular, differentiation of mental illness and of people with mental health problems was very common, as briefly mentioned in the section on causation of mental health problems in Chapter 5. Some clients on Spring Ward set themselves apart from other clients, whom they saw as more disturbed and less understandable, a more extreme version of what they themselves might be going through.

However, it was rare to find clients who set themselves apart from *all* other clients, as has been found in some other studies (Hayward & Bright, 1997; Maia de Nobrega, 1999): only a handful of clients, most of them at Winter Centre, saw themselves as completely normal or well, and all other clients as ill or abnormal. Instead, most grouped themselves and some other clients together, differentiating to a more subtle degree, for example, between conditions, a finding paralleled elsewhere (Hall & Cheston, 2002).

Differentiation between services, however, was almost universal: clients would talk about how clients at other services were very different from themselves, usually with the emphasis on the comparative strangeness of the other location. As Goffman (1961) says:

while restricting himself to the off-ward grounds community of paroled patients, he may feel, as some patients do, that life in the locked wards is bizarre; and while on locked admission or convalescent ward, he may feel that chronic 'back' wards are socially crazy places. But he need only move his sphere of sympathetic participation to the 'worst' ward in the hospital, and this, too, can come into social focus as a place with a liveable and continuously meaningful social world.   (p. 121)

This would certainly seem to be the case for many clients within this study. Clients at the Winter Day Centre would talk about the differences between themselves and patients at the hospital.

DUNCAN: *Spring Ward was very relaxing years ago.*
I: *Yeah*
DUNCAN: *Now it's kind of like ... they're taking in worse people ... and people that are very mentally disturbed ...*

(Interview with Duncan, Winter Day Centre)

Conversely, clients on Spring Ward often had similar views about clients at the Winter Centre, and other drop-in facilities.

> We talk about the fact that I did some research at the Winter Centre, and he says 'that must have been hard'. He also says he used to use the [user-led movement], but it's 'like a time-bomb waiting to go off' as there are some 'very unwell' people. (Spring Ward)

This differentiation, however, was not something that was divided exclusively along the lines of community facility/hospital. Clients at the Winter Centre might also see clients at other day facilities in the area as more unwell than themselves, even when the facilities were considered by professionals to deal with very similar client groups.

I: *And do you think the people that go to [another drop-in centre] are different to the people that come here?*
PAULA: *They're more, erm ... poorly.*
I: *Right*
PAULA: *They seem to be, erm, ... quite a lot of illness. You know, people hearing voices and things like that.*

(Interview with Paula, Winter Day Centre)

Participants also made comparisons between clients in Spring Ward and clients on other wards, both those within the hospital and others in which they had been patients in the past.

> She talks about a couple of locked wards she's been on, and talks about really 'upset' people, and 'real loony bins'. She says that Spring Ward is a hotel compared to them. (Spring Ward)

Differentiation between clients with different conditions, or with different diagnoses, was also apparent, both in the services and also in the newsletter data. For some clients, it is not possible to equate all kinds of mental health problem with one another, and there are important differences. This was also a common position for clients in the services participating in this research, especially for those at Spring Ward and at Summer Day Centre.

> Chris says he recognises the depressives, and the psychosis and what have you. I ask if this means he thinks some people suffer from different types of mental health problems, and he says definitely, and that some people suffer from 'very real ... there are different levels of mental illness, some are severe, enduring types of psychosis where you are a risk to yourself and others and you need powerful medication and support'. (Interview with Chris, Spring Ward)

It seems, then, that in matters of differentiation of mental health problems, there might be some common ground between clients and the general public (Foster, 2001), with clients seeing mental illness as differentiated along lines of severity.

On Spring Ward, clients undergoing detoxification programmes for alcoholism were, to some extent, set apart by the other clients: this separation did not manifest itself socially, as clients in 'detox' were treated in a similar fashion to other clients. However, on occasions, the division was obvious.

> The patients' phone rings a few times during a discussion in the smoking room, and two clients tell the person answering it to say that they aren't here if it's for them. Anna says 'The alcoholics never want to answer the phone.' (Spring Ward)

It is interesting, then, that the clients I met on Spring Ward who were undergoing detox programmes were all keen to emphasise their other problems, such as anxiety, depression and paranoia. It seems that the clients in detox themselves were also differentiating between alcoholism and other forms of mental health problem, and were keen to align themselves with other problems, not merely alcoholism. This might be because of the particular stigma that is attached to alcoholism. As one client said, doctors were more unsympathetic about drinking problems than other kinds of mental health problem because 'it's that attitude of nobody pours it down your neck'. However, clients in this position were still keen to accept that alcoholism was a mental health problem in itself.

In addition, differentiation also occurs *within* conditions. This is particularly common in some of the newsletter data. For example, some clients believe that there are different kinds of depression or manic depression and that there is insufficient recognition of this amongst the public and mental health profession. Differentiation might even be encouraged by the user movement as a way of combating the stigma associated with some conditions: for example, the diversity of voice hearing might be stressed in an attempt to promote the view that it is not always the result of schizophrenia. This issue has also received attention from critical professionals: Leudar and Thomas (2000) trace six historical cases of voice hearing through the ages (from Socrates to a young man named Anthony Smith in the mid-1990s), examining different interpretations of their experiences.

I believe that the possibility of differentiating between types of mental health problem and types of client, and within particular conditions, plays an important role in the identity work of an individual. It can allow clients to distance themselves from certain types of experience or from representations of mental illness held by the public, thereby maintaining a more positive identity for themselves.

Definitions with reference to staff

Many of the ideas which will be discussed in this section relate back to the issues of power and of the relationship between professionals' and clients' representations discussed in Chapter 5. However, it is worth reiterating some important points. Clients define themselves within the mental health services with reference to staff, and this process forms a crucial part of the identity work in which they engage. Much of this client/staff identity work stems from the particular way in which a client approaches their journey through mental ill health, for example, how much responsibility they aim to take within their mental health.

Three different ways of defining the self with reference to mental health professionals were discernible in both the services and newsletters involved in this study: clients as inferior to staff, clients and staff as equals, and clients as superior to staff.

Inevitably the power structures within the mental health services affect the actualisation of these ideas and determine whether or not they will be of any particular consequence.

Some clients seem content to view the staff with whom they come into contact as superior to them in some way and capable of more understanding of mental health issues. Contrary to the ideas presented by Tajfel (1981) in social identity theory, this construction of client identity as inferior does not seem to promote any dis-equilibrium on the part of the client: in fact, it seems to enable some clients to continue their journeys through mental illness in symbiosis with professionals. Indeed, professionals can be imbued with a kind of super-client ability to deal with mental health, and some clients might be particularly grateful for this.

I: *So if I say Winter [Centre], what do you think of when you think about the Winter [Centre]?*

MELANIE: *Erm ... what do I think of? An elephant.*

I: *An elephant? OK, why do you say that?*

MELANIE: *Well, because people on the staff have a good memory, I know they're very intelligent, and they have a good memory, they can sort of ... I don't know if I'm idealising the staff, or anything ... but the staff, I know you all take notes, so I suppose you could look it up in your notes, but I always think that, erm ... we're all here suffering from schizophrenia, the staff are one step ahead of the schizophrenia, and would remember, erm ... I had a panic attack, or how to help in the given situation I was in.*

(Interview with Melanie, Winter Day Centre)

However, in many ways this position is a minority one. By far the most predominant perspective is that staff and clients are equal. Clients might go to considerable lengths to point out that they are no different from the mental health professionals with whom they come into contact. In fact, on occasions their skills in other areas might exceed those of the professionals.

I: *[word association] ... Nurses*

BOB: *Nurses ... they're not better than me.*

(Interview with Bob, Winter Day Centre)

Scott talks again about his chess talents and the fact that he can beat all the staff where he lives. He says he likes proving his intellectual superiority over them. He says he's said to them many times that he doesn't look up to them, just because they're staff and he has a mental illness. (Summer Day Centre)

It is, of course, notable that clients feel the need to voice their equality with staff in the first place.

Problems arise for clients within this position in that their efforts to demonstrate their equality with staff are often thwarted by the staff themselves, and by other elements within the power structures of the mental health services. This was often most obvious on Spring Ward: clients would express their frustration with a system within which important issues might not be communicated to them, such as changes to PRN medication, discussed in Chapter 5. Many clients, especially men, also expressed anger at the fact that their consultant would generally not shake hands with them: this was seen by clients as an important mark of equality, and the consultant was seen as denying the client respect by refusing. This, in turn, might lead to clients expressing themselves in an antagonistic fashion in an attempt to assert their equality with staff, something advocated by some of the more political service user newsletters.

The more political sections of the user movement are the main proponents of the final position of client/professional identity found in this data. Here, clients might define themselves as superior to staff, especially in matters of understanding of mental health. To some extent, this position has already been alluded to in earlier chapters: clients are the 'experts by experience', the 'ones going through it'; they are the ones who are able to offer a different, and possibly more effective, form of care and understanding. Some of this superiority may come from the mere fact that clients have the experience and professionals do not. Alternatively, the professional's involvement with a coercive or even, on occasions, violent mental health system might make the client morally superior as well as more learned in issues of mental health. Again, this tended to be a position advocated almost exclusively by the more overtly political sections of the mental health service user movement and was not something which was discussed in the services that took part in this study.

Other ways of identifying the self

In this study, there were also some interesting instances of clients using me as the researcher to define and negotiate their identities. In the main, these occurred on Spring Ward and involved a gentle mockery of my own identity, through which clients might portray me as the one in need of help from the mental health services, emphasising their own relative 'normality' in the process.

> As I start to eat my lunch, Al asks me what I've got in my sand-wiches, and when I can't remember, although I did make them, he pretends to call the doctor, saying that I should be admitted to the ward.   (Spring Ward)

> We talk about what makes us cry, and I say I can cry even just watching 'Neighbours':[4] Mandy says 'God, you do need help' and Anna says 'See, I told you you should be in here'. (Spring Ward)

The proximity of my identity to that of the clients seemed to be an important issue for some clients on Spring Ward. It sometimes seemed that by emphasising the common ground between my identity and theirs, clients could project a more positive identity for themselves and also make fun of me. However, this was some-thing that was maintained in a humorous way, and in many other ways clients emphasised the differences between me and them. For example, at clients' request I wore a badge identifying myself as 'Juliet – Researcher', which one client decorated for me. When I left the ward I would take it off. This led to the following exchange on one occasion when I had accompanied three clients on a brief visit to a nearby supermarket.

> As we get closer to the supermarket, Matthew and Rufus ham it up a bit about being 'mental patients' again, and say that I should be careful, as I've not got my badge on, so no-one will

know who I am. The implication is that I might be seen as 'one of them'. (Spring Ward)

Collective identities: the sociogenetic level and 'the first great civil liberties movement of the twenty-first century'[5]

The role of the growing mental health service user movement, detailed in Chapter 3, in the identity work of the mental health services client is an important one. In this section, I will examine this process more closely, considering in particular the way that user groups might employ social creativity and social change (Tajfel, 1981) in order to develop and maintain more positive identities for mental health service clients. Both social creativity and social change fit in with the aims and activities of many user groups (Wallcraft et al., 2003). I will then go on to consider the process of resistance of the identities that are imposed upon clients by existing representations: this resistance and re-articulation of identity can be actualised at three levels (Duveen, 2001), which will be discussed in more detail.

According to Tajfel's (1981) theory of social identity, individuals seek to maintain group memberships which contribute to a positive social identity (Turner, 1975). If, in comparing his or her own group with another, an individual finds that his or her own group is of a lower status, and therefore likely to contribute to a negative social identity, problems occur. The individual might display in-group denigration and out-group preference: several studies in the past have confirmed this pattern, from Clark and Clark's (1947) early work with black children, to Lambert, Hodgson, Gardner and Fillenbaum's (1960) study of French Quebecois, and Tajfel's (1981) own work with Glaswegian children. This in-group denigration and out-group preference is supported by some of the earlier work using semantic differential tests with mental health patients discussed in Chapter 2 (e.g. Giovanni & Ullmann [1963]) and potentially by some of the comments made by clients about themselves and other clients discussed above.

However, these are not the only options open to the individual whose social identity threatens their self-esteem. Tajfel also discusses possibilities which are dependent upon the particular society and groups involved: if there is considerable flexibility in the boundaries between groups, social mobility might be an option; if it is not, passing might be possible (paralleling some of the work undertaken by Goffman, discussed earlier). If, however, there is a rigid stratification such that members of the lower status group may not pass into the higher status group, a role may develop for social movements, who might engage in social creativity, renegotiating the meanings and definitions of their social identity, or social change, in the form of mobilisation of the minority group for the purposes of altering the social structure that currently oppresses them. This parallels Breakwell's (1983) work on responses to threatened identity, in which she discusses reconstrual (of threat or identity), mobility or change, and adds a further option of inertia.

Many sections of the user movement, both the more and less political, concern themselves with the redefinition of the identity of the mental health service user, which might be termed social creativity. The redefinition of the term 'Mad', especially by the Mad Pride organisation, is one example, albeit a more radical one than most.

For some clients and survivors, 'Madness' is a term that needs to be employed, and to be employed by the 'Mad' themselves. This process, also discussed in Chapter 3, seems to fit under the banner of social creativity: as such, survivors of the mental health services attempt to redefine what it is to be 'Mad', emphasising the more positive and the more political aspects of the experience, rejecting and challenging accepted professional and public ideas in the process. This has led to the establishment of the Mad Pride organisation: some sections of the user movement are engaged in a struggle to reclaim vocabulary that has acted as an instrument of oppression in the past, and to redefine it. The user movement itself draws parallels between this and the work undertaken by the women's movement and some ethnic minority groups. Their rationale seems to parallel that expressed in Stuart Hall's statement regarding his ethnicity:

> We said, 'You have spent five, six, seven hundred years elaborating the symbolism through which Black is a negative factor. Now I don't want another term. I want that term, that negative one,

that's the one I want. I want a piece of that action. I want to take it out of the way it has been articulated in religious discourse, in ethnographic discourse, in literary discourse. I want to pluck it out of its articulation and re-articulate it in a new way'. (Hall, 1991, p. 54)

However, the Gay Pride movement seems to provide many sections of the user movement with the best analogy. Several of the newsletters, including the less radical A Single Step, refer to the need to 'come out of the closet' in public and openly acknowledge mental health service use.

However, how far this particular form of social creativity extends to wider communities of clients is debatable, and there appears to be some discrepancy between these arguments within the mental health service user movement and the clients who participated in my own study: how far clients at 'ground level' are engaged in any redefinition of the vocabulary surrounding 'madness' is less clear. This, perhaps, reflects some of the tensions between the user movement and users in general, raising, once again, questions about its representativeness (Wallcraft et al., 2003).

Indeed, there is a general absence of the word 'mad' or 'madness' in the data from the services involved in my study. Although absence can, of course, be as telling as presence (Gervais, Morant & Penn, 1999), here I feel it is more an indication that many clients at ground level are not prepared to call themselves mad (or Mad) or to refer to their problems as madness. Indeed, many expressed this notion explicitly: they were not mad and should not be referred to as such.

> I had 18 months, two year section when I went in there. When I first went in there. There was Dr M- sitting where you was, and he called me mad ... I said 'Who's mad?' [makes threatening movement – laughter] like that. (Interview with Bob, Winter Day Centre)

> OK, researcher, you're about to see something really exciting for your research, a first in the NHS. Because they've said a person who's not mad is a madman, and I'm going to sue, and lots of people are going to lose their jobs. (Spring Ward)

Following the earlier discussion of differentiation, however, madness is a term that might sometimes be applied to others, especially by clients on Spring Ward. It might be that problems with defining the self as mad lie partially in a representation of madness as the most extreme form of mental illness, and the mad as the most mentally ill of all the mentally ill, something that can be found in public representation (Foster, 2001). The term madness is not as widely used in English as, for example, 'la folie' is in French: Morant (1996) found that French mental health professionals would employ the term in a way in which professionals from the United Kingdom would not, although Pradeilles (1992) claims that the word has similar derogatory connotations in France too. It might be that the representation of 'madness' still owes more to archaic ideas of total loss of reason and Otherness, rather like the 'canonic themata' discussed by Moscovici (1993; 2000), which continue to shape and constrain today's representations (Foster, 2006a).

> The clients in the lounge talk about the closure of the old Victorian section of the hospital, and about where other patients might have gone, the 'really mad'.   (Spring Ward)

> He says he thinks Spring Ward isn't necessarily the best place for everyone, but it's fine for him, because he's not mad, but he's just mad in the legal sense, so it's fine for him to sit and smoke and drink coffee, and get given drugs. He says it's brought him onto a more even keel. I ask what mad in the real sense as opposed to the legal sense means, and he says it's like the Mental Health Act states that you are dangerous to yourself or to other people. That's really mad.   (Interview with Rufus, Spring Ward)

The above section of Rufus' interview is especially interesting: Rufus clearly makes a distinction between the 'mad in the legal sense' and the 'really mad'. His differentiation is based upon the risk that the individual presents to him or herself and to others: those who are dangerous (to themselves or to others) are the 'really mad'. However, this *is* the legal definition of 'madness' under the Mental Health Act, 1983, which Rufus was being detained under at the time of the interview. Rufus later argued that 'real madness' was more inherently physical in its causation.

Occasionally, clients on Spring Ward would refer to themselves as mad, usually within the context of humour or subversion. This might be seen in Goffman's terms as a way of expressing ambivalence towards the self. However, it was often done in an affectionate manner: the implication seemed to be that clients were using such vocabulary as a result of an awareness of public representations of patients within mental hospitals as 'mad', a way of coping with stigma through humorous solidarity (Manktelow, 1994). Clients might mockingly play along with this: reclaiming and redefinition did not appear to be the purpose behind it.

> Later someone calls on the patients' phone for Laura. Matthew, who answers it, finds out she's not on the ward and tells the caller this. The caller asks who they are speaking to, and Matthew light-heartedly replies 'Oh, just another mad patient'.   (Spring Ward)

> Al asks Chris if 'they've found out what's wrong with you yet' and Chris says he believes the technical term is 'mad as a box of frogs' and then everyone laughs and comes up with other slang terms for having mental health problems.   (Spring Ward)

To some extent, then, social creativity in the form of redefinition or reclaiming of vocabulary may be an important strategy for clients of the mental health services at the level of the service user movement, but how far this strategy translates to other clients in services is debatable and brings into question the overall success of such attempts at redefinition.

Social change is also a goal of much of the mental health service user movement, both at the national and more local level (Wallcraft et al., 2003). Some of this takes the form of lobbying political organisations for practical changes to the mental health services, for example, with regard to the proposed changes to the Mental Health Act (Foster, 2006a). In particular, this latter campaign resulted in the formation of the Mental Health Alliance, an unprecedented coalition of user and carer groups, professionals, lawyers, church groups and various other interested parties.

The mental health service user movement, including more radical groups such as Mad Pride and Reclaim Bedlam, also seeks to change public and professional perceptions of mental health service users and to change their position within society.

Some of the clients I met in the services that participated in my research were also involved in projects such as advocacy groups that sought to improve services and so forth. These are clear examples of attempts to bring about social change in an attempt to improve the representations surrounding issues of mental ill health and to address their stigmatising consequences.

The concepts of social creativity and social change might therefore be important aspects of identity work for mental health service clients. However, they still do not seem to provide a full consideration of the way that the mental health service client approaches issues of identity and mental ill health, especially at the more 'grass-roots' level of the mental health services. In addition, what of the wider socio-political context of the group and its identity? In other areas, such as the study of ethnic minority groups, there has been a reaction against psychological theories, especially those that view actors within a social movement as frustrated and marginal, and a move towards theories that attempt to appreciate the socio-economic and political exclusion of groups, and organisational issues within them (Sudbury, 2001). Resource mobilisation theory is one theory that seeks to act as an antidote to overly psychological theories of social movements (McCarthy & Zald, 1977), focusing especially on the aggregation of resources by social movements, the organisation within those groups and the wider infrastructure of outside agencies. Social movement organisations combine to form social movement industries: here this could be interpreted as organisations such as Depression Alliance and MIND forming the wider social movement industry of the mental health service user movement.

Resistance and negotiation: representations and identity

Perhaps a more comprehensive framework for considering the identity work of the client, both at the level of mental health services and the mental health service user movement, is the framework suggested by Duveen (2001) on resistance within identity: here resistance is: 'the point where an identity refuses to accept what is proposed by the communicative act, that is, it refuses to accept an attempt at influence' (p. 19).

In other words, individuals within a social group refuse to accept the identity that society assigns to them, refuse to accept the representations that others hold of them. Resistance is then articulated first at the microgenetic level of conversation; here, clients discuss amongst themselves their problems with public representations and the identities imposed upon them by these representations. In articulating their dissatisfaction with these representations and their implications, they employ and develop alternative ideas about mental ill health and what it is to be diagnosed with a mental health problem. Resistance then operates at the ontogenetic level, as these identities are restructured in light of alternative ideas, and in turn influence the identities of other clients: this is clear in my own study, in that the three mental health services had their own 'cultures', and clients influenced each others' journeys through mental illness and ideas regarding their mental health. Finally resistance manifests itself at the sociogenetic level, as these representations and identities have a wider impact on the social world, through the efforts of the mental health service user movement.

In this light, clients of the mental health services, unhappy with both their treatment and the perceptions of them found amongst the public, organise themselves into more formal networks, which in many ways parallel the more informal networks of the mental health services. Within these networks, clients take on particular shared projects and strive to renegotiate representations of mental health and illness, based on their collective experiences and beliefs, and maybe incorporating elements from public and professional representations as necessary. These new forms of knowledge are, of course, created against a background of socially shared, and to some extent constrained, knowledge: they will come into contact with other forms of knowledge and might clash with them. They will be implicated in the journeys through mental health problems in which the groups engage. Within this framework, however, there is also room for a consideration of the wider issues of cultural, political, economic context, and the way that they will influence the development and influence of different forms of understanding.

Conclusions

In this chapter, I have considered the effects of being diagnosed with a mental health problem, and considered mentally ill by others, on the identity of an individual. I have revisited the influential theories of Scheff and Goffman, suggesting that, while there is still value in many aspects of their arguments, the main problem is that these theories seem to assume that clients of the mental health services will share the ideas, beliefs and representations about mental ill health held by the wider public. I have suggested that a more comprehensive picture of client understanding shows that this is not the case, and that clients, and survivors, of the mental health services are engaged in a variety of strategies of identity work involving a multiplicity of other individuals and are directly related to their own journeys through mental illness. I have also discussed the role of the service user movement in this process, drawing on the theories of Tajfel and Duveen.

Ultimately, as Duveen (2001) has argued, representations create and sustain identities, and consequently, without representation, there can be no identity (Jovchelovitch, 1996). The representations to which a client subscribes, and the journey through mental health problems on which he or she embarks, will indeed create and sustain a particular identity, which will feed back into the way the client approaches his or her journey. Taking this into consideration allows us to consider the identity of the mental health service client, both at an individual and group level. It allows us to move away from the notion that the identity of a mental health service client is automatically, and somewhat passively, spoiled or labelled and introduces the possibility of negotiation and resistance of identity, within an active journey undertaken by an active client.

7 Representing mental ill health

Introduction

This chapter will begin to draw some conclusions about client understandings of mental ill health, in particular from the results of my own study, but also from other work in this area. It will introduce the idea that, overall, clients can represent mental health problems along two dimensions – controllability and location. Clients might take different positions within these dimensions at different times as their journeys through mental health problems progress. The positions that can be taken within this structure will be discussed, and the implications of these with regards to outcome briefly considered.

However, in-keeping with the discussion in Chapter 5 regarding the interaction between client and professional understandings and agendas, another kind of control also comes into the equation: this relates to the extent to which these representations of mental illness can be exercised by a client. Symbols, and those that hold them, must be recognised if they are to be of any consequence (Bourdieu, 1991). As discussed in the last chapter, a client might not have sufficient control to assert a particular representation of mental illness in the first place, for example, if his or her own ideas come into conflict with more powerful ideas, such as those of the mental health profession. This idea will be returned to in the final chapter, when the implications of this work will be considered from the perspective of the provision of mental health services.

Mental ill health was represented by the clients in this study along two dimensions, those of controllability and of location (see Figure 7.1). As such, it is possible for the client to see their mental health problem in various ways, at various points in their journey through mental illness: clients might see a mental health problem as either something that can be controlled or as something that is in control of them; similarly, it might be something which remains external to the client or something that is more

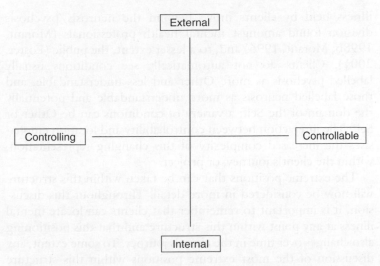

Figure 7.1   Representing mental illness in terms of control and of location

internal. Different positions might be taken as the client's journey develops and changes, as the client's experiences develop and as he or she interacts with other clients, professionals and others.

The notion of Otherness, discussed in Chapter 2, as so central to the representations of mental illness found amongst the general public (Jodelet, 1991), and to a lesser extent, those of mental health professionals (Morant, 1996), is therefore much more complex within the representations of mental illness held by the clients in my own study. Certainly, the Otherness of mental illness plays a role at some points within this structure: to represent mental health problems as external and controlling, for example, would maintain the construction of Otherness. However, defining client representations of mental ill health solely in these terms is overly simplistic. A more complex, and evolving, interaction between the level of controllability and location assigned to mental illness is at play in the representations held by clients.

Although in many ways the more common positions within this representational structure are mental illness as controlling/ external, or controllable/internal, some clients advocate controlling/internal and controllable/external positions. This also provides further evidence that representations of mental illness held by clients move beyond the neurosis/psychosis division found amongst mental health professionals (Morant, 1998b; Morant, 1996) and, to a lesser extent, the public (Foster, 2001). Clients do not automatically see conditions usually labelled psychosis as more Other and less understandable, and those labelled neurosis as more understandable and potentially the domain of the Self: a variety of conditions can be Other or Self. The interaction between controllability and location emphasises the increased complexity of this changing representation, within the client's journey, or project.

The extreme positions that can be taken within this structure will now be considered in more detail. Throughout this discussion, it is important to remember that clients can locate mental illness at any point within this structure and that this positioning also changes over time in the client's journey. To some extent, any discussion of the most extreme positions within this structure will involve painting an overly caricatured picture of clients' representations.

Mental illness as controlling and external

In many ways, a representation of mental illness as both controlling and external has elements in common with aspects of representations of mental illness found amongst the general public, exemplified in the work of Jodelet (1991) and many others and discussed in Chapter 2. At this extreme, mental illness is very much something Other, something which exists outside the client; it might inhabit a location in close proximity to the client but remains distinct and separate. However, it also exercises control over the client from this location.

Two issues are of particular note within this position: first, objectification of mental illness through use of metaphors of place, and second, objectification of mental illness as some kind of entity, which might involve elements of anthropomorphism or animation. Within this latter type of objectification, the personification of the voices a client might hear is especially important.

In objectifying mental illness as a place, the client seems to be able to maintain the notion that mental illness is external to him or her and to avoid taking possession of it in anyway. The issue of control becomes relevant once more when the range of place metaphors used to refer to mental illness is considered: mental health organisation newsletters in particular describe the experience as a pit, the woods, a tunnel, a prison, a black hole, a trap. Similar metaphors were found in Torpor's (2001) study of client understanding (cited in Bracken & Thomas [2005]). The control remains with the mental health problem: it is the place, the external entity, that is in control in most of these examples, not the person within it. The client remains somewhat helpless, even trapped, and at the mercy of the location.

> She says that [user-led movement] is full of men smoking, and the women who are there are encased in their own illnesses. (Summer Day Centre)

Objectification of mental illness as some kind of (potentially living) external entity might also occur when mental illness is represented as both external and controlling. Again, a distinction is maintained between the client and his or her mental health problem, even if the proximity of the Other, in this case, the object, the generally malicious Other, is acknowledged. Numerous examples of this can be found in the newsletter data. Sometimes the mental illness seems like another person or living thing: as such it follows you, you know it, you see it, and so on. This is especially common in A Single Step and Signpost, furthering the argument that conditions usually seen as more understandable, and more the domain of the Self, by professionals or the public, that is, depression and eating disorders, are not always represented as such by clients. This separation of self from 'the depression' is something which Karp (1992) also found in his study of a depression self-help group.

The notion of mental health problems as some kind of living thing, almost stalking the client is particularly striking.

> He asks me if I had a nice Christmas, and says that 'the illness messed mine up', as he was in hospital, although the staff made an effort. (Winter Day Centre)

> We're all here suffering from schizophrenia, the staff are one step ahead of the schizophrenia. (Interview with Melanie, Winter Day Centre)

This was often particularly evident when clients talked about the voices that they heard. It was very rare in my data to find clients who took possession of the voices that they heard and referred to 'my voices', although this did occur very occasionally. There is also often a sense of passivity in the way clients describe voice-hearing experiences. Clients would discuss 'getting' and 'having' voices as well as hearing them, emphasising their very minimal role in the process, even at a sensory level.

ELLEN: *Well, he [consultant] said to me just before Christmas he asked me 'You haven't been receiving any symptoms again?' that I used to have and it was a long while back, when I was first admitted, and I said, 'Oh, I think I'd have told you, Dr M-', yes ... yeah ...*

I: **So what sort of symptoms did you used to get?**

ELLEN: *I thought I'd got voices when I was first admitted ... . I might have got it wrong ...*

(Interview with Ellen, Winter Day Centre)

And I often get voices ... I've had voices since 1980. (Interview with Mark, Winter Day Centre)

For many clients, the voices take on the status of a real person, external to the client, and in control of him or her.

Alex talks about how he's not feeling so good, and says he didn't sleep at all last night, and C- [nurse] says he must be really exhausted. He says he is, and it's because of the voices. ... Alex says at the moment he feels just like he's got someone sitting next to him talking to him all the time. (Summer Day Centre)

PAULA: *... if you've been used to hearing voices for years and years, when they go, you actually miss them.*

I: **Do you?**

PAULA: *Because you've been used to ... it's like having company in your head ... that you've always got somebody with you.*

(Interview with Paula, Winter Day Centre)

Continuing from this is the idea that the voices themselves are responsible for a client's experience: it is the voices themselves that 'do' things to the client. This seems to be an extension of the fact that many clients are told to do unpleasant or dangerous things by the voices they hear. The voices themselves are animated, becoming the mental illness.

> And the voices said ... erm ... you're never going to eat them, put the taste in my mouth and said you're never going to eat them again. And what they were doing, the voices, was they were black-mailing me to suicide. (Interview with Mark, Winter Day Centre)

> I ask her how she felt when she first heard the voices, and she says she was on the dole and quite bored, so to start off it was quite interesting, but then they took control of her, and she couldn't stop them.   (Interview with Sarah, Spring Ward)

In most of these cases, the client refers to the voices taking control and then maintaining that control over the client. 'The voices' provide a very concrete objectification of mental illness for many clients. Taken to its extreme, then, getting better might only be possible when the voices will allow it.

> She says that she's feeling 'very well' at the moment, though, and that 'the voices are finally leaving me alone'.   (Winter Day Centre)

Mental illness as controlling and internal

I: *Mental illness [word association]*
HAYLEY: *Not being well inside myself.*
              (Interview with Hayley, Winter
                                  Day Centre)

An alternative perspective is that mental illness controls you, but also somehow gets inside you and becomes internal. At this extreme, it is possible for mental illness either to remain Other within the body, or to become part of the Self.

If it remains Other within the body, it still often represents an engulfment and leads to significant changes in a person's Self. It is almost as if mental illness takes over the client's body: it might then successfully take over the Self or might succeed merely in suppressing it. Suppression seemed to be regarded as more common.

Clients might therefore talk about the changes that they have experienced in themselves which result from mental health problems: mental illness might prevent a client from being him or herself.

This relates significantly to the idea of 'coming round', the journey or project, in which the clients at the Winter Centre were engaged. Within this journey, as discussed in Chapter 5, mental illness seems to parallel a state of unconsciousness: clients are not themselves and are not capable of being themselves. They can, however, come round from the experience and begin to re-establish themselves: in this way, we see that mental illness, although it takes one away from what one might otherwise be, does not necessarily annihilate the Self altogether; rather it suppresses it into a state of dormancy, until it has the opportunity to return to control the body.

MARK: *And I absconded [from hospital] once, I had done before, and went to E- ...*
I: *Oh, OK*
MARK: *And I was coming round, I thought to myself, 'Now, am I doing the right thing here?'*
                    (Interview with Mark, Winter Day Centre)

If mental illness takes over the self, a degree of distance between the self and self as mentally ill is possible; past behaviours can be reflected upon with hindsight, as mentioned in Chapter 5. Clients at the Winter Centre were not alone in this.

Marion says she's just come out of hospital, as she was on Spring Ward until last Wednesday. She says she was there for six weeks, as she says they wouldn't let her out, but she says she was doing some pretty stupid things when she was taken in, so it's probably best.   (Summer Day Centre)

For some clients, mental illness was something that not only took away or took over aspects of one's self but also, effectively, took away one's life, albeit temporarily in some cases. This idea was also implicit within the discussions clients had about how their plans for their lives had been thwarted by mental health problems.

He says that the Winter Centre has 'restored my life'. (Interview with Adam, Winter Day Centre)

It is interesting to note the passivity in the above example. This is common within the representation of mental illness as something controlling: mental illness takes away life and plans, and one needs help in order to be given them back. However, this does not prevent some clients from trying to play a more active role on some occasions within certain aspects of their life. A loss of control in one area of life does not always involve a loss of control in every area, and, as already mentioned, it is not the case that these representations of control are stagnant and unchanging. As clients try to take more control, they might move to a position whereby they see mental illness as more controllable in general.

However, at the most extreme level within this representation of mental illness as both in control and internal is the idea that mental illness is not only capable of taking away the self, taking away life as a client would want to live it, but is something that might also take away a client's very humanity. This risks subscribing to the age-old idea that those with mental health problems degenerate to an almost bestial level (De Rosa, 1987; Lucas & Barratt, 1995).

Alternatively the mental health problem might remain separate from the client's self but still exist within that client, controlling them. An interesting example of this can be found in the representation of eating disorders within Signpost. Here, eating disorders are seen as existing within the client, controlling him or her, but still remain Other, and separate from the client, almost like some kind of internal parasite.

Dealing with controlling mental illness

Although the two dimensions under discussion here, controllability and location, are both important, the dimension of controllability seems to have more immediate significance in influencing how the client might deal with mental health problems. Discussion centred on efforts to overcome mental illness divides more neatly according to whether the mental health problem is seen as controlling or controllable; the internal/external divide seems to have less relevance here, although obviously the interaction between the two dimensions means it remains implicated in numerous ways.

How, then, do clients deal with mental health problems if they represent them as something in control, which can take on the mantle of a living thing or can be equated with a difficult place? For many clients who subscribe to this representation, the only approach is to fight the mental illness, to try to subdue it, taking its control away. The use of metaphors of battle, also evident elsewhere in understandings of health (Lupton, 1994), is common once again in A Single Step and in Signpost but was also employed by other clients and has been found in other studies, such as that of Barham and Hayward (1991), who discuss clients' war with voices. In some ways, parallels can be drawn between some of the language which is used to describe how a client can approach a mental health problem, in terms of fighting it, battling with it, conquering it and so on, and that which is often used to describe the process of having, and fighting, cancer, as described by Sontag (1978). Indeed, other parallels can be drawn in that mental illness can be represented as a malevolent alien presence within the body, threatening to take it over.

I: *So how would you describe, to someone who didn't know anything about it, how would you describe being unwell? What's it like?*
ERIC: *Ermm ... well ... it's a sort of battle in the brain.*
I: *Right ...*
ERIC: *Trying to stay sane at the same time as being unwell. So it's quite difficult, you know.*

(Interview with Eric, Winter Day Centre)

It is perhaps because of this need to fight mental ill health that an important aspect of the mental health services for many clients is safety: at all three services clients talked about how they saw the service as a safe haven, a day centre with security (Winter Day Centre), a refuge, a safe place (Spring Ward) and a sanctuary (Summer Day Centre). Safety is essential to the success of a mental health service, something echoed in other studies (Gordon, Alexander & Dietzan, 1979). Clients need a safe place to begin, or to continue, their battle with mental ill health.

Inevitably, the question arises as to the amount of responsibility a client should take for a mental health problem and within the process of dealing with it. Two positions are clearly discernible amongst clients who seem to subscribe, in the main, to representations of mental illness as controlling. The first is that this controlling nature of mental ill health absolves the client of any responsibility.

The debate on control and responsibility echoes discussion as to the parallels which can be drawn between physical and mental ill health: if a client 'suffers from' depression in the same way that an individual might 'suffer from' diabetes, how much control can that client have over that condition? Such arguments, of course, assume that those who suffer from physical ailments are not seen as responsible for their conditions, something which some theorists argue is not universally the case, especially in an increasingly secular society in which health might be said to have taken the place of religion in defining goodness and morality (Crawford, 1994).

The alternative perspective on responsibility is much more common, and in many ways leads naturally to the next extreme position within the representational structure which will be discussed, with mental illness being regarded as something which can be controlled by the client: this perspective holds that while mental illness is mostly in control of a client, the client must take responsibility in whatever ways are possible, even if only by taking medication.

> They talk about one person who is in hospital and has been for a long time, and Eve says it's his own fault, as he won't take his medication. She says you have to take your medication for your own sake. Ken says that he thinks it is half the fault of this person, but half something else, as he was retired from his job, so there must have been something wrong. (Summer Day Centre)

Another much less common position, generally expounded only by the more 'radical' sections of the mental health service user movement, was the need for client and mental health problem to develop a symbiotic relationship. The client, it was argued, should learn to stop fighting their mental ill health and instead should live with it in a more harmonious way, thereby sharing control. This is evident in some discussions surrounding voice hearing, in which clients are encouraged to learn to deal with their voices, and in some ways, to share control with their mental ill health. In many ways, this implies a need for the client to realise that equal control between self and mental health problem, at the very least, is possible. This leads to the other extreme of the control dimension, at which clients see themselves as having more control over mental ill health.

Mental illness as controllable and external

Mental illness can be seen as something which remains external to the client but is also controllable by the client. This extreme position within the representational structure is best exemplified by some of the less negative place metaphors used, many of which begin to use images of movement: in line with the notion of a journey through mental ill health, the client does not stay in one place but rather moves from one place to another. Pendulum, in particular, refers to tightrope walks and roller-coasters, both of which imply more activity, or at the very least movement, on the part of the client.

Similarly, the vocabulary used to describe the process of getting better might be more active, even in cases where the 'place' described is one that leaves the client with little room for control: clients might, for example, discuss the need to 'climb' out of depression, or how to journey or pull through it. This emphasises yet again the need to guard against an overly simplistic view of control within representations of mental illness: at different times in a client's journey either the mental illness or the client might be more in control, and a representation of mental illness as in control at one point does not preclude the client taking back control at a later date.

Mental illness as controllable and internal

It might also be that when mental illness is represented as more controllable, mental health problems are located more firmly within the person himself or herself and regarded as internal. This location within the person can manifest itself in different ways: it might be that the mental health problem is a part of the individual's character or nature; alternatively it might be contained within the individual in a more abstract way, yet still controllable.

SIMON: ... ... *mental illness ... ... it just makes me feel sad really.*
I: *Right.*
SIMON: *Having struggled with it for so long.*
I: *Yeah.*
SIMON: *It's actually a part of my character now.*
I: *OK*
SIMON: *I feel as if it is. It's part of me, it's part of my make-up. It's in who I am ... . But yeah, it makes me feel sad.*
(Interview with Simon, Summer Day Centre)

This quotation from Simon's interview is particularly telling: it supports the idea that clients might hold different representations of mental illness at different points in their lives: Simon now sees mental ill health as being much more a part of himself, given the length of his experience. It has grown to be a part of him, although he implies that this was not always the case.

However, a client need not regard mental ill health as an implicit part of his/her character in order to subscribe to this representation of mental illness as an internal, controllable entity. The crucial aspect is that the client takes possession of the mental health problem, rather than it taking possession of him/her. This ties in with many arguments on recovery made by the mental health service user movement and some professionals, discussed in Chapter 5 (e.g. Coleman [1999]).

While there might be an occasional sense of passivity in being controlled by mental illness, this contrasts sharply with the activity needed to take control of mental ill health and to maintain this control. There are obvious parallels here between this active process of taking control of mental illness and the journeys or projects of clients discussed in Chapter 5, especially the project of 'getting it together' in which clients on Spring Ward were engaged.

Dealing with controllable mental illness

Much of this process of gaining control over mental illness is associated, in the newsletter data, with knowing and understanding one's own mental health. This is particularly noticeable in the more political sections of the mental health service user movement; Openmind made frequent references to the importance of this process.

Dealing with mental illness within this perspective often focuses on the notion of maintaining a balance, which seems to reflect movement along the dimension of mental illness or client in control. The client needs to ensure that a balance is maintained.

Work directed by MDF – the Bipolar Organisation – is a good example of this emphasis on the need for self-awareness and self-knowledge in the process of taking control of one's own mental health. The MDF self-management programme is a clear illustration of this: the programme is run by other clients or former clients of the mental health services with a diagnosis of bipolar disorder and focuses on enabling clients to maintain a healthy lifestyle but to also recognise their own particular 'warning signs' that might indicate the onset of a crisis and consider what steps they can take to manage these situations themselves.

Within the MDF's own description of the self-management programme are many of the elements found elsewhere in this data, for example, the notions of process and of project, but above all the possibility of active control of mental illness on the part of the client is highlighted. Other relevant subjects discussed by MDF include the introduction of 'mood diaries' for clients to record their own progression through mental health and ill health, and discussion of Advance Directive Orders, in which clients accept that an episode of mental ill health is possible and state what they themselves would like to be done in this event, for example, preferred medication, unhelpful treatment and so on.

Control plays an important role within this process. The client believes that he or she has the potential to control the situation and the mental health problem through a number of elements. The most significant of these seems to be accepting responsibility for one's condition and life. Thus personal effort is required in the process of dealing with mental illness, and not merely medication or professionals.

However, Pendulum and MDF are not the only locations of such ideas. They are contained within the journeys of clients on Spring Ward, 'getting it together', which was also expressed as sorting yourself out, and getting a life. Again, the emphasis was on the client to act in order to gain and maintain control. This was also echoed by clients in other services on occasions.

> He says mind over matter is very important: he says 'the Lord up top and medication both help' and that 'I try to the best of my ability.' He says 'you've got to have faith to keep going.'
> (Interview with Adam, Winter Day Centre)

Many of the elements contained within this representation of mental illness as controllable return once more to the debate surrounding recovery or cure. Recovery, as discussed in Chapter 5, is seen as a key element by much of the mental health service user movement: it represents a holistic and responsible approach to one's own mental health and, it is claimed, is not currently sufficiently recognised as a possibility by mental health service professionals in the United Kingdom, who remain more orientated towards maintenance of mental illness (Coleman, 1999). Certainly, to adopt a model of mental illness as something that can be actively controlled in a number of ways by the client themselves is to support this model of recovery, as opposed to the more passive notion of cure. These ideas also tie in with work by the Mental Health Foundation in their Strategies for Living project, which seeks to find out what clients find helpful in their lives and mental health problems, taking as holistic a perspective as possible.

However, according to some sections of the user movement, clients need not only gain control over themselves individually but must also gain wider control of mental health, possibly through becoming active in the mental health service user movement itself and campaigning for change.

It is clear that clients might encounter problems when attempting to exercise control over their own mental health: the way that clients might be thwarted in their attempts to engage in their own projects with regard to their mental health by professionals or the general public, discussed in Chapter 5, are clear examples of this. Indeed, as we saw in Chapters 1 and 2, the very right of a client to hold representations of mental ill health in the first place might be questioned. Some of these issues will be discussed in more detail in the next chapter.

Summary and conclusions

In this chapter I have argued that the dimensions of controllability and of location are crucial to a client's representation of mental health problems and that different positions can be taken on these dimensions. These positions are by no means fixed, and clients might move from controlling to controllable, external to internal positions, or vice versa, during their journeys through mental health problems. I have argued that these dimensions extend the notion of Otherness, found in representations held by the public and professionals, and demonstrate a more complex representational structure, within which Otherness plays varying roles at different positions. I have also argued that the dimension of controllability appears to have significant effects in influencing how a client might go about attempting to overcome mental health problems and in journeying through mental illness.

To actualise and exercise a representation, however, requires that the representer be in a position of relative power. It involves recognition from others that the individual has the right to a representation about a particular thing and that that representation is valid, to whatever extent. Mental health service clients are rarely in such a position. On a material level, they often have fewer resources, given the poverty and unemployment that many contend with; on a more theoretical level, their ideas are often derided and dismissed. What, the familiar question goes, is the point of listening to a mental health service client, when his or her thoughts will be nothing more than the product of a disturbed or irrational mind?

I do not wish to deny that, for many clients, delusions and hallucinations are part of their experience and of their distress, but this does not imply that *anything* a client *ever* says on *any* topic is a product of delusory thinking. It certainly does not negate that client's beliefs about his or her own mental ill health and treatment. In my own study, as in others in this area, clients have very definite, lucid and well-thought-through ideas about their experiences and future.

Mental health professionals, then, have a significant amount of control over the actualisation of any representation held by a client. For example, a client might see a mental health problem as controllable and believe that a variety of actions are helpful, from taking vitamin supplements to seeing a complementary therapist, whereas the professional might see the client's mental health problem as out of control, and in need of closer supervision, for example, in the form of hospitalisation. This then compromises the client's ability to sustain and act on his or her own representation. This was evident in Chapter 5, when the thwarting and supporting of client projects by professionals was discussed.

The next, and final, chapter will move on from this brief discussion of controlling representations of control, and attempt to discuss the theoretical and practical implications for the mental health services of the results and conclusions of my own, and other, studies.

8 Conclusions and implications

Summary

Throughout this book I have argued that, contrary to some claims and assumptions, clients and former clients of the mental health services have well-developed understandings of mental health and ill health and that they develop these communally with other clients as they move through different mental health services and as their own experiences change and develop. These understandings centre around the notion of mental ill health as a journey, and clients embark upon projects in order to progress through this journey in different ways. The activity needed by the client to engage in this journey, the aims of it and the strategies employed may differ, but clients at the same services engage in similar projects, and certain aspects of a journey are seen as key by most clients. Within these journeys, mental ill health might be represented as something internal or external, and as something controllable or controlling: these representations are likely to change as the client progresses through his or her journey.

The implications of these arguments are manifold: in this final chapter, I would like to focus on two, the theoretical and the practical. Theoretically, considering client understanding of mental ill health allows us to pay closer attention to the interaction between different forms of knowledge. I will discuss this opportunity first in greater depth, drawing in particular on work from the field of the sociology of scientific knowledge (SSK), in addition to social representations theory, to consider the possibilities afforded by such interaction. This leads to the next implication, the practical: here, I will consider some of the ways in which the mental health services might incorporate client understanding and adapt or change accordingly.

Multiple understandings: challenges and possibilities

It is clear from the work reviewed and discussed in the course of this book that clients are engaged in maintaining and developing understandings about mental ill health that, while they may have elements in common with those of the public and of professionals in some ways, differ in important ways from other forms of understanding. In particular, the construction of mental health problems as less Other, and more potentially controllable are significant and meaningful divergences.

However, what is equally as important as the content of clients' understanding is their labelling of it as, at the very least, just as valid as that of professionals or the general public, and potentially much more valid. In this way, clients are holders of a different, and possibly alternative, form of *expert* knowledge: they are, after all, 'the ones going through it' (Summer Day Centre), the 'experts by experience' (Pendulum, 15[4]), or even 'the primary experts' (Mental Health Foundation, 1997) on their own particular cases. It is certainly not the case that mental health is the only forum within the health services in which such challenges to expert knowledge are occurring. Indeed, the NHS in the United Kingdom now even runs an 'expert patient's programme', which organises online and face-to-face courses run by other patients aimed at promoting self-management of a variety of long term conditions (see http://www.expertpatients.nhs.uk for more details). Hardey (1999) maintains that such deprofessionalisation of medical knowledge has increased significantly with the development of the internet as a lay resource. Popay and Williams (1996) conclude that 'through a more or less systematic process whereby experience is checked against life events, circumstances and history, lay people acquire an 'expert' body of knowledge, different from but equal to that of professionals in the public health field' (Popay & Williams, 1996, p. 760). The way that such alternative *expert* knowledge might interact with what is traditionally seen as expert knowledge regarding mental health (i.e. professional understanding) should be of particular interest to social scientists.

A number of theoretical approaches could be taken to examining this question. First, in line with many of the theoretical arguments made within this book, we could employ the theory of social representations. Moscovici's (1961) early work focused on the way that understandings of psychoanalysis developed amongst various groups within French society: as a part of this, he discussed the way that scientific knowledge from the reified universe filtered into common sense understanding within the consensual universe, where it changed and developed (Moscovici, 1984a). Within social representations theory, however, there has so far been less consideration of the transformation of knowledge in the opposite direction, that is, the way in which other forms of knowledge might influence scientific understanding. Indeed, this facet of social representations theory has been much misunderstood (Foster, 2003), with many critics claiming that it reinforces the idea of a hierarchy between knowledges, with science portrayed as unadulterated truth and common sense as a bastardisation of it. While I would argue that this is indeed a misunderstanding, I would agree that there is a need to emphasise the interaction between knowledges from different domains or perspectives in all directions – that is, common sense might influence thinking in scientific domains just as it is influenced by them (Flick, 1998c). The concept of the representational project (Bauer & Gaskell, 1999) discussed throughout this book allows for this: this theoretical perspective allows us to examine the ways in which different projects – for example, the project of a psychiatrist and the project of a client, interact, influence and clash with one another.

However, as yet little work using social representations theory seems to have taken up the challenge of examining this interaction between health-related knowledges. Perhaps a useful contribution here comes from work in the field of SSK, which Bloor (2001) uses to consider the doctor/patient relationship. There are many parallels between the SSK approach to lay understanding and that of social representations theory: neither denigrates public understanding, and instead both seek to demonstrate its richness and coherence.

Many studies in SSK have focused on the way in which patients, or the general public, approach health issues and the interaction between these groups and professionals, whether doctors or research scientists. It seems to me that much of this work can be divided into two groups. The first considers the understandings that the public or patients have of various issues and parallels much work in the area of social representations theory: these studies aim to highlight the coherence and logic of public understanding (Williams & Popay, 1994), the way it differs from scientific knowledge but is just as rich and useful to the individuals concerned. Examples of such work include Bloor, Monaghan, Dobash and Dobash's (1998) work on steroid use among bodybuilders, who become 'ethnopharmacologists' through their knowledge and experience, Lambert and Rose's (1996) consideration of the ways in which patients make sense of genetic metabolic disorder through general knowledge, observations, and family and general history, and Irwin's (1995) analysis of the public's understanding of various health issues, including pesticides, BSE and petrochemical factory accidents.

Sociology of scientific knowledge (SSK) studies in the second group, however, seek not only to explore the understandings held by patients or the public but also to examine the interaction of these knowledges with those of professional scientists and doctors. Epstein (1996), for example, details the way in which activists in the United States influenced the development of treatments for HIV/AIDS; Arksey (1998) focuses on the attempts of people with Repetitive Strain Injury to have the condition officially recognised, and Bloor (2000) examines the role of miners themselves in gaining official recognition that coal dust alone caused miners' lung. What is clear from all of this work, however, is that while patient understandings *can* have an impact on professional understanding and treatment of an issue, this process has tended to be painfully slow, partial and very complicated.

It seems, then, that it is quite one thing to recognise that patients, clients and the public might have their own well-developed, logical and rational understandings of health and illness (Herzlich & Pierret, 1987) and that these might have implications in the decisions that they make with regard to their lives but quite another to accept that these forms of knowledge should be considered equal to professional medical discourse, even to influence health professionals. Whether a shift in the mental health services is possible, such that clients' understandings might be seen in this light, and might influence treatment and services, is a complex issue. Epstein (1996) points out that the AIDS activists in his study were largely white, educated, middle-class gay men, who fought the scientific establishment through learning more about biomedicine and using this knowledge to challenge accepted notions.

Mental health service clients, who are likely to be in poorer situations materially, whose knowledge is so often derided and denigrated, and whose understandings are not necessarily founded on biomedicine, are unlikely to find influencing professionals uncomplicated.

However, recent discussions amongst mental health professionals have brought many of these issues to the fore, and the remainder of this chapter will discuss these more practical implications in more depth. In my view, it is insufficient merely to comment on the interaction between professional and client knowledge in a disinterested manner from a theoretical perspective: what is also needed is an attempt to alter current imbalances in the situation (Rogers & Pilgrim, 1993).

Implications for the mental health services

Where, then, does all of this discussion leave the mental health services? Can the mental health services really take into consideration the views and opinions of clients at all times? What, if anything, is the role for mental health professionals in a mental health crisis? Although we have unarguably seen an increasing interest in client perspectives in the social sciences and in the mental health services in the past decade, this has been accompanied by parallel moves towards greater surveillance and control of people considered to have a mental health problem (Beresford, 2005), and an increasing focus on dangerousness and risk within the mental health services (Beresford, 2005; Laurance, 2003; Ramon, 2005). Is it possible for the mental health services to both empower and regulate at the same time (Beresford, 2005), to allow clients control over their mental health and also to maintain public confidence? Some of these problems, and perhaps, more importantly, potential solutions, will now be discussed. However, as will become obvious, the debate is far from over.

It would seem from much of the work discussed in this book that clients of the mental health services often have more socially based models of mental health problems than some professionals, both in terms of their understanding of what causes mental illness, and the treatment and other strategies that they believe will help them in their journeys. Clients are, of course, not alone in this: the general public seems to share similar social models (Leff, 2001), as do many mental health professionals. While it is still probably fair to say that biomedical understanding continues to dominate psychiatry, especially with recent increases in interest in the genetics of mental health (Leff, 2001), psychiatrists have always relied on using multiple models in practice (Double, 2005; Tyrer & Steinberg, 2005), and current multi-disciplinary mental health teams have clearly had an important influence on professional thinking about mental health (Miller & Rose, 1986; Sampson, 1995), whatever tensions might exist in the actuality of such teams (Griffiths, 1998).

The problem arises in that, as Tew (2005b) points out, while there is a groundswell of interest in social ideas about mental health problems, these are not organised into a coherent model like the dominant medical model. Double (2005) supports this view, claiming that, while the user movement and research within it have had important effects, many of these centre more upon listening to the voices of people with mental health problems, and not on the establishment of a clear model or philosophy.

The lack of a more coherent 'social' model of mental health problems has important implications when it comes to designing and implementing policy, when 'social' can come to be regarded purely as an issue of practicalities, such as housing. Instead of this more piecemeal approach, Tew (2005c) argues that the mental health services need to make a commitment to a holistic approach to treatment and, perhaps most importantly, engage in a partnership with clients which takes their perspectives seriously *on their own terms*. In this way, mental distress might come to be seen as an internalisation or acting out of stressful social experiences, or as a coping/survival strategy. A social model, then needs to start with the lived experience of a client, to be holistic, to take issues of power seriously, and to move from 'care' to 'action planning' (Tew, 2005c).

Many of these issues are also discussed by Bracken and Thomas (2001; 2005) in their proposals to create a system of 'post-psychiatry', an approach which is regarded by some as the best example of critical psychiatry, the only serious challenge to psychiatric dominance since the anti-psychiatry movement of the 1960s and 1970s (Double, 2005). Bracken and Thomas (2005) see current ideas within psychiatry as rooted within modernism and the Enlightenment, and therefore increasingly inadequate in a post-modern world. They state that we should instead move from reductionism to an emphasis on hermeneutics: as such, the focus within post-psychiatry (Bracken & Thomas, 2001) is an emphasis on the context of an individual and his or her experience, on ethics over technology (i.e. on the meaning of an experience to an individual) and on rethinking the issue of coercion within the mental health services. Service users are placed centre-stage throughout.

Repper and Perkins (2003) also produce a number of very useful concrete ideas for adapting the mental health system in order to incorporate client understanding more fully. They maintain that in the current system too much emphasis is placed on disorders and deficits, and that this arises because mental health problems are described by people who have never experienced them. Instead, in line with many of the other theorists discussed above, and drawing on the social disability model, they claim that there should be a greater focus on possibilities, and on people, and on developing services to enable people to use and develop their skills, and to pursue their aspirations. Such an approach would encourage social inclusion, and place greater emphasis on the citizenship of mental health service users (Bracken & Thomas, 2005).

Within any mental health service, there must be room for recovery: this concept was integral to many of the ideas expressed by clients in the studies in this book. Recovery, however, should be defined by clients, not by professionals, and include ideas of recovery from the psychiatric system and from the experience of stigma as well as from mental health problems (Wallcraft, 2005). This is not to say that professionals have no role to play within recovery: instead, they can play an active role in encouraging a client to take control and to work towards their goal of recovery, inspiring hope in clients rather than preventing change and development (Bracken & Thomas, 2005; Repper & Perkins, 2003), as we saw in Chapter 5 when professionals thwarted clients' own strategies and projects.

It almost goes without saying that any mental health system must take user involvement that is more than purely tokenistic seriously at all levels, from that of individual service use to local service planning to national policy formation. At the individual level, this entails professionals properly engaging with clients, for example, in devising Care Plans, something which studies suggest is not necessarily currently the case (Healthcare Commission, 2004; Rose, 2001); at the local level, it means meaningful consultation with clients over changes and developments to services, and at the more national level, it involves full discussion with clients over wider changes in policy regarding the treatment of mental health problems, over how to address issues of stigma and so on. However, this point must be emphasised: the recent debates surrounding the Mental Health Bill and opposition to it by user groups rightly highlight the inevitable problems that arise when clients' views are sampled and then ignored in policy making (Foster, 2006a).

A more controversial issue is the role of the mental health professional in the future mental health services. For some clients, including many in the studies reviewed in this book, there will always be problems associated with a system that employs individuals who have no direct experience of mental health problems to provide services for those that do. However, I return to a quotation used in a different context in Chapter 1: as Repper and Perkins (2003) point out,

> knowing things and having skills is good. There is nothing wrong with expertise per se, nor is there anything wrong with seeking confirmation of our expertise. It is the way in which this expertise is used, and the places in which we look to confirm it, that can be problematic. (Repper & Perkins, 2003, p. 74)

The final sentence of this quotation is key, calling as it does on mental health professionals to reflect and act on issues of power and practice. Many of the ways in which professionals might be able to alter the ways in which they use their expertise so as to incorporate client understanding to a greater extent into the mental health services they provide would not need to be revolutionary: discussing changes in medication, service provision and so forth with a client, listening to a client's preferences and so on are not new concepts and for many are already cornerstones of mental health practice. Similarly, adopting procedures that support clients in taking control of their mental health problems, for example, in the form of Advance Directive Orders or in encouraging participation in self-management programmes, are hardly revolutionary.

This is not to underestimate the problems associated with these approaches: to accept the representations of clients and to act on them is a challenge for the mental health services, given the frequent (and perhaps even implicit) professional conviction that clients of the mental health services, by definition, often do not know what is 'best' for them, due to their lack of insight. The mental health service power structure is founded upon this, and this is confounded by the fact that many clients themselves often agree that at points within their journey through mental health problems they have indeed not been capable of taking control or of making their own decisions. Similarly, a policy shift towards treating client understanding as equal to that of professionals also relies on political, and therefore (theoretically) public, support for such a move. This is not a given, when we consider the public's conviction that the majority of those with mental illness, when left to their own devices in the community, turn into rampaging murderers (Rose, 1998), despite evidence to the contrary (Taylor & Gunn, 1999).

However, whatever the problems of the actuality of altering services to incorporate client understanding to a greater extent, what also seems clear from the work reviewed and discussed in this book is that mental health professionals have a lot to learn from clients, former clients and survivors of the mental health services. Perhaps the easiest place to begin to address this is in the training of mental health professionals. Although there are limited numbers of mental health professionals who discuss their experiences of mental health problems, as reviewed in Chapter 3, these experiences are usually seen as incidental, and less directly relevant to their employment in the mental health field. In contrast, a small number of clients and users of the mental health services are now involved directly in training mental health professionals: Livingston and Cooper (2004) found two in their recent review. As one of these user professionals argues, 'having a diagnosis is a qualification for the job' (Rose, 2003, p. 1331), albeit a complicated and often tense experience juggling user and professional status. There seems to be far more scope for clients to become involved in the training of mental health professionals, drawing on their own expertise and experience.

Sadly, the conclusions of this book are not new: John Perceval asserted that the patient knew more about madness than the doctor or public in the middle of the nineteenth century (Bateson, 1961), and there have been calls to see the client as a colleague for more than a generation (Gordon et al., 1979). Ultimately, however, it must be recognised that to understand the experience of mental ill health, to understand how clients themselves come to understand mental ill health and how this then influences them in their lives and service use, we need not only to talk to and listen to clients, but to act upon what they tell us, recognising that they are, in fact, different, yet equal, kinds of experts. Clients of the mental health services embark upon active journeys through mental illness, developing their own ideas about what works and what does not when it comes to mental health, reacting to their own experiences and to interactions with those around them, especially the other clients with whom they come into contact: mental health professionals and members of the general public alike have much to learn from these journeys.

Appendix – methods

The aim of this Appendix is to provide a little more methodological background to the main study discussed in this book.

The study took a qualitative approach to the research questions, something that has been seen as particularly appropriate in studies using social representations theory (Flick, 2001; Flick & Foster, in press) and in studies that aim to access the meaning of a concept to a group (Bauer, Gaskell & Allum, 2000; Flick, 1998b). It also took a multi-method approach, again recommended in social representations studies (De Rosa, 1987), in an attempt to address issues of multiple perspective.

Consequently, fieldwork was carried out at three mental health services in one urban area. After consultation with a clinical psychologist and a psychiatrist familiar with the services, two day centres and one acute ward were chosen, in order to gain access to as wide a variety of clients as possible within the timeframe of the study. I then met first with each consultant psychiatrist with clients at the three services and subsequently with the manager or nurse-in-charge of each service to discuss the study further. Once these individuals had consented, I also met with other members of staff from the three services, giving them the opportunity to ask any questions that they had. In parallel with this, ethical approval was also negotiated with the Local Research Ethics Committee of the NHS Trust. Once this had been granted, I was able to arrange meetings with the clients themselves to discuss the study and seek their consent. Service users were provided with information sheets and signed witnessed consent forms, showing that they understood the structure and purpose of the project and agreeing to their participation. Two sets of information sheets and consent forms were used, one for the ethnographic phase of the research and one for the interviews. Given that the fieldwork lasted between six and eight weeks at each location, consent was necessarily an ongoing process (Applebaum, Lidz & Meisel, 1987): clients had the opportunity at any point of the research to decline to participate, and staff were also able to raise any concerns they had about involving any clients who were particularly distressed. In fact, across all three services, only two clients declined to participate, and staff only expressed concerns about one individual participating, meaning that over eighty clients participated in the project overall.

The fieldwork comprised ethnography and interviewing. These methods are both in-keeping with the research questions and theoretical perspective of the study (Duveen & Lloyd, 1993; Farr, 1982) and complement one another (Agar, 1980): interviews can allow the researcher the opportunity to check details or to ask questions that cannot be answered from the ethnography, while ethnography can allow access to non-verbal expression of representations in the forms of routines, practices and artefacts. Ethnography is particularly useful in studies that seek to access the meaning of health and illness to a client in a medically dominated situation (Charmaz & Olsen, 1997). The methods were also appropriate for practical and ethical reasons: engaging in ethnographic work for a number of weeks before asking clients if they would take part in an interview meant that clients were more familiar with me, and the research study, and that we had had the opportunity to get to know each other and discuss the study in a number of different contexts. As Charmaz (1999) has pointed out, it is hard to establish trust in the context of one interview. Some clients were also uncomfortable with more formal interviews, associating them with discussions with mental health professionals but were happy to answer questions similar to those I asked other clients in interview in the more informal context of the ethnography. Twenty-five clients participated in more formal narrative-style interviews.

Interviews were broadly narrative in style, in that I invited clients first to tell me how they came to be using the service. This was then followed up as appropriate, and a number of other semi-structured questions were asked, including, for example, whether the client used any other services. Finally, clients were presented with some word association tasks.

Comprehensive notes were taken during the ethnographic phase of the research, and interviews were taped and transcribed. In some cases, clients preferred not to be taped, and so notes were taken during the interview.

The fieldwork in the three services represented an attempt to access representations and ideas circulating at the microgenetic level (Duveen & Lloyd, 1990), that is, conversations and interactions between individuals and small groups in everyday life. However, it has also been pointed out that representations circulate at the sociogenetic level, that is, the level of wider society (Duveen & Lloyd, 1990). Many studies of social representations include a content analysis of the media in order to sample such representations (Farr, 1993b). Given the role of newspapers, television and films in the maintenance and propagation of negative images of mental ill health (Philo, 1996), it seemed highly unlikely that a sample of the mainstream media would contain substantial contributions from clients or former clients of the mental health services. I therefore decided to turn, instead, to the mental health service user movement. As discussed in Chapter 3, substantial developments in this movement over the past 15 years have led to them becoming an important resource for mental health service users. I therefore sampled all newsletters produced by four organisations in 1999. The organisations (MIND, The Eating Disorders Association, Depression Alliance and MDF – the Bipolar Organisation) were chosen to represent a diverse cross-section of mental health issues and perspectives.

All material written in these four newsletters by individuals who had experienced mental health problems were therefore sampled, and documents analysed, along with ethnographic notes and interview transcripts and notes, with the aid of the Atlas-ti computer-aided qualitative data analysis programme (Muhr, 1997).

The qualitative coding of data is a cyclical, iterative procedure (Bauer, 2000) and is, of course, not an end in itself. However, in order to ensure transparency, a discussion of the coding process is essential. A coding frame was developed that was partially inductive, in that certain key themes that had proven to be important in previous studies on social representations of mental ill health were examined, and partially deductive, in that it incorporated codes that emerged from the data during the analysis. All documents were coded twice at different times, in an attempt to ensure that the coding frame was used consistently throughout. After the initial coding, the relationship between themes was examined in greater depth, and similarities and differences between the different forms of data, the different services and different clients were considered.

Efforts were made throughout the research to maintain an awareness of the way that my own perspective as a researcher affected my understanding of the situation. As such, I attempted to position myself as a 'learner' (Flick & Foster, in press; Howarth, Foster & Dorrer, 2004). I also returned to the two day centres to discuss some of the themes that had emerged from my data and sent summaries to interested clients who had been interviewed while on the acute ward: I responded to any comments made by the clients as a result of this and incorporated their ideas into my analysis.

The research was guided by the principles of coherence and consistency (Duveen & Lloyd, 1993) throughout, maintaining an awareness of the appropriateness of, and links between, research questions, methods, analysis and discussion of results.

Notes

1 Allowing madness vox

1. See Clark (1996) for a fascinating discussion of the history, daily life and development of one asylum, Fulbourn Hospital, near Cambridge.
2. This is not to imply that studies with the general public are automatically easier to conduct: Wolff et al. (1999) note that their research into community attitudes to local mental health care facilities was rejected by several area ethics committees.

2 Perspectives from psychology, psychiatry and other disciplines

1. On 23rd March, 2006, the government announced that it was dropping the Mental Health Bill. This was widely recognised to be in response to the unprecedented opposition it had faced and an increasing recognition of the problems with the bureaucratic structure that the Bill called for. However, the issues raised in the Bill were once again introduced in the Queen's Speech at the Opening of Parliament on 15th November, 2006.
2. Both these phrases are in English in the original text.
3. This term, coined by Cooper (1967), is used collectively here: however, it should be noted that it does not apply equally well to all the theorists discussed. It has been claimed that R. D. Laing, for example, did not consider himself to be an 'anti-psychiatrist' (Laing, 1994).
4. All the studies reviewed here consist of a male psychiatric patient and a female spouse.
5. Forgetting of the self.

3 Perspectives from clients and the mental health service user movement

1. Priory Healthcare runs a number of private mental health facilities, including acute and secure units, neuro-rehabilitation centres and specialist educational services.

2. See also Bracken and Thomas (2005) for a discussion of the way in which pharmaceutical companies financially aid client and carer organisations. They claim that, in the absence of being allowed to advertise directly to potential consumers in the United Kingdom, this provides the pharmaceutical industry with an important channel for promoting their products.
3. Individuals who have not had experience of mental health problems or used mental health services, but who have an interest in mental health and are sympathetic to the aims of the organisation, e.g. researchers, professionals, carers etc.
4. The Sainsbury Centre for Mental Health is a charitable organisation, set up in 1985, funded by the Gatsby Charitable Foundation. Although affiliated to the Institute of Psychiatry, it maintains its independence.
5. Similar discrepancies between qualitative and quantitative data have been noted in work on service user views, leading some theorists to suggest that quantitative work masks much client dissatisfaction (Crawford & Kessel, 1999; Letendre, 1997).
6. Introduced in 1991, the Care Programme Approach (CPA) aims to co-ordinate the mental health care that an individual will receive. It involves an initial assessment and then meeting between all professionals involved in a client's care, the client and a friend or family member of the client, if they wish, at which social and medical needs are discussed, and a programme of how to address these, is drawn up. A keyworker amongst the professionals is appointed to oversee the delivery of this programme. The client should then be given a copy of their care programme, and this should be subject to regular review.

4 Defining mental health problems by and through experience

1. Pseudonyms will be used for people and places throughout this book. Some personal details have also been changed in order to preserve the anonymity of participants.
2. This refers to compulsorily detention of a client in hospital for assessment or treatment under a section of the Mental Health Act, 1983, for a period from seventy-two hours up to six months and beyond.
3. Both extracts from interviews and from my ethnographic field notes will be included to illustrate the points being made. These extracts are

chosen to represent the broader themes that were often raised by many clients. Pseudonyms have been used, and some personal details have been changed to protect anonymity and confidentiality. Interview extracts with clients are identified as such; extracts from my ethnographic notes are identified by a reference to the mental health service in which they were written.
4. Interestingly, there now seems to be less emphasis on this method of trying to destigmatise mental health problems. 'Shift', the five-year campaign set up by the National Institute for Mental Health in England in 2004 focuses instead on emphasising the positive contribution made to society by people with mental health problems, and tackles stigma at a variety of levels, including through education of young people and through tackling media representations.
5. A small minority of patients at Spring Ward were undergoing programmes of detoxification from alcohol.

5 The journey through mental illness

1. See also discussion of Rose et al.'s (2003) user-led review of attitudes toward Electro-Convulsive Therapy (ECT), which suggests that results are influenced, among other things, by the identity of the researcher and when the research is carried out in relation to the administration of ECT.
2. National Vocational Qualifications.
3. Work also suggests that this mismatch between client and professional notions of recovery exists in other countries (Tooth et al., 2003).
4. In 2000, a general practitioner named Harold Shipman, from Greater Manchester in the United Kingdom, was convicted of the murder of 15 of his patients.
5. This stands for 'Pro re nata', although I did not hear any client or professional call it by anything other than its initials. PRN is written on prescriptions for medication which may be taken as and when the client desires.
6. The bedboard is a list of all clients on the ward, on which staff recorded the whereabouts of each client on an hourly basis. It was sometimes referred to by staff and clients as 'join the dots'.
7. See Repper and Perkins (2003) for a discussion of such 'distancing' measures employed by mental health staff.
8. See, for example, Whitehead and Williams' (2001) discussion of the often problematic attempts of women with Lupus to negotiate with doctors and play an active role in determining their care.

6 Labelled, spoiled, negotiated and rejected: issues of identity

1. For example, Scheff maintained that residual rule-breaking might stem from four diverse sources – the organic, the psychological, external stress and volitional acts.
2. Temporary, sometimes unqualified care workers, who move from service to service, depending on staffing levels and needs.
3. Staff meetings at the beginning of each shift in which the Nurse in Charge will run through the recent events on the ward, the current patients, and pass on information to the incoming staff as necessary.
4. An Australian soap opera, not generally associated with good-quality acting of emotional storylines.
5. The mental health service user movement is referred to in these terms in the jacket description of the book *Mad Pride* (Curtis et al., 2000).

References

Agar, M. H. (1980). *The professional stranger: an informal introduction to ethnography*. New York: Academic Press.

Amaturo, E. (1987). Contribution des techniques d'analyse multidimensionnelle a d'étude des représentations sociales: le cas de la représentation de la maladie mentale. In G. Bellelli (ed.), *La représentation sociale de la maladie mentale*. Naples: Liguori.

Anderson, M. (2003). 'One flew over the psychiatric unit': mental illness and the media. *Journal of Psychiatric and Mental Health Nursing*, 10(3), 297–306.

Angermeyer, M. C. (1992). 'Trop de stress!' Comment des patients atteints de psychoses fonctionnelles se représentent les causes de leur maladie. In U. Flick (ed.), *La perception quotidienne de la santé et de la maladie: théories subjectives et représentations sociales* (pp. 143–155). Paris: L'Harmattan.

Angermeyer, M. C., Matschinger, H. & Hotzinger, A. (1998). Gender and attitudes towards people with schizophrenia: results of a representative survey in the Federal Republic of Germany. *International Journal of Social Psychiatry*, 44(2), 107–116.

Anon. (1955). An autobiography of a schizophrenic experience. *Journal of Abnormal and Social Psychology*, 51, 677–689.

Applebaum, P. S., Lidz, C. W. & Meisel, A. (1987). *Informed consent: legal theory and clinical practice*. Oxford: Oxford University Press.

Appleby, L. & Wessley, S. (1988). Public attitudes to mental illness: the influence of the Hungerford Massacre. *Medicine, Science and the Law*, 28(4), 291–295.

Arksey, H. (1998). *RSI and the experts: the construction of medical knowledge*. London: UCL Press Ltd.

American Psychiatric Association. (2000). *Diagnostic and statistical manual of mental disorders IV-TR*. Washington: American Psychiatric Association.

Awad, A. G. & Vorugarti, L. N. P. (1999). Quality of life and new anti-psychotics in schizophrenia: are patients better off? *International Journal of Social Psychiatry*, 45(4), 268–275.

Ayestran Etxeberria, S. (1987). Représentation sociale et attribution de causalité. In G. Bellelli (ed.), *La Représentation sociale de la maladie mentale* (pp. 121–131). Naples: Liguori.

Backner, B. L. & Kissinger, R. D. (1963). Hospitalised patients' attitudes toward mental health professionals and mental patients. *Journal of Nervous and Mental Disease*, 136, 72–75.

Barham, P. & Hayward, R. (1991). *From the mental patient to the person.* London: Tavistock/Routledge.

Barnes, M. & Berke, J. (1971). *Mary Barnes: two accounts of a journey through madness.* London: MacGibbon and Kee Ltd.

Barnes, M. & Bowl, R. (2001). *Taking over the asylum: empowerment and mental health.* Basingstoke: Palgrave.

Barrymore, D. & Frank, G. (1957). *Too much too soon.* London: Frederick Miller Ltd.

Bassman, R. (2001). Whose reality is it anyway? Consumers/survivors/ex-patients can speak for themselves. *Journal of Humanistic Psychology, 41*(4), 11–35.

Bastide, R. (1972). *The sociology of mental disorder.* London: Routledge and Kegan Paul.

Bastounis, M. (1996). *La folie mise en scène: le cas de la télévision grecque.* Unpublished doctoral thesis, Ecole des Hautes Etudes en Sciences Sociales, Paris.

Bates, J. (1968). Attitudes toward mental illness. *Mental Hygiene, 52,* 250–253.

Bateson, G. (ed.). (1961). *Perceval's narrative: a patient's account of his psychosis 1830–1832.* Stanford, CA: Stanford University Press.

Bauer, M. & Gaskell, G. (1999). Towards a paradigm for research on social representations. *Journal for the Theory of Social Behaviour, 29*(2), 163–186.

Bauer, M. W. (2000). Classical content analysis: a review. In M. W. Bauer & G. Gaskell (eds), *Qualitative researching with text, image and sound.* London: Sage.

Bauer, M. W., Gaskell, G. & Allum, N. A. (2000). Quality, quantity and knowledge interests: avoiding confusion. In M. W. Bauer & G. Gaskell (eds), *Qualitative researching with text, image and sound* (pp. 3–17). London: Sage.

Becker, H. (1963). *Outsiders.* New York: Free Press.

Beeforth, M., Conlan, E. & Gravley, R. (1994). *Have we got views for you: user evaluation of case management.* London: Sainsbury Centre for Mental Health.

Bellelli, G. (ed.). (1987a). *La représentation sociale de la maladie mentale.* Naples: Liguori.

Bellelli, G. (1987b). Prototypes et représentations sociales de la maladie mentale. In G. Bellelli (ed.), *La représentation sociale de la maladie mentale.* Naples: Liguori.

Bentz, W. K. & Edgerton, J. W. (1971). The consequences of labelling a person as mentally ill. *Social Psychiatry, 6*(1), 29–33.

Beresford, P. (2005). Social approaches to madness and distress: user perspectives and user knowledges. In J. Tew (ed.), *Social perspectives in mental health* (pp. 32–52). London: Jessica Kingsley.

Bethlem and Maudsley NHS Trust. (1997). *Beyond Bedlam*. London: Bethlem and Maudsley NHS Trust.

Bloor, M. (2000). The South Wales Miners Federation, miners' lung and the instrumental use of expertise 1900–1950. *Social Studies of Science*, *30*(1), 125–140.

Bloor, M. (2001). *On the consulting room couch with citizen science: a consideration of the sociology of scientific knowledge perspective on practitioner–patient relations*. Paper presented at the British Sociological Association Medical Sociology Group 33rd Annual Conference, University of York 21–23 September 2001.

Bloor, M., Monaghan, L., Dobash, R. P. & Dobash, R. E. (1998). The body as a chemistry experiment: steroid use among South Wales bodybuilders. In S. Nettleton & J. Watson (eds), *The body in everyday life*. London: Routledge.

Bourdieu, P. (1991). *Language and symbolic power*. Cambridge: Polity Press.

Bowden, W. D. (1993). First person account: the onset of paranoia. *Schizophrenia Bulletin, 19*(1), 165–167.

Bracken, P. & Thomas, P. (2001). Postpsychiatry: a new direction for mental health. *British Medical Journal, 322*, 742–747.

Bracken, P. & Thomas, P. (2005). *Postpsychiatry: mental health in a postmodern world*. Oxford: OUP.

Breakwell, G. M. (1983). Formulations and searches. In G. M. Breakwell (ed.), *Threatened identities*. Chichester: John Wiley and Sons.

Brockington, I. F., Hall, P., Levings, J. & Murphy, C. (1993). The community's tolerance of the mentally ill. *British Journal of Psychiatry, 162*, 93–99.

Burr, V. (2003). *Social constructionism*. London: Routledge.

Bury, M. (2001). Illness narratives: fact or fiction? *Sociology of Health and Illness, 23*(3), 263–285.

Busfield, J. (2000). Introduction: rethinking the sociology of mental health. *Sociology of Health and Illness, 22*(5), 543–558.

Byrne, P. (1997). Psychiatric stigma: past, passing and to come. *Journal of the Royal Society of Medicine, 90*(11), 618–621.

Byrne, P. (1999). Stigma of mental illness: changing minds, changing behaviour. *British Journal of Psychiatry, 174*, 1–3.

Callan, A. & Littlewood, R. (1998). Patient satisfaction: ethnic origin or explanatory model? *International Journal of Social Psychiatry, 44*(1), 1–11.

Campbell, P. (2005). From little acorns: the mental health service user movement. In A. Bell & P. Lindley (eds), *Beyond the water towers: the unfinished revolution in mental health services 1985–2005*. London: Sainsbury Centre for Mental Health.

Caudill, W. (1958). *The psychiatric hospital as a small society*. Cambridge, MA: Harvard University Press.

Caudill, W., Redlich, F., Gilmore, H. & Brody, E. (1952). Social structure and interaction processes on a psychiatric ward. *American Journal of Orthopsychiatry, 22*, 314–334.

Chadwick, P. K. (1993). The stepladder to the impossible: a first hand phenomenological account of a schizoaffective psychotic crisis. *Journal of Mental Health, 2*(3), 239–251.

Chadwick, P. K. (1997a). Learning from patients. *Clinical Psychology Forum, 100*(February), 5–10.

Chadwick, P. (1997b). Recovery from psychosis: learning more from patients. *Journal of Mental Health, 6*(6), 577–588.

Chadwick, P. (1997c). *Schizophrenia: the positive perspective.* London: Routledge.

Charmaz, K. (1999). Stories of suffering: subjective tales and research narratives. *Qualitative Health Research, 9*(3), 362–381.

Charmaz, K. & Olsen, V. (1997). Ethnographic research in medical sociology. *Sociological Methods and Research, 25*(4), 452–494.

Chastko, H. E., Glick, I. D., Gould, E. & Hargreaves, W. (1971). Patients' posthospital evaluations of psychiatric nursing treatment. *Nursing Research, 20*, 333–338.

Clark, D. H. (1996). *The story of a mental hospital: Fulbourn 1858–1983.* London: Process Press.

Clark, K. & Clark, M. (1947). Racial identification and preference in Negro children. In T. M. Newcomb & E. L. Hartley (eds), *Readings in social psychology.* New York: Holt.

Cleary, M., Freeman, A., Hunt, G. & Walter, G. (2005). What patients and carers want to know: an exploration of information and resource needs in adult mental health services. *Australian and New Zealand Journal of Psychiatry, 39*(6), 507–513.

Coate, M. (1964). *Beyond all Reason.* London: Constable.

Coleman, R. (1999). *Recovery: an alien concept.* Gloucester: Handsell Publishing.

Condor, S. (1997). And so say all of us? Some thoughts on 'experiential democratization' as an aim for critical social psychologists. In T. Ibáñez & L. Íñiguez (eds), *Critical Social Psychology* (pp. 111–146). London: Sage.

Cook, J. A. & Wright, E. R. (1995). Medical sociology and the study of severe mental illness: reflections on past accomplishments and directions for future research. *Journal of Health and Social Behavior, 36*(Extra issue), 95–114.

Cooper, D. (1967). *Psychiatry and Anti-psychiatry.* London: Tavistock Publications.

Cormack, S. & Furnham, A. (1998). Psychiatric labelling, sex role stereotypes and beliefs about the mentally ill. *International Journal of Social Psychiatry, 44*(4), 235–247.

Corrigan, P. W. & Watson, A. C. (2002). The paradox of self-stigma and mental illness. *Clinical Psychology: science and practice, 9*(1), 35–53.

Coursey, R. D., Keller, A. B. & Farrell, E. W. (1995). Individual psychotherapy and persons with serious mental illness: the clients' perspective. *Schizophrenia Bulletin, 21*(2), 283–301.

Crawford, M. J. & Kessel, A. S. (1999). Not listening to patients – the use and misuse of patient satisfaction studies. *International Journal of Social Psychiatry, 45*(1), 1–6.

Crawford, R. (1994). The boundaries of the Self and the unhealthy Other: reflections on health, culture and AIDS. *Social Science and Medicine, 38*(10), 1347–1365.

Crocetti, G. M., Spiro, H. & Siassi, I. (1974). *Contemporary attitudes toward mental illness*. Pittsburgh: University of Pittsburgh Press.

Crumpton, E., Weinstein, A. D., Acker, C. W. & Annis, A. P. (1967). How patients and normals see the mental patient. *Journal of Clinical Psychology, 23*, 46–49.

Crumpton, E. & Groot , H. (1966). What mental illness labels mean to schizophrenics. *Psychological Reports, 19*, 927–933.

Cumming, E. & Cumming, J. (1957). *Closed ranks: an experiment in mental health education*. Cambridge, MA: Harvard University Press.

Curtis, T., Dellar, R., Leslie, E. & Watson, B. (eds). (2000). *Mad Pride: a celebration of mad culture*. London: Spare Change Books.

Cutcliffe, J. R. & Hannigan, B. (2001). Mass media, 'monsters' and mental health clients: the need for increased lobbying. *Journal of Psychiatric and Mental Health Nursing, 8*(4), 35–321.

D'Arcy, C. & Brockman, J. (1976). Changing public recognition of psychiatric symptoms? Blackfoot revisited. *Journal of Health and Social Behaviour, 17*, 302–312.

Davison, G. C. & Neale, J. M. (1994). *Abnormal psychology (sixth edition)*. New York: John Wiley and Sons Ltd.

De Rosa, A. S. (1987). The social representations of mental illness in children and adults. In W. Doise & S. Moscovici (eds), *Current issues in social psychology*. Cambridge: Cambridge University Press.

Delange, W. (1962). Conceptions of patient role by patients and staff in a state mental hospital. *Comprehensive Psychiatry, 3*, 174–180.

Di Giacomo, J. P. (1987). Fonctions sociales et individuelles des représentations sociales. In G. Bellelli (ed.), *La représentation sociale de la maladie mentale*. Liguori, Naples.

Double, D. (2005). Beyond biomedical models: a perspective from critical psychiatry. In J. Tew (ed.), *Social perspectives in mental health: developing social models to understand and work with mental distress* (pp. 53–70). London: Jessica Kingsley.

Duveen, G. M. (2000). Introduction: the power of ideas. In S. Moscovici (ed.), *Social representations: explorations in social psychology* (pp. 1–17). Cambridge: Polity Press.

Duveen, G. M. (2001). Representations, identities, resistance. In K. Deaux & G. Philogène (eds), *Representations of the social: bridging theoretical traditions.* Oxford: Blackwell.

Duveen, G. M. & Lloyd, B. (1986). The significance of social identity. *British Journal of Social Psychology, 26,* 219–230.

Duveen, G. M. & Lloyd, B. (1990). Introduction. In G. Duveen & B. Lloyd (eds), *Social representations and the development of knowledge* (pp. 1–10). Cambridge: Cambridge University Press.

Duveen, G. M. & Lloyd, B. (1993). An ethnographic approach to social representations. In G. Breakwell & D. Canter (eds), *Empirical approaches to social representations.* Oxford: Oxford University Press.

Epstein, S. (1996). *Impure science: AIDS, activism and the politics of knowledge.* Berkeley: University of California Press.

Estroff, S. E. (1981). *Making it crazy: an ethnography of psychiatric clients in an American community.* Berkeley: University of California Press.

Fainzang, S. (1995). L'alcool, les nerfs, le cerveau et le sang. *L'Homme, 135,* 109–125.

Farina, A. (1981). Are women nicer people than men? Sex differences and the stigma of mental disorders. *Clinical Psychology Review, 1,* 223–243.

Farr, R. M. (1982). Interviewing: the social psychology of the inter-view. In F. Fransella (ed.), *Psychology for occupational therapists* (pp. 151–170). London: Macmillan.

Farr, R. M. (1987). Social representations: a French tradition of research. *Journal for the Theory of Social Behaviour, 17*(4), 343–369.

Farr, R. M. (1993a). Theory and method in the study of social representations. In D. Canter & G. Breakwell (eds), *Empirical approaches to social representations.* Oxford: Clarendon Press.

Farr, R. M. (1993b). Common sense, science and social representations. *Public Understanding of Science, 2,* 189–204.

Faulkner, A. & Thomas, P. (2002). User-led research and evidence-based medicine. *British Journal of Psychiatry, 180,* 1–3.

Feder, L. (1980). *Madness in literature.* Princetown, NJ: Princetown University Press.

Finlay, W. M. L., Dinos, S. & Lyons, E. (2001). Stigma and multiple social comparisons in people with schizophrenia. *European Journal of Social Psychology, 31*(5), 579–592.

Fitzpatrick, R. & Hopkins, A. (eds). (1993). *Measurement of patients' satisfaction with their care.* London: Royal College of Physicians.

Flick, U. (1998a). The social construction of individual and public health: contributions of social representations theory to a social science of health. *Social Sciences Information, 37*(4), 639–662.

Flick, U. (1998b). *An introduction to qualitative research.* London: Sage.

Flick, U. (1998c). Everyday knowledge in social psychology. In U. Flick (ed.), *The psychology of the social* (pp. 41–59). Cambridge: Cambridge University Press.

Flick, U. (2000). Qualitative inquiries into social representations of health. *Journal of Health Psychology, 5*(3), 315–324.

Flick, U. (2001). Interpretative social psychology: qualitative methods in the study of social representations. In F. Buschini & N. Kalampalikis (eds), *Penser la vie, le social, la nature: mélanges en l'honneur de Serge Moscovici* (pp. 201–218). Paris: Editions de la Maison des Sciences de l'Homme.

Flick, U. & Foster, J. L. H. (in press). Social representations. In C. Willig & W. Stainton-Rogers (eds), *The handbook of qualitative research in psychology.* London: Sage.

Foster, J. L. (1998). *Unification and differentiation: a study of the social representations of mental illness.* Unpublished MSc thesis, London School of Economics, London.

Foster, J. L. H. (2001). Unification and differentiation: a study in the social representation of mental illness. *Papers on social representations 10*, 3.1–3.18. Online at http://www.psr.jku.at/PSR2001/10_3Foste.pdf

Foster, J. L. H. (2003). Representational projects and interacting forms of knowledge. *Journal for the Theory of Social Behaviour, 33*(3), 231–244.

Foster, J. L. H. (2004). 'I believe the technical term is mad as a box of frogs': mental health service clients representing mental ill health. *Social Psychological Review 6*(2), 59–70.

Foster, J. L. H. (2006a). Media discussion of the Mental Health Act and representations of mental ill health. *Journal of Community and Applied Social Psychology 16*, 285–300.

Foster, J. L. H. (2006b). *The development of the mental health service user movement and research into mental health: challenges and opportunities.* Paper presented at the Communities and Change Workshop, Institute of Social Psychology, London School of Economics, 26 June, 2006.

Foucault, M. (1961). *Madness and civilisation.* London: Routledge.

Foucault, M. (1976). Two lectures. In C. Gordon (ed.), *Power/knowledge: selected interviews and other writings 1972–1977.* New York: Pantheon Books.

Freeman, C. P. L. & Kendell, R. E. (1980). ECT: I Patients' experiences and attitudes. *British Journal of Psychiatry, 137*, 8–16.

Freud, S. & Breuer, J. (1955). *Studies on Hysteria.* (1991 edition). London: Penguin.

Furlong, F. W. (1991). Credibility of patients in psychiatric research. *American Journal of Psychiatry, 148*(10), 1423.

Gelder, M. (1983). *Oxford textbook of psychiatry.* Oxford: Oxford Medical Publications.

Gellner, E. (2003). *The psychoanalytic movement.* Oxford: Blackwell.

Gervais, M.-C., Morant, N. & Penn, G. (1999). Making sense of 'absence': towards a typology of absence in social representations theory and research. *Journal for the Theory of Social Behaviour, 29*(4), 419–444.

Gilman, S. L. (1985a). *Difference and pathology: stereotypes of sexuality, race and madness.* New York: Cornell University Press.

Gilman, S. L. (1985b). *Seeing the insane.* New York: John Wiley and Sons Ltd.

Gilman, S. L. (1988). *Disease and representation: images of illness from madness to AIDS.* Ithaca: Cornell University Press.

Giovanni, J. & Ullmann, L. (1963). Conceptions of mental health held by psychiatric patients. *Journal of Clinical Psychology, 19*, 398–400.

Gittins, D. (1998). *Madness in its place: narratives of Severalls Hospital, 1913–1997.* London: Routledge.

Goffman, E. (1959a). The moral career of the mental patient. *Psychiatry, 22*, 123–142.

Goffman, E. (1959b). *The presentation of the Self in everyday life.* Harmondsworth: Penguin.

Goffman, E. (1961). *Asylums.* (1991 edition). Harmondsworth: Penguin.

Goffman, E. (1968). *Stigma: notes on the management of spoiled identity.* Englewood Cliffs, NJ: Prentice Hall.

Gordon, D., Alexander, D. A. & Dietzan, J. (1979). The psychiatric patient: a voice to be heard. *British Journal of Psychiatry, 135*, 115–121.

Gray, A. J. (2002). Stigma in society. *Journal of the Royal Society of Medicine, 95*(February), 72–76.

Greenfeld, D., Strauss, J. S., Bowers, M. B. & Mandelkern, M. (1989). Insight and interpretation of illness in recovery from psychosis. *Schizophrenia Bulletin, 15*(2), 245–252.

Griffiths, L. (1998). Humour as a resistance to professional dominance in community mental health teams. *Sociology of Health and Illness, 20*(6), 874–895.

Guimelli, C. (2000). Structures des représentations sociales de la dépression et pratiques médicales. In M. Chaib & B. Orfali (eds), *Social representations and communicative processes* (pp. 188–195). Jönköping: Jönköping University Press.

Guzé, S. B. (1957). Theory and observation in psychiatric research. *Human Organisation, 16*(4), 4–6.

Gynther, M. D. & Brilliant, P. J. (1964). Psychopathology and attitudes towards mental illness. *Archives of General Psychiatry, 11*, 48–52.

Hall, P., Brockington, I. F., Levings, J. & Murphy, C. (1993). A comparison of responses to the mentally ill in two communities. *British Journal of Psychiatry, 162*, 99–108.

Hall, S. (1991). Old and new identities, old and new ethnicities. In A. D. King (ed.), *Culture, globalization and the world system*. New York: Macmillan.

Hall, S. & Cheston, R. (2002). Mental health and identity: the evaluation of a drop-in centre. *Journal of Community and Applied Social Psychology, 12*, 30–43.

Hallam, A. (2002). Media influences on mental health policy: long-term effects of the Clunis and Silcock cases. *International Review of Psychiatry, 14*(1), 28–33.

Hardey, M. (1999). Doctor in the house: the Internet as a source of lay health knowledge and the challenge to expertise. *Sociology of Health and Illness, 21*(6), 820–835.

Harrow, M., Fox, D. & Detre, T. (1969). Self concept of the married psychiatric patient and his mate's perception of him. *Journal of Consulting and Clinical Psychology, 33*, 235–239.

Harrow, M., Fox, D. A. & Markhus, K. L. (1968). Self-concept of the married psychiatric patient and his mate's perception of him. *Journal of Nervous and Mental Disease, 147*(3), 152–159.

Hayward, P. & Bright, J. A. (1997). Stigma and mental illness: a review and critique. *Journal of Mental Health, 6*(4), 345–354.

Healthcare Commission. (2004). *Mental health survey* (Patient survey report). London: Healthcare Commission.

Herman, N. J. & Musolf, G. R. (1998). Resistance among ex-psychiatric patients: expressive and instrumental rituals. *Journal of Contemporary Ethnography, 26*(4), 426–449.

Herzlich, C. (1973). *Health and illness*. London: Academic Press.

Herzlich, C. & Pierret, J. (1987). *Illness and Self in society*. Baltimore, MD: The Johns Hopkins University Press.

Hill, R. G., Hardy, P. & Shepherd, G. (1996). *Perspectives on manic depression: a national survey of the Manic Depression Fellowship*. London: Sainsbury Centre for Mental Health.

Hollingshead, A. B. & Redlich, F. C. (1958). *Social class and mental illness*. New York: John Wiley and Sons Ltd.

Howarth, C., Foster, J. & Dorrer, N. (2004). Exploring the potential of the theory of social representations in community-based health research – and vice versa? *Journal of Health Psychology, 9*(2), 229–243.

Humphries, B., Mertens, D. M. & Truman, C. (2000). Arguments for an 'emancipatory' research paradigm. In C. Truman, D. M. Mertens & B. Humphries (eds), *Research and inequality*. London: UCL Press.

Huxley, P. (1993a). Location and stigma: a survey of community attitudes to mental illness – Part II. Community mental health facilities – anonymity or invisibility. *Journal of Mental Health, 2,* 157–164.

Huxley, P. (1993b). Location and stigma: a survey of community attitudes to mental illness – Part I. Enlightenment and stigma. *Journal of Mental Health, 2,* 73–80.

Imre, P. & Wolf, S. (1962). Attitudes of patients and personnel toward mental hospitals. *Journal of Clinical Psychology, 18,* 232–234.

Imre, P. D. (1962). Attitudes of volunteers toward mental hospitals compared to patients and personnel. *Journal of Clinical Psychology, 18,* 516.

Irwin, A. (1995). *Citizen Science: a study of people, expertise and sustainable development*. London: Routledge.

J. T. (ed.). (1904). *The house of quiet: an autobiography*. London: John Murray.

James, R. S. P., Zahl, A. & Huws, J. C. (2001). First-hand accounts of emotional experiences in autism: a qualitative analysis. *Disability and Society, 16*(3), 393–401.

Jamison, K. (1995). *An unquiet mind: a memoir of moods and madness*. London: Picador.

Jamison, K. R. (1996). *Touched with fire: manic depressive illness and the artistic temperament*. London: Simon and Schuster Ltd.

Jodelet, D. (1991). *Madness and social representations* (trans., Tim Pownall). Hemel Hempstead: Harvester Wheatsheaf.

Joffe, H. (1996). AIDS research and prevention: a social representational approach. *British Journal of Medical Psychology, 69,* 169–190.

Joffe, H. (1999). *Risk and 'the Other'*. Cambridge: Cambridge University Press.

Johannsen, W. J. (1969). Attitudes toward mental patients: a review of the empirical research. *Mental Hygiene, 49,* 218–228.

Johnson, S. & Orwell, M. (1995). Insight and psychosis: a social perspective. *Psychological Medicine, 25,* 515–520.

Jones, N. F., Kahn, M. W. & MacDonald, J. M. (1963). Psychiatric patients' views of mental illness, hospitalisation and treatment. *Journal of Nervous and Mental Disease, 136,* 82–87.

Jovchelovitch, S. (1996). In defence of social representations. *Journal for the Theory of Social Behaviour, 26*(2), 121–135.

Jovchelovitch, S. (2006). *Knowledge in context: representations, community and culture*. London: Routledge.

Kahn, M. W., Jones, N. F., MacDonald, J. M., Conners, C. K. & Burchard, J. (1963). A factorial study of patient attitudes towards mental illness and psychiatric hospitalisation. *Journal of Clinical Psychology, 19*, 235–241.

Karmel, M. (1969). Total institutions and self-mortification. *Journal of Health and Social Behaviour, 10*, 134–141.

Karp, D. A. (1992). Illness ambiguity and the search for meaning: a case study of a self-help group for affective disorders. *Journal of Contemporary Ethnography, 21*(2), 139–170.

Kaysen, S. (2000). *Girl, interrupted*. London: Virago.

Kennard, D. (1974). The newly admitted psychiatric patient as seen by self and others. *British Journal of Medical Psychology, 47*, 27–41.

Kleinman, A. (1988). *The illness narratives*. New York: Basic Books.

Kotin, J. & Schur, J. M. (1969). Attitudes of discharged mental patients toward their hospital experiences. *Journal of Nervous and Mental Disease, 149*, 408–414.

Krause Jacob, M. (1992). 'Je commence à croire que j'ai une névrose.' La modification des théories subjectives dans l'interaction avec les conseillers professionnels. In U. Flick (ed.), *La perception quotidienne de la santé et de la maladie: théories subjectives et représentations sociales* (pp. 238–258). Paris: L'Harmattan.

Kutchins, H. & Kirk, S. A. (1999). *Making us crazy: DSM – the psychiatric bible and the creation of mental disorders*. London: Constable.

Laine, A. & Lehtinen, V. (1973). Attitudes toward mental illness and their relationship to social structure and mental hospital bed utilisation in two Finnish rural communities. *Social Psychiatry, 8*, 117–123.

Laing, A. C. (1994). *R. D. Laing: a life*. London: Harper Collins.

Laing, R. D. (1960). *The divided Self*. (1969 edition) Harmondsworth: Penguin.

Laing, R. D. & Esterson, A. (1964). *Sanity, madness and the family*. (1990 edition) Harmondsworth: Penguin Books.

Lakoff, G. & Johnson, M. (1980). *Metaphors we live by*. Chicago: University of Chicago Press.

Lally, S. J. (1989). Does being in here mean there is something wrong with me? *Schizophrenia Bulletin, 15*(2), 253–265.

Lambert, H. & Rose, H. (1996). Disembodied knowledge? Making sense of medical science. In A. Irwin & B. Wynne (eds), *Misunderstanding science? The public reconstruction of science and technology* (pp. 65–83). Cambridge: Cambridge University Press.

Lambert, W. E., Hodgson, R. C., Gardner, R. C. & Fillenbaum, S. (1960). Evaluational reactions to spoken languages. *Journal of Abnormal and Social Psychology, 60*, 44–51.

Lapsley, H., Nikora, L. W. & Black, R. (2002). *'Kia Mauri Tau!' Narratives of recovery from disabling mental health problems* (Report of the University of Waikato Mental Health Narratives Project). Wellington: Mental Health Commission.

Laurance, J. (2003). *Pure madness: how fear drives the mental health system*. London: Routledge.

Leff, J. (2001). *The unbalanced mind*. London: Weidenfeld and Nicholson.

Lemaku, P. & Crocetti, G. (1962). An urban population's opinion and knowledge about mental illness. *American Journal of Psychiatry, 118*, 692–700.

Letendre, R. (1997). The everyday experience of psychiatric hospitalisation: the users' viewpoint. *International Journal of Social Psychiatry, 43*(4), 285–297.

Leudar, I. & Thomas, P. (2000). *Voices of reason, voices of insanity*. London: Routledge.

Leventhal, H. & Benyamini, Y. (1997). Lay beliefs about health and illness. In A. Baum, S. Newman, J. Weinman, R. West & C. McManus (eds), *Cambridge handbook of psychology, health and medicine*. Cambridge: Cambridge University Press.

Leventhal, H., Benyamini, Y., Brownlee, S., Diefenbach, M., Leventhal, E. A., Patrick-Miller, L. & Robitaille, C. (1997). Illness representations: theoretical foundations. In K. J. Petrie & J. A. Weinman (eds), *Perceptions of health and illness: current research applications*. Amsterdam: Harwood Academic.

Levey, S. & Howells, K. (1995). Dangerousness, unpredictability and the fear of people with schizophrenia. *Journal of Forensic Psychiatry, 6*(1), 19–39.

Lewis, S. G. (1995). A search for meaning: making sense of depression. *Journal of Mental Health, 4*(4), 369–382.

Lloyd, B. and Duveen, G. M. (1992). *Gender identities and education*. Hemel Hempstead: Harvester Wheatsheaf.

Link, B. G. (1987). Understanding labelling effects in the area of mental disorders: an assessment of the effects of expectations on rejection. *American Sociological Review, 52*, 96–112.

Link, B. G., Cullen, F. T., Struening, E., Shrout, P. E. & Dohrenwend, B. P. (1989). A modified labelling theory approach to mental disorder: an empirical assessment. *American Sociological Review, 54*, 400–423.

Link, B. G. & Phelan, J. C. (2001). Conceptualising stigma. *Annual Review of Sociology, 27*, 363–385.

Linn, L. S. (1968). The mental hospital from the patient perspective. *Psychiatry, 31*, 213–223.

Littlewood, R. & Lipsedge, M. (1989). *Aliens and alienists*. London: Routledge.

Livingston, G. & Cooper, C. (2004). User and carer involvement in mental health training. *Advances in Psychiatric Treatment, 10*, 85–92.

Lucas, R. H. & Barratt, R. J. (1995). Interpreting culture and psychopathology: primitivist themes in cross-cultural debate. *Culture, Medicine and Psychiatry, 19,* 287–326.

Lukes, S. (1973). *Individualism.* Oxford: Blackwell.

Lupton, D. (1994). *Medicine as culture: illness, disease and the body in Western society.* London: Sage.

Maclean, U. (1969). Community attitudes to the mentally ill in Edinburgh. *British Journal of Preventative and Social Medicine, 23,* 45–52.

Maia de Nobrega, S. (1999). *Représentations sociales de la folie par les familles de malades mentaux au nord-est du Brésil (le cas de Joao Pessoa).* Unpublished doctoral thesis, Ecole des Hautes Etudes en Sciences Sociales, Paris.

Manis, M., Houts, P. S. & Blake, J. B. (1963). Beliefs about mental illness as a function of psychiatric status and psychiatric hospitalisation. *Journal of Abnormal and Social Psychology, 67*(3), 226–233.

Manktelow, R. (1994). *Paths to psychiatric hospitalisation: a sociological analysis.* Aldershot: Avebury.

Marková, I. (1990). Self and other awareness of the risk in HIV/AIDS in people with haemophilia and implications for behavioural change. *Social Science and Medicine, 31,* 73–79.

Marková, I. (1996). Towards an epistemology of social representations. *Journal for the Theory of Social Behaviour, 26*(2), 177–193.

Marková, I. (2003). *Dialogicality and social representations.* Cambridge: Cambridge University Press.

Marková, I., Moodie, E., Farr, R. M., Drozda-Senkowska, E., Gros, F., Plichtova, J., Gervais, M. -C., Hoffmanova, J. & Mullerova, O. (1998). Social representations of the individual in a post-communist perspective. *European Journal of Social Psychology, 28*(5), 797–830.

Mayo, C. & Havelock, R. G. (1970). Attitudes toward mental illness among mental hospital personnel and patients. *Journal of Psychiatric Research, 7,* 291–298.

McCabe, R., Heath, C., Burns, T. & Priebe, S. (2002). Engagement of patients with psychosis in consultation: conversation analytic study. *British Medical Journal, 325,* 1148–1151.

McCarthy, J. D. & Zald, M. N. (1977). Resource mobilisation and social movements: a partial theory. *American Journal of Sociology, 82,* 1212–1241.

McIntyre, K., Farrell, M. & David, A. S. (1989). What do psychiatric patients really want? *British Medical Journal, 298,* 159–160.

McIver, S. (1991a). *An introduction to obtaining the views of users of health services.* London: Kings Fund Centre for Health Services Development.

McIver, S. (1991b). *Obtaining the views of users of mental health services.* London: Kings Fund Centre for Health Services Development.

Mead, G. H. (1977). *On social psychology.* Chicago: University of Chicago Press.

Mechanic, D. (1962). Some factors in identifying and defining mental illness. *Mental Hygiene, 42,* 66–74.

Mies, M. (1983). Towards a methodology for feminist research. In G. Bowles and R. Duelli Klein (eds), *Theories of women's studies* (pp. 117–139). London: Routledge and Kegan Paul.

Miles, A. (1987). *The mentally ill in society.* (second edition). Oxford: Blackwell.

Miller, P. & Rose, N. (1986). Introduction. In P. Miller & N. Rose (eds), *The power of psychiatry* (pp. 1–11). Cambridge: Polity Press.

Mills, E. (1962). *Living with mental illness.* London: Routledge and Kegan Paul.

Mental Health Foundation, (1997). *Knowing our own minds: a survey of how people in emotional distress take control of their lives.* London: Mental Health Foundation.

Molvaer, J., Hantzi, A. & Papadatos, Y. (1992). Psychotic patients' attributions for mental illness. *British Journal of Clinical Psychology, 31,* 210–212.

Morant, N. J. (1995). What is mental illness? Social representations of mental illness among British and French mental health professionals. *Papers on Social Representations, 4*(1), 41–52.

Morant, N. J. (1996). *Social representations of mental illness: a study of British and French mental health professionals.* Unpublished PhD, University of London, London.

Morant, N. J. (1998a). Representations, communities and health: an introduction. *Social Sciences Information, 37*(4), 633–637.

Morant, N. J. (1998b). The social representations of mental ill-health in communities of mental health practitioners in the UK and France. *Social Science Information, 37*(4), 663–685.

MORI. (1979). *Public attitudes to mental illness: research study conducted for the Mental Health Appeal.* London: MORI.

Moscovici, S. (1961). *La psychanalyse: son image et son public.* (1976 edition). Paris: Presses Universitaires de France.

Moscovici, S. (1972). Theory and society in social psychology. In J. Israel & H. Tajfel (eds), *The context of social psychology.* London: Academic Press.

Moscovici, S. (1973). Preface. In C. Herzlich (ed.), *Health and illness.* London: Academic Press.

Moscovici, S. (1984a). The phenomenon of social representations. In R. M. Farr & S. Moscovici (eds), *Social representations* (pp. 3–69). Cambridge: Cambridge University Press.

Moscovici, S. (1984b). The myth of the lonely paradigm. *Social Research* *51*, 939–967.

Moscovici, S. (1987). Answers and questions. *Journal for the Theory of Social Behaviour 17*(4), 513–529.

Moscovici, S. (1993). Introductory address. *Papers on Social Representations*, *2*, 160–170.

Moscovici, S. (1998). The history and actuality of social representations. In U. Flick (ed.), *The Psychology of the Social* (pp. 209–247). Cambridge: Cambridge University Press.

Moscovici, S. (2000). The concept of themata. In G. Duveen (ed.), *Social representations: explorations in social psychology* (pp. 156–183). Cambridge: Polity.

Moscovici, S. & Hewstone, M. (1983). Social representations and social explanations: from the 'naïve' to the 'amateur' scientist. In M. Hewstone (ed.), *Attribution theory: social and functional extensions* (pp. 98–125). Oxford: Blackwell.

Moscovici, S. & Marková, I. (1998). Presenting social representations: a conversation. *Culture and Psychology, 4*(3), 371–410.

Muhr, T. (1997). Atlas-ti: the knowledge workbench (Version 4.2 Build 055). Berlin: Scientific Software Development.

Murray, M. (2000). Levels of narrative analysis in health psychology. *Journal of Health Psychology, 5*(3), 337–347.

Murray, M. (2004). Challenging narratives and social representations of health, illness and injury. In M. Murray (ed.), *Critical health psychology* (pp. 173–187). Basingstoke: Palgrave.

National Institute for Mental Health in England. (2004). *2004–2009: A strategic plan to tackle stigma and discrimination on mental health grounds: from here to equality.* Leeds: National Institute for Mental Health in England.

Nieradzik, K. & Cochrane, R. (1985). Public attitudes towards mental illness – the effects of behavior roles and labelling. *International Journal of Social Psychiatry, 31*(1), 23–33.

Nugent, C. (2001). *Not waving but drowning: telling survivor stories.* Paper presented at the British Sociological Association Medical Sociology Group 33rd Annual Conference, University of York, September, 2001.

Nunnally, J. C. (1961). *Popular conceptions of mental illness: their development and change.* New York: Holt, Rinehart and Winston.

Office for National Statistics. (1999). *Labour force survey.* London: Office for National Statistics.

Office for National Statistics. (2003). *Attitudes towards mental illness.* London: Department of Health.

O'Hagan, M. (1993). *Stopovers on my way home from Mars.* London: Survivors Speak Out.

Olmstead, D. W. & Durham, K. (1976). Stability of mental health attitudes: a semantic differential study. *Journal of Health and Social Behaviour, 17*, 35–44.

O'Mahony, P. (1980). *Public, professional and patient perceptions of the mentally ill.* Unpublished PhD thesis, Trinity College, Dublin.

Onken, S. J., Dumont, J., Ridgway, P., Dornan, M. S. & Ralph, R. O. (2002). *Mental health recovery: what helps and what hinders? A national research project for the development of recovery facilitating system performance indicators* (Phase one research report). Alexandria, VA: National Technical Assistance Center for State Mental Health Planning.

Oyserman, D. & Swim, J. K. (2001). Stigma: an insider's view. *Journal of Social Issues, 57*(1), 1–14.

Paez Rovira, D. (1987). Représentation sociale, cognition sociale et maladie mentale: convergences et divergences théoriques. In G. Bellelli (ed.), *La représentation sociale de la maladie mentale* (pp. 133–143). Naples: Liguori.

Pankejeff, S. (1972). *The Wolf Man and Sigmund Freud.* London: Hogarth Press and the Institute for Psychoanalysis.

Pembroke, L. R. (1992). *Eating distress: perspectives from personal experience.* London: Survivors Speak Out.

Penn, D. L. & Nowlin-Drummond, A. (2001). Politically correct labels and schizophrenia: a rose by any other name? *Schizophrenia Bulletin, 27*(2), 197–203.

Peterson, D. (ed.). (1982). *A mad people's history of madness.* Pittsburgh: University of Pittsburgh Press.

Petrillo, G. (1987). Représentations naïves et professionnelles de la maladie mentale. In G. Bellelli (ed.), *La Représentation sociale de la maladie mentale.* Naples: Liguori.

Philo, G. (1996). The media and public belief. In G. Philo (ed.), *Media and mental distress.* London: Longman.

Philo, G., McLaughlin, G. & Henderson, L. (1996). Media content. In G. Philo (ed.), *Media and mental distress.* London: Longman.

Pilgrim, D. (2005). Protest and co-option: the voice of mental health service users. In A. Bell & P. Lindley (eds), *Beyond the water towers: the unfinished revolution in mental health services 1985–2005.* London: Sainsbury Centre for Mental Health.

Popay, J. & Williams, G. (1996). Public health research and lay knowledge. *Social Science and Medicine, 42*(5), 759–768.

Porter, R. (1987). *A social history of madness.* London: Weidenfeld and Nicholson.

Porter, R. (ed.). (1991). *The Faber book of madness.* London: Faber.

Powell, R. A. (1992). Credibility of patients in psychiatric research. *American Journal of Psychiatry, 149*(8), 1126–1127.

Pradeilles, C. (1992). *La représentation sociale de la maladie mentale en Lozère.* Unpublished doctoral thesis, Université de Provence.

Prior, L. (1991). Mind, body and behaviour: theorisations of madness and the organisation of therapy. *Sociology, 25*(3), 403–421.

Prior, R. M. (1995). Surviving psychiatric institutionalisation: a case study. *Sociology of Health and Illness, 17*(5), 651–667.

Proctor, G. (2001). Listening to older women with dementia: relationships, voices, power. *Disability and Society, 16*(3), 361–376.

Quadagno, J. S. & Antonio, R. J. (1975). Labelling theory as an over-socialised conception of man: the case of mental illness. *Sociology and Social Research, 60*, 33–45.

Rabkin, J. (1974). Public attitudes toward mental illness: a review of the literature. *Schizophrenia Bulletin, 10*, 9–33.

Rabkin, J. G. (1972). Opinions about mental illness: a review of the literature. *Psychological Bulletin, 77*(3), 153–171.

Ramon, S. (2005). Approaches to risk in mental health: a multidisciplinary discourse. In J. Tew (ed.), *Social perspectives in mental health: developing social models to understand and work with mental distress* (pp. 184–199). London: Jessica Kingsley.

Raphael, W. (1977). *Psychiatric hospitals viewed by their patients.* London: King Edward's Hospital Fund for London.

Räty, H. (1990). A world without mental illness: concepts of mental health and mental illness among a student group. *Social Behaviour, 5*(5), 315–326.

Read, J. & Reynolds, J. (Eds.). (1996). *Speaking our minds: an anthology.* Basingstoke: Palgrave.

Read, S. (1989). *Only for a fortnight: my life in a locked ward.* London: Bloomsbury.

Reda, S. (1996). Public opinion about the preparation required before closing psychiatric hospitals. *Journal of Mental Health, 5*(4), 407–420.

Reid, D., Ryan, T. & Enderby, P. (2001). What does it mean to listen to people with dementia? *Disability and Society, 16*(3), 377–392.

Repper, J. & Perkins, R. (2003). *Social inclusion and recovery: a model for mental health practice.* Philadelphia: Elsevier Science.

Rippere, V. (1977). Common sense beliefs about depression and anti-depressive behaviour: a study of social consensus. *Behaviour, Research and Therapy, 15*, 465–473.

Rippere, V. (1981). How depressing: another cognitive dimension of common sense knowledge. *Behaviour, Research and Therapy, 19*, 169–181.

Robertson, D. W. (1996). Ethical theory, ethnography and differences between doctors and nurses in approaches to patient care. *Journal of Medical Ethics, 22*, 292–299.

Rogers, A. & Pilgrim, D. (1991). Pulling down churches: accounting for the British mental health users' movement. *Sociology of Health and Illness, 13*(2), 129–148.

Rogers, A. & Pilgrim, D. (1993). Service users' views of psychiatric treatment. *Sociology of Health and Illness, 15*(5), 612–631.

Rogers, A. & Pilgrim, D. (1997). The contribution of lay knowledge to the understanding and promotion of mental health. *Journal of Mental Health, 6*(1), 23–36.

Rogers, A. & Pilgrim, D. (2001). *Mental health policy in Britain.* Basingstoke: Macmillan Press Ltd.

Rogers, A., Pilgrim, D. & Lacey, R. (1993). *Experiencing psychiatry: users' views of services.* London: Macmillan, in association with MIND Publications.

Rollason, K., Stow, J. & Paul, J. (2000). People in the smoke room. *Community Care* (14–20 December), 20–21.

Romme, M. & Escher, S. (1993). *Accepting voices.* London: MIND.

Rose, D. (1996a). *Representations of madness on British television: a social psychological analysis.* Unpublished PhD thesis, University of London, London.

Rose, D. (1996b). *Living in the community.* London: Sainsbury Centre for Mental Health.

Rose, D. (1998). Television, madness and community care. *Journal of Community and Applied Psychology, 8*, 213–228.

Rose, D. (2001). *Users' voices: the perspectives of mental health service users on community and hospital care.* London: Sainsbury Centre for Mental Health.

Rose, D. (2003). Having a diagnosis is a qualification for the job. *British Medical Journal, 326*(14 June), 1331.

Rose, D., Fleischmann, P., Wykes, T., Leese, M. & Bindman, J. (2003). Patients' perspectives on electroconvulsive therapy: systematic review. *British Medical Journal, 326*, 1363.

Rose, D., Ford, R., Lindley, P. & Gawith, L. (1998). *In our experience: user-focused monitoring of mental health services.* London: Sainsbury Centre for Mental Health.

Rose, D. & Muijen, M. (1998). Twenty-four nursed care: users' views. *Journal of Mental Health, 7*(6), 603–610.

Rosenhan, D. L. (1973). On being sane in insane places. *Science, 179*, 250–258.

Round, A., Bray, C., Polak, S. & Graham, L. (1995). Divergent views – patient, carer and staff perceptions of diagnosis and reasons for psychiatric admission to a district general hospital. *International Journal of Social Psychiatry, 41*(3), 210–216.

Sainsbury Centre for Mental Health (2003). *Doing it for real.* London: Sainsbury Centre for Mental Health.

Sampson, C. (1995). The fractioning of medical dominance in British psychiatry. *Sociology of Health and Illness, 17*(2), 245–268.

Sarbin, T. & Mancuso, J. (1970). Failure of a moral enterprise: attitudes of the public toward mental illness. *Journal of Consulting and Clinical Psychology, 35*(2), 159–173.

Sayce, L. (2000). *From psychiatric person to citizen: overcoming discrimination and social exclusion.* Basingstoke: Palgrave.

Scambler, G. (1998). Stigma and disease: changing paradigms. *The Lancet, 352*(26 September), 1054–1055.

Scheff, T. (1966). *Being mentally ill.* Chicago: Aldine Publishing Company.

Schoeneman, T. J., Clark, S., Gibson, C., Routbort, J. & Jacobs, D. (1994). Seeing the insane in textbooks of abnormal psychology: the use of art in histories of mental illness. *Journal for the Theory of Social Behaviour, 24*(2), 111–141.

Schreber, D. P. (1988). *Memoirs of my nervous illness.* Cambridge, MA: Harvard University Press.

Schurmans, M. -N. (1990). *Maladie mentale et sens commun.* Lausanne: Delachaux et Niestle.

Schurmans, M. -N. & Duruz, N. (1999). 'Co-operating', 'fighting against' or 'letting go' in the therapeutic context: social logic of parents with psychologically disturbed children. In J. Guimon, W. Fischer & N. Sartorius (eds), *The image of madness: the public facing mental illness and psychiatric treatment* (pp. 72–84). Basel: Karger.

Serino, C. (1987). Entre 'normal' et 'différent': aspects du lien soi/autrui dans le processus de représentation sociale. In G. Bellelli (ed.), *La Représentation sociale de la maladie mentale* (pp. 89–105). Naples: Liguori.

Sevigny, R., Wenying, Y., Peiyan, Z., Marteau, J., Zhouyun, Y., Lin, S., Guowang, L., Dang, X., Yanling, W. & Haijun, W. (1999). Attitudes towards the mentally ill in a sample of professionals working in a psychiatric hospital in Beijing (China). *International Journal of Social Psychiatry, 45*(1), 41–55.

Shelley, R. (ed.). (1997). *Anorexics on anorexia.* London: JKP.

Shepherd, G., Murray, A. & Muijen, M. (1994). *Relative values: the differing views of users, family carers, and professionals in services for people with schizophrenia in the community.* London: Sainsbury Centre for Mental Health.

Smith, K. & Sweeney, M. (eds). (1997). *Beyond Bedlam: poems written out of mental distress.* London: Anvil Press.

Social Exclusion Unit (1998). *Rough sleeping.* London: Social Exclusion Unit.

Sommer, R. & Osmond, H. (1960). Autobiographies of former mental patients. *Journal of Mental Science, 106*, 648–667.

Sommer, R. & Osmond, H. (1983). A bibliography of mental patients' autobiographies. *American Journal of Psychiatry, 140*, 1051–1054.

Sonn, M. (1977). Patients' subjective experiences of psychiatric hospitalisation. In T. C. Manschreck & A. M. Kleinman (eds), *Renewal in psychiatry: a critical rational perspective*. New York: John Wiley and Sons Ltd.

Sontag, S. (1978). *Illness as metaphor*. New York: Farrar, Straus and Giroux.

Stanton, A. H. & Schwarz, M. S. (1954). *The mental hospital: a study of institutional participation in psychiatric illness*. London: Tavistock.

Stockdale, J. & Purkhardt, S. C. (1993). Multi-dimensional scaling as a technique for the exploration and description of a social representation. In D. Canter & G. Breakwell (eds), *Empirical approaches to social representations*. Oxford: Clarendon Press.

Styron, W. (1991). *Darkness visible: a memoir of madness*. London: Jonathan Cape.

Sudbury, J. (2001). (Re)constructing multi-racial blackness: women's activism, difference and collective identity in Britain. *Ethnic and Racial Studies, 24*(1), 29–49.

Sutherland, S. (1976). *Breakdown: a personal crisis and a medical dilemma*. London: Weidenfeld and Nicolson.

Svedberg, B., Backenroth-Ohsako, G. & Lützén, K. (2003). On the path to recovery: patients' experience of treatment with long-acting injections of antipsychotic medication. *International Journal of Mental Health Nursing, 12*, 110–118.

Swanson, R. & Spitzer, S. P. (1970). Stigma and the psychiatric patient career. *Journal of Health and Social Behaviour, 11*, 44–57.

Szasz, T. (1961). *The myth of mental illness*. London: Secker and Warburg Ltd.

Tajfel, H. (1981). *Human groups and social categories: studies in social psychology*. Cambridge: Cambridge University Press.

Taylor, P. J. & Gunn, J. (1999). Homicides by people with mental illness: myth and reality. *British Journal of Psychiatry, 174*, 9–14.

Taylor, S. M. & Dear, M. J. (1981). Scaling community attitudes toward the mentally ill. *Schizophrenia Bulletin, 7*(2), 225–240.

Temerlin, M. K. (1968). Suggestion effects in psychiatric diagnosis. *Journal of Nervous and Mental Disease, 147*(4), 349–352.

Tew, J. (2005a). Power relations, social order and mental distress. In J. Tew (ed.), *Social perspectives in mental health: developing social models to understand and work with mental distress* (pp. 71–89). London: Jessica Kingsley.

Tew, J. (2005b). Core themes of social perspectives. In J. Tew (ed.), *Social perspectives in mental health: developing social models to understand and work with mental distress* (pp. 13–31). London: Jessica Kingsley Publishers.

Tew, J. (2005c). Social perspectives: towards a framework for practice. In J. Tew (ed.), *Social perspectives in mental health: developing social models to understand and work with mental distress* (pp. 216–227). London: Jessica Kingsley.

Tones, K. & Tilford, S. (1994). *Health education: effectiveness, efficiency and equity.* London: Chapman and Hall.

Tooth, B., Kalyanasundaram, V., Glover, H. & Momenzadah, S. (2003). Factors consumers identify as important to recovery from schizophrenia. *Australasian Psychiatry, 11*(Supplement), S70–S77.

Trauer, T., Duckmanton, R. A. & Chiu, E. (1998). A study of the quality of life of the severely mentally ill. *International Journal of Social Psychiatry, 44*(2), 79–91.

Truman, C. (2000). New movements and social research. In C. Truman, D. M. Mertens & B. Humphries (eds), *Research and Inequality.* London: UCL Press.

Turner, J. (1975). Social comparison and social identity: some prospects for intergroup behaviour. *European Journal of Social Psychology, 5,* 5–34.

Tyrer, P. & Steinberg, D. (2005). *Models of mental disorder: conceptual models in psychiatry.* Chichester: John Wiley and Sons Ltd.

Wahl, O. F. (1995). *Media madness: public images of mental illness.* New Brunswick: Rutgers University Press.

Wahl, O. F. (2003). Depictions of mental illnesses in children's media. *Journal of Mental Health, 12*(3), 249–258.

Walker, M. (1992). *Surviving secrets.* Buckingham: Open University Press.

Wallace, A. F. C. (1972). Mental illness, biology and culture. In F. L. Hsu (ed.), *Psychological Anthropology.* Cambridge, MA: Schenkman Publishing Co. Inc.

Wallcraft, J. (2005). Recovery from mental breakdown. In J. Tew (ed.), *Social perspectives in mental health: developing social models to understand and work with mental distress* (pp. 200–215). London: Jessica Kingsley.

Wallcraft, J., Read, J. & Sweeney, A. (2003). *On our own terms: users and survivors of mental health services working together for support and change.* London: Sainsbury Centre for Mental Health.

Warner, R., Huxley, P. & Berg, T. (1999). An evaluation of the impact of clubhouse membership on quality of life and treatment utilisation. *International Journal of Social Psychiatry, 45*(4), 310–320.

Weinreich, P. (1983). Emerging from threatened identities: ethnicity and gender in redefinitions of ethnic identity. In G. Breakwell (ed.), *Threatened identities* (pp. 149–185). Chichester: John Wiley and Sons Ltd.

Weinstein, R. (1972). Patients' perceptions of mental illness: paradigms for analysis. *Journal of Health and Social Behaviour, 13,* 38–47.

Weinstein, R. M. (1981). Mental patients' attitudes toward hospital staff: review of quantitative research. *Archives of General Psychiatry, 38,* 483–489.

Weinstein, R. M. (1983). Labelling theory and the attitudes of mental patients: a review. *Journal of Health and Social Behaviour, 24,* 70–84.

Weinstein, R. M. & Brill, N. Q. (1971). Conceptions of mental illness by patients and normals. *Mental Hygiene, 55*(1), 101–108.

Whitehead, K. & Williams, J. (2001). Medical treatment of women with Lupus: the case for sharing knowledge and decision-making. *Disability and Society, 16*(1), 103–121.

Wield, C. (2006). *Life after darkness: a doctor's journey through severe depression.* Oxford: Radcliffe Medical Press.

Williams, B. (1994). Patient satisfaction: a valid concept. *Social Science and Medicine, 38*(4), 509–516.

Williams, G. & Popay, J. (1994). Lay knowledge and the privilege of experience. In D. Kelleher & G. Williams (eds), *Challenging medicine* (pp. 118–139). London: Routledge.

Wing, J. K. (ed.). (1975). *Schizophrenia from within.* London: National Schizophrenia Fellowship.

Wolff, G., Pathare, S., Craig, T. & Leff, J. (1999). Public education for community care: a new approach. In J. Guimon, W. Fischer & N. Sartorius (eds), *The image of madness: the public facing mental illness and psychiatric treatment* (pp. 105–117). Basel: Krager.

Wolfson, P. M. & Paton, C. (1996). Clozapine audit: what do patients and relatives think? *Journal of Mental Health, 5*(3), 267–273.

Wood, E. C., Rakusin, J. M. & Morse, E. (1960). Interpersonal aspects of psychiatric hospitalisation: I: the admission. *Archives of General Psychiatry, 3*, 632–641.

World Health Organisation, (1992). *The ICD10 classification of mental and behavioural diagnostic criteria for research.* Geneva: World Health Organisation.

Wurtzel, E. (1996). *Prozac nation: young and depressed in America – a memoir.* London: Quartet Books.

Zani, B. (1987). Stratégies thérapeutiques et représentations sociales de la maladie mentale. In G. Bellelli (ed.), *La Représentation sociale de la maladie mentale* (pp. 107–120). Naples: Liguori.

Zani, B. (1993). Social representations of mental illness: lay and professional perspectives. In D. Canter & G. Breakwell (eds), *Empirical approaches to social representations.* Oxford: Clarendon Press.

Zittoun, T., Duveen, G., Gillespie, A., Ivinson, G. & Psaltis, C. (2003). The use of symbolic resources in developmental transitions. *Culture and Psychology, 9*(4), 415–448.

Index